Tropical Pioneers

Human Agency and Ecological Change in the Highlands of Sri Lanka, 1800–1900

JAMES L. A. WEBB, JR.

OHIO UNIVERSITY PRESS
Athens

Ohio University Press, Athens, Ohio 45701

© 2002 by Ohio University Press
Printed in the United States of America

Ohio University Press books are printed on acid-free paper ♾™

10 09 08 07 06 05 04 03 02   5 4 3 2 1

Maps 2, 3, 4, and 5 are based on those in *Atlas of Sri Lanka*
(Arjuna Consulting Co. Ltd., Dehiwala, Sri Lanka, 1997), edited by T. Somasekaram,
M. P. Perera, M. B. G. de Silva, and H. Godellawatta.
They appear by permission of T. Somasekaram.

Library of Congress Cataloging-in-Publication Data

Webb, James L. A.
    Tropical pioneers : human agency and ecological change in the highlands of Sri
Lanka, 1800–1900 / James L. A. Webb, Jr.
        p. cm. — (Ohio University Press series in ecology and history)
    Includes bibliographical references (p.).
    ISBN 0-8214-1427-5 (alk. paper) — ISBN 0-8214-1428-3 (pbk. : alk. paper)
    1. Rain forest ecology—Sri Lanka—History—19th century. 2. Agricultural
ecology—Sri Lanka—History—19th century. 3. Human ecology—History—19th
century. 4. Nature—Effect of human beings on—Sri Lanka—19th century.
I. Title. II. Series.

QH183.5 .W435 2002
577.34'095493'09034—dc21

                                                          2001058810

For Elizabeth and Isaac

Contents

Figures, Maps, and Tables   ix

Acknowledgments   xi

List of Abbreviations   xv

Note on Climatological and Elevational Zones   xvii

INTRODUCTION   1

CHAPTER 1   4
*The Natural Ecology of the Island and Processes of Early
Ecological Change*

CHAPTER 2   25
The Highland Ecologies in the Early Nineteenth Century

CHAPTER 3   53
Early-nineteenth-century Processes of Change

CHAPTER 4   76
The Transformation of the Middle Highlands

CHAPTER 5   108
Into the Upper Highlands

CONCLUSION   147

APPENDIX 1   153
*Sir Joseph Banks, Director of Kew Gardens, on the Principles on
Which a Colonial Botanic Garden in Ceylon Should Be Founded
[c. 1810]*

APPENDIX 2   155
    Sir Joseph Banks's Instructions to William Kerr, First Gardener
    of the Royal Botanic Garden, Ceylon [1812]

APPENDIX 3   157
    Burning the Forest

APPENDIX 4   159
    Cinchona Harveting

APPENDIX 5   161
    Superintendents, Assistant Directors, and Directors of the Royal
    Botanic Garden, Peradeniya, in the Nineteenth Century

Notes   163

Bibliography   207

Index   235

Figures, Maps, and Tables

FIGURES

2.1 Photograph of Samuel Daniell's Drawing "The Water Carrier"   44

5.1 *Cinchona officinalis* (colored plate by W. Fitch)   119

5.2 *Cinchona succirubra* (colored plate by W. Fitch)   119

5.3 Propagation by Layers   120

5.4 Propagation by Cuttings and Buds   121

5.5 Forest Being Felled Preparatory to a Burn and Planting, 1875   128

5.6 Tea, Coffee, and Cinchona Nurseries   129

5.7 View of a Nineteenth-century Coffee Plantation   129

5.8 Cinchona Growing at Elevation of 5,200 feet, 1875   130

5.9 Plantation Bungalow Set Amid Imported Trees   130

5.10 Picking Coffee   131

5.11 "Pulping the Cherries" [coffee cherries]   131

5.12 Drying and Cleaning Parchment Coffee   132

5.13 Transporting Coffee by Bullock Cart   132

5.14 Tea Fields in the Highlands [1999]   140

MAPS

1 South India and Sri Lanka   5

2 Elevational Zones   6

3 Agro-ecological Zones   9

4 Towns, Rivers, and Subregions   58

5   Change in the Extent of Coffee Plantations   109
between 1863 and c. 1880

6   Enlarged Detail of Coffee Plantations   110

Tables

i   Climatological and Elevational Zones   xviii

3.1   Estimate of Extent of Forest Land Newly Opened by   70
Kandyan Farmers for Coffee Production, 1812–1845

3.2   Acreage of Crown Land Sold, 1833–1886   72
With graph

4.1   Average Annual Arrivals of South Indian Laborers in Sri Lanka,   90
by Decade, 1840–1887

4.2   Rice Imports in Bushels, 1837–1899   91
With graph

4.3   Volume and Value of Cattle Imports, 1837–1886   96
With two graphs

4.4   Volume and Value of Elephant Exports, 1863–1899   101
With two graphs

5.1   Volume and Value of Coffee Exports, 1849–1899   113
With two graphs

5.2   Varieties and Quantities of Cinchona Plants Sold at   126
Hakgala Garden, 1876–1880

5.3   Volume and Value of Cinchona Exports, 1877–1900   126
With two graphs

5.4   Highland Acreage in Coffee, Cinchona, and Tea, 1867–1900   134
With graph

5.5   Coffee, Cinchona, and Tea as Percentages of   136
Major Highland Exports, 1878–1901
With graph

5.6   Volume and Value of Tea Exports, 1873–1900   137
With two graphs

Acknowledgments

*I*n the mid-1990s, the prospect of writing a book in South Asian environmental history beckoned to me somewhat unexpectedly. Trained as a historian of West Africa with a specialization in economic history, I had just finished a first book that explored the social and economic consequences of a long-term trend in aridity along the southern shore of the Sahara in the period 1600–1850.[1] I was casting about for a new research topic in West African environmental history and writing up some articles that were spin-offs from the book.

One day an administrator from a consortium of U.S. liberal arts colleges called to ask whether I would be willing to be considered for the resident directorship of a program in Sri Lanka, and I began to give serious thought to a research project in South Asia. I had spent a brief, but highly influential period of my teenage life at the Kodaikanal School in the Palni Hills in Tamilnadu, India, and, even more briefly, living and traveling there with medical missionaries, and I had always wanted to return to South Asia. I began to undertake some initial research into the ecological history of the highlands of Sri Lanka. In 1998, I was offered, and accepted, the position mentioned above—to direct for an academic year the Intercollegiate Sri Lankan Education (ISLE) Program, a junior-year, study-abroad program for U.S. undergraduates, based in Kandy and affiliated with the University of Peradeniya.

The ISLE program has enjoyed broad success since its inception in 1983 largely because of its engagement with a group of committed scholars in the Faculty of Arts at the University of Peradeniya. I would like to thank in particular Ranjith Amarasinghe, Ashley Halpé, Udaya Meddegama, P. B. Meegaskumbura, P. D. Premasiri, Sudarshan Seneviratne, and Tudor Silva for all the good work that they have done for the ISLE program. I owe a personal debt of thanks to these scholars as well. I have been enriched through conversations with them and enlightened by attendance at their academic lectures.

Over the course of my year as ISLE director and the year sabbatical that followed, I became endebted to other Sri Lankan scholars for their professional assistance and personal generosity. Kingsley M. de Silva, professor emeritus at the University of Peradeniya and Sri Lanka's outstanding political historian of the British and independence periods, was continuously supportive. He graciously extended to me the facilities and the aegis of the International Centre for Ethnic Studies in Kandy, where he is the executive director. At a later date, Kingsley read the entire draft manuscript and helpfully pointed out instances where I had lost sight of the forest for the trees. Colleagues in the Department of Geography at the University of Peradeniya introduced me to some of the core problems in the historical geography of the highlands. I am grateful to C. M. M. Bandara, Gerald H. Peiris, and Nimal Wickramaratne for their willingness to share their ideas and perspectives . A very special thanks is owed to P. Wickramagamage, who shared unstintingly his ecological knowledge of the highlands and used his expertise in GIS technology to map the extent of the coffee estates in the second half of the nineteenth century.

Another debt of gratitude is owed to the archivists and librarians in Sri Lanka, the United Kingdom, and the United States who facilitated my access to historical documentary materials. In Sri Lanka, the archivists and staff at the National Archives in Colombo and in Kandy were unfailingly helpful. They made the seasons of research fruitful and enjoyable. The staff at the Department of Agriculture Library at Gannaruwa made useful suggestions and graciously provided office space. The staff of the Royal Asiatic Society–Ceylon Branch (Colombo) and of the Ceylon Room at the University of Peradeniya were courteous and helpful. Dr. Siril Wijisundera, the acting director at the Royal Botanic Garden, Peradeniya, provided me regular access to the institutional library and kindly arranged introductions for me at the Royal Botanic Gardens at Kew. In the United Kingdom, the staff at the new British Library, the British Library–Newspaper Annex in Colindale, the Royal Botanic Gardens at Kew, and the Public Records Office–Kew were models of efficiency. In the United States, the dedicated Interlibrary Loan staffs at the College of William and Mary in Williamsburg, Virginia, and at Colby College in Waterville, Maine, played a critical role in the success of this project.

I would like to thank my colleagues at Colby for their ongoing support through the college's Social Science Grants Committee. These funds have allowed me to travel to the United Kingdom on numerous occasions and to defray my research expenses there. I would also like to thank James McCord, chair of the Department of History at the College of William and Mary, for graciously extending a professional appointment during the spring semester of my 1999–2000 sabbatical year. Tony Anemone, chair of the Department of Modern Foreign Languages at William and Mary, and his wife Vivie Pyle arranged for a marvelous sabbatical house and generally helped to make life enjoyable during our sojourn in tidewater Virginia.

I have written this book in an effort to engage some of the larger themes that are emerging in the field of global environmental history. In addition to the critical commentary by Sri Lankanists, I have benefitted greatly from thoughtful readings of this manuscript by colleagues who are specialists in the environmental history of other areas of the world and/or in global environmental history. Their advice has been provocative, and if I have failed to heed every suggestion they will undoubtedly recognize in this book the influence of their ideas. Christopher Conte, José Drummond, James McCann, and John McNeill incisively interrogated the text and coaxed more thought and more research from me. I am grateful.

I have presented the arguments in this book in various states of evolution at a university faculty seminar and a Department of Geography seminar at the University of Peradeniya, the Third World Economic History and Development Workshop at the London School of Economics, the Contemporary History Institute at Ohio University, and at a panel on Tropical Forests and Environmental History at the American Society for Environmental History. The ideas and challenges that arose in these venues likewise contributed to the final version.

The debts that one incurs in writing a book cannot be tallied solely within the bounds of academe. A final and profound debt of caring and forbearance is owed to my family. This project would not have taken wing without the willingness of my wife, Alison, to put her consulting business "in mothballs" and to move our family to the highlands of Sri Lanka for an extended stay. My first book was dedicated to Alison. This second book I dedicate to our children, Elizabeth and Isaac, who, when placed in a schooling environment in which the language of instruction was Sinhala, rose to the occasion magnificently.

Abbreviations

AGA	Assistant Government Agent
ARC	Administration Reports, Ceylon
BPP	British Parliamentary Paper
CAR	Ceylon Administrative Reports
CC	*Ceylon Chronicle*
CF	*Ceylon Forester*
CGG	*Ceylon Government Gazette*
CHGA	*Ceylon Herald and General Advertiser*
CJHSS	*Ceylon Journal of Historical and Social Sciences*
CO	*Colombo Observer*
COCA	*Colombo Observer and Commercial Advertiser*
COOFPCI	*Colombo Overland Observer, & Fortnightly Precis of Ceylon Intelligence*
COOFS	*Colombo Overland Observer & Fortnightly Summary*
CS	Colonial Secretary
GA	Government Agent
KHPWC	*Kandy Herald and Planters' Weekly Chronicle*
JRASCB	*Journal of the Royal Asiatic Society, Ceylon Branch*
OOFSI	*Overland Observer & Fortnightly Summary of Intelligence*
OOMPCI	*Overland Observer and Monthly Precis of Ceylon Intelligence*
PRO	Public Record Office (Kew)
RBG	Royal Botanic Garden
RBG Kew	Archives of the Royal Botanic Gardens at Kew
SLNA	Sri Lankan National Archives, Colombo
SLNA, KB	Sri Lankan National Archives, Kandy Branch
SP	*Sessional Paper* [Government of Ceylon]
TA	*Tropical Agriculturalist*

Note on Climatological and Elevational Zones

C ontemporary agro-ecologists define the highly complex ecological mosaic of the highlands by reference to soil types, patterns of precipitation, and average temperature, which are all critical determinants of the possibilities of agricultural land use. Even today, however, the delineation of contemporary agro-ecological zones is only approximate and cannot do full justice to the ecological reality of the highlands. For example, there has never been a detailed soil survey of the highlands, at least in part because the complexity and patchwork nature of the soils would render the expense of an accurate soil survey prohibitive.

In the nineteenth century, British scientists and planters understood soil types and rainfall patterns to be critically important. But for much of the period under study, they made financial and agronomic decisions without the benefit of even a rudimentary soil survey or local meteorological data. They placed considerable confidence in the cruder measures of elevation above sea level and on the orientation of the mountainside vis-à-vis the southwestern monsoon.[1] They generally considered the highlands as divisible into three elevational zones; and the orientation of the terrain they saw as either facing the southwestern monsoon or lying in its shadow. This yielded a matrix of six different climato-elevational zones in the highlands, defined by elevation and seasonal rainfall patterns.

Table i: *Climatological and Elevational Zones*

	Altitude	Monsoon Pattern
Lower highlands	500–2,000 feet	Rainface/double monsoons (SW and NE)
		Rainshadow/single monsoon (NE)
Middle highlands	2,000–4,500 feet	Rainface/double monsoons (SW and NE)
		Rainshadow/single monsoon (NE)
Upper highlands	above 4,500 feet	Rainface/double monsoons (SW and NE)
		Rainshadow/single monsoon (NE)

This schema is a variant of that employed by C. R. Panabokke in his *Soils and Agro-Ecological Environments of Sri Lanka.*[2] It accords with the vision of the nineteenth-century British planters. The decisions they made on this basis helped to reshape the ecology of the highlands.

Introduction

S urrounded by the warm tropical waters of the Indian Ocean, the island of Sri Lanka lies only forty miles or so off the southeastern coast of the southern tip of India. This proximity to the South Asian mainland is a principal key to the island's earliest ecological history. Over deep time, its flora and fauna developed in a common garden with the flora and fauna of the South Asian mainland. In more recent millennia, its human populations have migrated in waves large and small from the mainland. Humans brought fire and with fire reworked the landscape and reordered the biological communities on the island. With their seeds, tools, animals, and ideas, the migrants extended the animal, plant, and disease environments of the mainland, most dramatically in the dry, northern reaches of the island. In this profound ecological sense, Sri Lanka is best understood as an extension of mainland South Asia, rather than as a world unto itself.[1]

Taking an even broader perspective, it is clear that Sri Lanka was also part of the vast ecological ecumene of Eurasia. Over the long millennia of experiments with agriculture and the domestication of animals, human populations across the landmass suffered through repeated bouts with deadly diseases, many of which adapted across species and moved from the Eurasian herds to the herders.[2] As a result, in Sri Lanka at the beginning of the era of European colonialism (1505–1948), the populations of the island had already inherited some degree of immunity that foreclosed the possibility of wholesale conquest through virgin-soil epidemic, such as that which resulted from the European contacts with the Americas and the Pacific islands.[3] Moreover, the island harbored tropical diseases and remained a largely unwelcoming epidemiological environment for its European colonizers, as did mainland South Asia.[4]

During the early millennia of long-distance exchange within the Indian Ocean world, the highlands remained sparsely populated. In the fifteenth century, larger settlements and a highland kingdom did begin to form, along the banks of the Mahaweli River, behind a dense belt of rainforest. But during the early centuries of European colonialism, the highlands remained relatively isolated. The Portuguese and the Dutch tried and failed repeatedly to establish their control in the highlands. They were forced to content themselves with their activities in the maritime zones of the island, even as they pioneered the first global sea routes of trade. Only in the nineteenth century did the British carve out permanent corridors through the dense belt of green rainforest that surrounded the kingdom of Kandy.

Tropical Pioneers investigates the ecological history of the highlands during this critical period of the nineteenth century. As the green canopies of the rainforest fell to the ax, the isolation of the highlands collapsed. New economic and ecological forces that had been generated far beyond the Indian Ocean world came to bear on the highlands. The abolition of slavery within the British Empire sent coffee and sugar planters far afield in search of new opportunities and ignited an explosive land rush in the Kandyan highlands. British planters put the highland forest mantle to the torch and accomplished the most extensive conversion of rainforest into tropical plantation agriculture to be seen anywhere in the British Empire in the nineteenth century. The British transferred the model of the "scientific" plantation from the Caribbean to make way for monocrop plantations of trees species from other mountainous zones around the world. They introduced the coffee tree originally from the Ethiopian highlands, the cinchona tree from the eastern slopes of the Andes mountains, and the tea tree from the foothills of the Himalayas.

The Kandyans not only bore the costs they also exploited the opportunities of these radical transformations. The only settled farmers in Asia to make extensive use of slash-and-burn agriculture, the highland villagers burned off by far an even larger extent of highland rainforest than did the plantation owners. They charred out new fields for dry grains, extending their land claims in order to establish tenure.[5] By the end of the nineteenth century, the ecological conversion of the highlands was complete. The natural endowment had been burned over. Only a few craggy corners and a few reserved mountain caps escaped the firestick.[6]

～

Tropical Pioneers is organized chronologically in five main chapters, with a brief summation in conclusion. Chapter 1 provides an overview of the natural-resource endowment of the island and early processes of ecological change, from early geological time up until 1800. Chapter 2 examines ecological processes at work within the highlands in the early decades of the nineteenth century. Chapter 3 addresses the ecological consequences of the opening up of the highlands following the British conquest of the Kandyan Kingdom in 1815. Chapter 4 explores both British and Kandyan ecological initiatives during the momentous upheavals of the mid-nineteenth century, when the middle highland rainforests rose in smoke and the new plantation regimes and dry grain fields took root. Chapter 5 explores the transformation of the upper highlands as the coffee sectors and then the cinchona sectors collapsed and tea cultivation spread dramatically into higher elevations.

~ CHAPTER 1 ~

The Natural Ecology of the Island and Processes of Early Ecological Change

T he island known today as Sri Lanka is ancient.[1] It is part of an original landmass that formed slowly during the geological era known as the Proterozoic, roughly 2.5 to 0.5 billion years ago, when it was part of the southern supercontinent of Gondwanaland, which included Africa, South America, and Australia, as well as what is today South Asia. In deep geological time, the land that would become Sri Lanka drifted north with the rest of the Indian land shield, which itself collided with the Eurasian landmass and created the Himalayan mountains. About twelve million years ago, the small Sri Lankan portion calved off the southern edge of the subcontinent of South Asia and shifted slowly into its present position in the Indian Ocean, some forty miles or so from the coast of southern India, near the equator.

Today, the basic form of the island is that of an extensive coastal erosion plain, out of which rises a central mass of mountains known as the central highlands.[2] These mountains, which dominate the south-central portion of the island, are themselves composed of two distinct erosion plateaus, composed of jumbles of peaks, ridges, plateaus, escarpments, valleys, and intermontane basins. As a whole, the central highlands make up a roughly triangular area. The terrain is highly uneven and highly dissected, which creates complex physiographic conditions that defy easy generalization. The highest peaks reach elevations of more than 7,500 feet, with one soaring higher than 8,200 feet, but most of the land surface in the mountains is much lower.[3]

The tropical warmth, high rainfall, and periodic winds that chiseled the

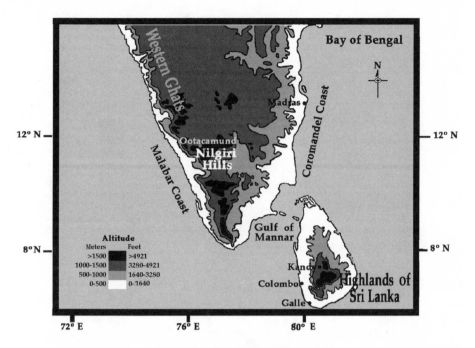

Map 1. *South India and Sri Lanka*

island's physiography also formed the island's soils. The product of aeons of deep weathering, enriched by organic humus and by the life activity of bacteria, the soils are comparatively poor. They are inferior, for example, in their fertility and mineral endowment to the more recently formed tropical igneous soils such as those of the island of Java. Within Sri Lanka, the soils of the central highlands, composed mostly of old lateritic materials, with a high iron content, are somewhat richer than those of the lowlands. And in the highlands of Sri Lanka, as elsewhere, these ancient soil endowments in more recent periods have had a profound impact on the possibilities of human land use. They have been critical determinants of the flora that could establish themselves and the types of plants that human beings would succeed or fail at growing.[4]

Elemental Forces

Over recent millennia, the climate of the island has been tropical and monsoonal, and the seasonal rhythms of rainfall distinct. These conditions are owing to the island's location near the equator, between six and ten degrees north

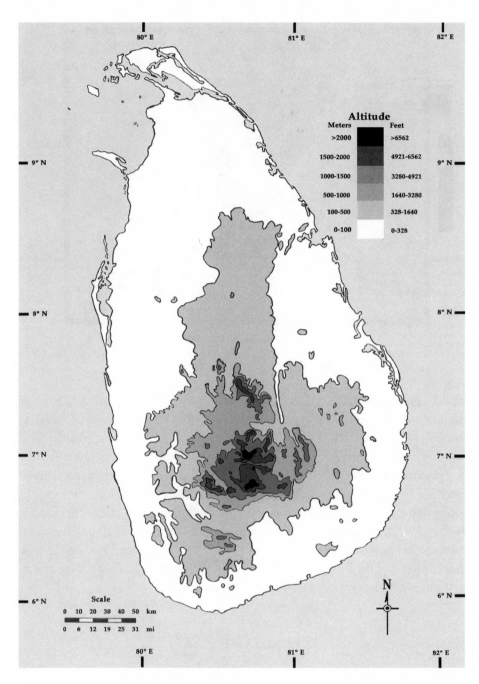

Map 2. *Elevational Zones*

latitude. The average diurnal temperatures on the island are high along the coast, and shade into more moderate averages at higher altitudes. There are two monsoons, or seasonal winds, that control the patterns of rainfall, and in between the two monsoons are light and variable winds that also bring rainfall to the highlands. The onset and decline of the summer monsoon and the period of the winter monsoon itself are marked by high winds. The beginning and ending of the summer monsoon is often marked by wind storms that blow between 20 and 38 miles per hour. The winter monsoon season produces even stronger storms. It is the period of cyclones, which reach intensities of 39 to 74 miles per hour, and occasionally higher.[5] The intensity and timing of the monsoons are determined by the pourings of two subtropical high-pressure systems into an atmospheric trough along the equator. This convergence of atmospheric pressure systems is unstable, and the Inter-Tropical Convergence Zone (ITCZ) moves north and south of the equator with the seasons, in an annual, if not entirely predictable, pattern.

The summer monsoon roars out of the southwest between May and September, when the ITCZ is above the equator. The summer monsoon drenches the southwestern quadrant of the island and releases even more of its rainfall in the highlands than along the coast. The highlands capture the rainfall and prevent it from showering on the leeward side of the mountains. This creates a remarkable summer monsoon effect on the far side of the mountains—a rainshadow governed by a warm, dry wind known as the Kachchan. It is followed by an intermonsoonal period from October to November during which rains fall over the entire island, but most heavily again on the southwestern quadrant. The winter monsoon cyclones out of the northeast from December through February. It drenches the other northeastern and southeastern quadrants of the island and releases sheets of rain in the highlands. But there is no rainshadow effect in the mountains during the winter monsoon. It in turn is followed by an intermonsoonal period from March to April during which most rainfall is concentrated again in the southwestern quadrant.

The spatial distribution of the rainfall across the island is thus highly varied. As a conventional shorthand, it is useful for heuristic purposes to characterize the island in terms of a Wet Zone in the southwestern quadrant, surrounded by an Intermediate Zone, which in turn is bounded by a Dry Zone over the rest of the island. In the Wet Zone, the highest annual rainfalls are in the mountains, and even there the variation is considerable. Some sections of the western slopes receive more than 200 inches of total annual rainfall, others 140 inches. The distribution of annual rainfall is also quite varied. Total rainfalls are highest on the western slopes, where there is no rainshadow, and most precipitation occurs during the summer monsoon. On the eastern slopes, cupped in a rainshadow, most rain falls during the winter monsoon. Interannual and interseasonal variability in rainfall are, however, substantial; "droughts" have occurred with some frequency over the past two centuries for which we have recorded observations.[6] Variations in the volume, spatial distribution, and timing of rainfalls, along with the variations in local soils, were fundamental parameters of the highland ecologies and set limits on the possibilities for ecological change.

The wetness of the climate in the highlands of Sri Lanka historically distinguished it from the nearby mountain ecologies of mainland South Asia. In this respect the highlands had more in common with the western regions of Malaysia and the eastern coastal region of Madagascar.[7] The high annual rainfalls and mild temperatures in the highlands also contrasted markedly with the Dry Zone plains to north and east. There, because of the pronounced dry season, the total productivity of the biological system was strongly determined by the distribution and timing of rainfall.

Average temperatures in the Wet, Intermediate, and Dry Zones of Sri Lanka were, as they still are today, remarkably constant throughout the year, the difference in temperature between the coldest and warmest months being only a matter of several degrees Fahrenheit. Average temperatures were, of course, highest along the coast. Temperatures decreased with altitude, at a rate of roughly three or four degrees Fahrenheit for every thousand feet of elevation. Thus the highlands of Sri Lanka, rising from 500 to more than 8,000 feet, were considerably cooler than the coastal plain. And in the Wet Zone, the biological productivity of the forested highlands was relatively constant year-round, governed both by the regularity of solar radiation and plenitude of rainfall.[8]

The patterns of rainfall, in conjunction with the island's geomorphology, meant that the principal source of fresh water in all three zones was surface flow. There were few natural lakes, and no ice caps, even on the highest peaks. Fresh water flowed in the rivers and streams around the year, however, and in the early millennia of human settlement, this had a profound influence on the distribution of both human communities and faunal populations, both of which were dependent upon surface water resources. In the Dry Zone, many millennia later, human communities eventually constructed shallow surface reservoirs to capture the freshwater that streamed out of the mountains. During the early historical period, these tanks were built on a vast scale. This engineering feat, the capture of run-off from the highlands in order to mitigate the uncertainty

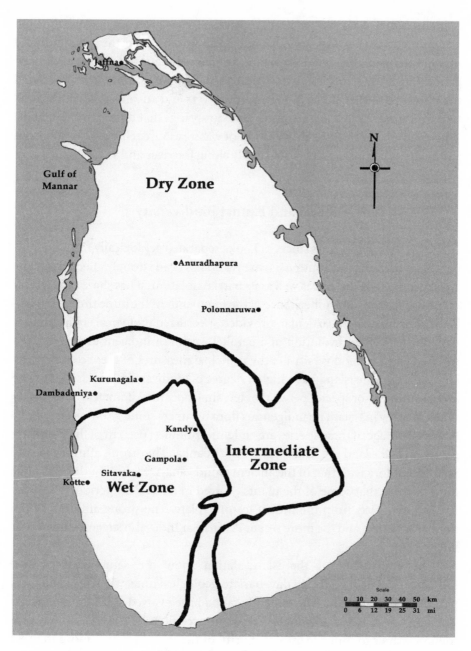

Map 3. *Agro-ecological Zones*

of interseasonal variability in rainfall, was the foundation upon which the high achievements of the early Dry Zone civilizations were based: the impoundment of water resources brought human and animal populations together at the irrigation tanks. By contrast, in the highlands, human communities restricted their areas of settlement to those near the rivers and streams that cut through the highlands, or close by the more than 120 springs that dotted the highlands. Thus, in the highlands the distribution of water resources brought human and animal populations together principally along the river and stream banks.

Floral and Faunal Biodiversity

In the twelve million years since Sri Lanka separated geologically from the subcontinent of mainland South Asia, the island has been strongly affected both by its proximity to India and as well as its partial isolation. It has shared the wealth of the floral and faunal inheritance of the mainland. At the same time, the highlands of Sri Lanka, in particular, provided specialized ecological environments that allowed for the evolution of a parallel wealth of indigenous species. The elevated levels of biodiversity are the principal measures of these complementary processes: the island has a higher degree of biodiversity—measured by the average number of species per grid of terrain (100 x 100 kilometers)—than any other country in Asia. The indigenous flora numbers some 7,500 species, and a large percentage of these species are endemic. About 25 percent of the flowering plants on the island are found only in Sri Lanka. The strong affinities of the relic-forest flora with that of the ancient Gondwana-Deccan (Southwest India) flora suggests that some of the plants evolved in an ancient period, before Sri Lanka rifted away from the Indian tectonic plate. The strong affinities of the flora of Sri Lanka and the more recent Peninsular India also suggest similar past linkages.[9]

The endemicity of the island fauna show the same patterns and influences. Some relict fauna date back to geological time, when Sri Lanka was part of Gondwanaland. The endemic fauna have evolved since the geological isolation of Sri Lanka, through the rise in oceanic water levels, some twelve million years ago. But the great majority of the island's fauna, more than 80 percent, are of relatively recent origin. This largest group of animals is traceable to immigrant ancestors who visited the island more recently during the ice ages, when increased cold drove animals south from the Himalayas, across a land bridge to Sri Lanka that appeared intermittently during geological upthrusts and disappeared under intermittent floodings. This grouping of animal immigrants is only about one million years old and thus has had only enough time in isolation to produce new subspecies, rather than to evolve new endemic species. The new subspecies, classified as "indigenous" animals, have common relatives on the Indian subcontinent. Most endemic species, too, have over time also developed distinctive morphological or other features. This is true, for example, of the Asian elephant, which in Sri Lanka has largely stopped producing ivory tusks, in contrast to its South Indian elephant cousin on the other side of the forty-mile-wide Gulf of Mannar.

The spatial distribution of the island's fauna can be best understood by considering the interaction of climate and soils, which produced specific vegetation zones. These zones in turn have had a major influence on which animals could live in which areas. Most of the endemic animals are found in two subzones—the Low Country Wet Zone and the Up Country Wet Zone. These were the areas least affected by geological change, and this allowed new species to evolve in relative isolation. In the highlands, the degree of endemism is greater than in the lowlands.

Early Human Presence and Ecological Change

The peopling of the island began many millennia ago. The earliest evidence suggests that, perhaps as early as 28,500 B.C.E., small bands may have crossed the Gulf of Mannar from southern India. The archaeological evidence indicates that these prehistoric peoples were transhumant and lived in the Wet, Intermediate, and Dry Zones. Their population densities per square kilometer are estimated to have been very low. These early peoples lacked the technology to make iron, and there has been virtually no evidence developed of technological change during the long millennia of the Stone Age. The early inhabitants of the island apparently did not practice settled agriculture. In a regional context, it appears, on the basis of evidence assembled by the archaeologist S. U. Deraniyagala, that Sri Lanka was a backwater of South Asia.[10] In good measure this can be attributed to the natural ecological endowment of the island. Although potable water was generally abundant, in this era a dense forest cover blanketed virtually the entire island (much as was the case on Sumatra and Borneo, for example) before the era of human settlement, and this forest cover was a difficult environment from which to extract resources. The thick green mat would have been a principal reason why human migrants were not drawn earlier or in larger numbers south across the Gulf of Mannar to Sri Lanka. Indeed, tropical rainforests around the globe virtually everywhere presented a hostile environment for hunters and gatherers.[11]

If the early human bands did not make large technological advances, they did have the ability to make fire. This ancient technology was itself revolutionary because it made possible the clearing of forest patches and the smoky conversion of green biomass to organic ash. This in turn facilitated the evolution of grasslands in the highlands, because grasses were generally successful at colonizing the newly burned-over soils. This early prehistoric ecological process, initiated by the striking of fire and the burning of biomass, might at first appear to have had only local, and extremely circumscribed, ecological effects, owing to the low human population densities in the island forests. But studies of the long-term impact of low-intensity human fire practices, as well as other economic activities of selection in agriculture, gathering, and hunting in rainforests elsewhere in the tropics, suggests a different, and probably more realistic, interpretation.[12]

Early fire practices would have had a considerable effect on the overall floral composition of the forest. In addition, the ecotones of burned-over patches colonized by grasses within the forest would have created a food bounty for grazers and small ruminants, and in turn these burgeoning faunal populations would have made prime game for human hunters. As A. Terry Rambo has argued in relation to the Malaysian rainforests, low-intensity hunting itself may well have initiated significant environmental change: through direct selection, human beings probably brought about the dispersion (flight) of animal groups, habitat modification, and, ultimately, the domestication of some animals. Human hunting and gathering practices would have brought about significant change in the population size of some species, and perhaps even extinction in some others, while resulting in coadaptive change in yet others.[13] These ecological transformations had important unforeseen consequences that were not limited to the floral and faunal communities. The biomass burn-offs left sunlit holes in the canopy that were new and ideal breeding grounds for mosquitos, which could carry malaria. This disease, likely introduced from the mainland, continues to plague human communities on the island into the present. Thus on the island of Sri Lanka, even before the historical migration of peoples from northern and southern India in the last three millennia, it is probable that human communities had a major and lasting impact on the floral and faunal composition of the rainforest environment.

Iron Age technologies came to the island from the mainland during the first millennium B.C.E. Iron implements, in combination with fire, made it possible for human groups to practice slash-and-burn agriculture, or *chena,* as it is known there today. The iron tools facilitated land clearance, and they thus allowed for the evolution of more land-extensive ecological change. But the adoption of iron tools did not alter the agricultural imperative for fire. Weed growth in the wet tropics was beyond the capacity of the shifting cultivator to tackle by any other means. Even with metal tools for weeding and clearing, the presence of tree stumps, constantly producing shoots, would have defeated these efforts. It was fire that grew grain.[14]

The clearing of burned-over forest patches and the planting of dry grain, although certainly more labor-intensive than hunting and gathering, yielded a bounty of calories that could support larger human populations. But chena agriculture exhausted the forest soils quickly, and human groups moved on to new forest patches after one, two, or three seasons. Adoption of this pattern of shifting agriculture in turn produced ecological changes that extended beyond population growth, the domestication of plants, and modification of habitat. The slow reversion to scrub forest of extensive chena agricultural lands may well have accommodated the presence of one of the wild cattle of South and Southeast Asia, the *Bos gaurus.* These cattle appear to avoid the undisturbed evergreen rainforest and to live near relatively open terrain that has been transformed by the human use of fire. In the late nineteenth century, they were still found in all the large forests of southern India.[15] Thus it may well be that, whatever the early habitat of this wild cow, the *Bos gaurus* followed the expansion of shifting cultivation into Sri Lanka, much as it apparently did in Malaysia.[16] If this is indeed the case, it would bring the Sri Lankan experience into close accord with the broader patterns of ecological change in Southeast Asia, where the areas under shifting cultivation were probably much larger a thousand or more years ago than they are today.[17]

Processes of Ecological Change in Early Historical Time

Many thousands of years after the earliest human bands established themselves on the island, larger settled communities began to form in the Dry Zone. Some shared the cultural attributes of the settled communities just across the Gulf of Mannar in areas that are today largely populated by Tamil Hindu communities; and with the arrival of new immigrants from northern India in the first millennium B.C.E., new communities began to emerge, although there is no scholarly consensus as to when the Sinhalese Buddhist ethnic group, today the majority community on the island, solidified its identity.[18] At least some of these groups burned and cleared the land in order to practice irrigated agriculture. Over time, coastal communities, too, began to stabilize around the entire perimeter of the island, burning the biomass to make an environment productive for cultivating grain and edible fruit, to supplement the nutritional wages of the fishing life. Other, smaller, groups known as Veddyas, who opted not to embrace these lifestyles, retreated to the forests, at some remove from the larger settled communities, and won their livelihoods from hunting, gathering, and slash-and-burn agriculture.

Eventually, small states began to form in the Dry Zone, and then larger states that specialized in the larger-scale control of water resources. This expanded the possibility for wet rice cultivation, which had been introduced from the South Asian mainland, probably during the beginning of the first millennium B.C.E.[19] The cultivation of wet rice spread rapidly where controlled water resources would allow. It produced a taxable surplus and generally assured the subsistence of the farming classes, although natural disasters are documented throughout the period.[20] Wet rice cultivation was the economic foundation for the evolution of political authority, and this process culminated in the high *rajarata* ("land of the kings") civilizations (sixth–thirteenth centuries C.E.).

Thus, the ecological foundation for the rajarata civilization was laid by countless generations of human communities of hunters and gatherers and dry grain and wet rice cultivators, who burned off the green canopy. This was probably most extensive in what is today the dry lowlands, although it is also probable that the fire-use practices of human communities in the intermediate and wet highlands led to the creation of grasslands, which were burned out of a formerly unbroken forest cover. Historical sources will not permit even a rough periodization of the destruction of the original forest cover by fire, but it seems clear that at least by the height of the rajarata period, by the middle of the first millennium C.E., most of the original vegetation in the rajarata zone had been burned away. During the rajarata period, the continuation of these fire-use practices and the extensive remaking of the landscape through the construction of reservoirs and irrigation channels took place under the aegis of Buddhist regimes. The greater concentration of political power meant that more large-scale engineering projects could be undertaken, and in line with the Buddhist doctrine of respect for all life-forms, the regimes harnessed the age-old techniques of ecological transformation and sought harmony in the management of nature.

Over time, the expansion of the scale of human efforts at ecological control had a number of significant consequences. Many endemic floral species were unable to adapt to the fire regimes and became restricted to a few pockets, remote from the possibilities of water control and fire use. The large-scale deforestation had been recent enough in the past that few if any endemic species of scrub bush or tree had had sufficient time to evolve to fire tolerance. The endemic flora retreated before the fire. The tangible evidence of this historical process is that the endemic flora of Sri Lanka are found today mostly in the Wet Zone, which was less amenable to colonization by human communities with their firesticks. In the Dry Zone itself, once burned, the lands were colonized by gregarious species from other terrains. The door was opened to large-scale invasion by flora that had enjoyed success within the more ancient human fire regimes of mainland South Asia. They arrived in their hundreds. In the irrigated lowlands of the Dry Zone, however, the low-elevation "jungle scrub," which replaced the "original" forest, was less biologically diverse. The net result was a loss of species diversity.

There were also important consequences for the lowland fauna, both endemic and indigenous. The loss of shelter habitat drove many of the large animals away from the human land-use regions, following a universal pattern of the displacement of large animals by human settlement. Because Sri Lanka was an island, the natural domains into which large animals could flee were limited. Some species saw their numbers sharply reduced. Other species made unusual adaptations; groups of elephants, for example, accommodated themselves to life in the forest shelter of the mountains, which was only possible because of the anthropogenically created grasslands that had taken root and that now provided food for the pachyderms.

Fire use in the Dry Zone evolved along with complex hydraulic works. As more land was claimed for cultivation, regular firings were needed to maintain it. The sheer biological productivity of the wild flora could not be otherwise contained. Indeed, foresters in the nineteenth and twentieth centuries identified the relentless encroachment of the natural world on the works of human communities as the principal dynamic force in the Dry Zone. Looking at the massive scrub forests in areas of the Dry Zone of Sri Lanka and on the South Asian mainland once cultivated and burned, historians judged that a tidal wave of jungle growth could in short order undo the achievements of generations of human effort.[21]

What is less certain is how and why this "jungle tide" proved victorious. Scholars have been able to reconstruct the outlines of the political history of the hydraulic civilizations, based upon the reigns of kings in the two principal centers of political authority, the cities of Anuradhapura (161 B.C.E.–1017 C.E.) and Polonnaruwa (1070–1215 C.E.). The historical record is replete with references to warfare between indigenous factions on the island and between the rajarata states and invading armies from South Asia. According to one interpretation, these wars eventually ruined the hydraulic works and brought about the collapse of the state. In the destruction of war, the great engineering hydraulic works were severely damaged, perhaps irreparably. With the breaching of the reservoir tanks, the control over irrigation for the rice fields was broken. The loss of the wet-rice irrigation systems resulted in a new and more profound dependence on chena cultivation, with its peculiar ability to create conditions conducive to malaria. The increased incidence of malaria brought about the virtual abandonment of the rajarata zone of civilization.[22] As in the case of the precipitous disintegration of the Lowland Mayan civilization, which had also been carved out of a rainforest environment, there were almost certainly many causes for the ecological collapse.[23] Whatever the exact dynamics, there seems little doubt about its extent. Population declined dramatically. The successors to the great hydraulic states drifted to the southwest, eventually into the Intermediate Zone, and then into the Wet Zone itself.

The collapse of the rajarata civilization and its irrigation works in the thirteenth century C.E. ushered in a period of political decline on the island of Sri Lanka. To be sure, there were Sinhalese states that attempted to fill the vacuum of political power, but these states, based successively in Dambadeniya, Kurunagala, and (again) Polonnaruwa, had limited reach. Into this vacuum moved both indigenous and foreign powers. During this same period (c.1250–c.1400 C.E.), the Tamil kingdom of Jaffna grew in importance in the northwestern reaches of the island and extended its hegemony south, even into the highlands themselves. The fifteenth century also saw a major intervention in the island's politics by the emperor of China, who sent two expeditions to Sri Lanka in an effort to secure tribute and obedience. The first expedition spirited away to China, against his will, the Sinhalese ruler. The second returned with the abducted king and a candidate designated by China as his replacement on the throne. In the midst of this chaos, a new Sinhalese Buddhist kingdom, known as Kotte, took root in the Wet Zone. During the lifetime of its founder, Kotte extended its authority throughout the island. Thereafter, succession struggles fragmented the polity.

In the late fifteenth century, a new political authority began to emerge in the highlands, at Gampola. It is uncertain if this new authority began as a satellite of Kotte, but at all events, the wielders of this new power succeeded in aggravating the political chaos occasioned by a succession crisis in Kotte, and a kingdom of Udarata (the Up-Country), which would be known as the kingdom of Kandy (Mountains) separated itself from a weakened Kotte in good order.[24] Within a generation or so, the Portuguese arrived on the southwestern coast of the island and inserted themselves into regional politics. From internal fissures, Kotte broke apart into three political units, and the largest of these three, Sitavaka, attempted to reassert control over the new kingdom of Kandy, which in turn sought assistance first from the Portuguese and then an accommodation with Sitavaka through marriage alliances. These were the first steps in the "crisis of the sixteenth century" that, by dint of complex succession politics and shifting alliances between the Portuguese, the Kandyan state, Kotte, and Sitavaka, eventually brought about the fall of Kotte. Sitavaka then enjoyed a brief period of regional power and waged war against the Portuguese and the Kandyan state. But at the death of its ruler, occasioned by a wound sustained in a campaign against the kingdom of Kandy, the state of Sitavaka collapsed. And at this point the highland kingdom, now seated at the town of Kandy, became the principal independent state on the island.[25]

The Ecological Impact of Portuguese and Dutch Maritime Trade

During the same centuries that the Kandyan kingdom took shape, new political and economic forces came into play throughout the coastal zone of the island. The broad outlines of the patterns of ecological change brought about by the new currents of maritime trade in the period 1500–1800 have yet to come fully into focus. It is clear that these centuries did see an intensification of the commercial and cultural contacts that had long linked the peoples of the island with those of southern and northern India and beyond, to Southeast Asia and the Middle East. In even earlier centuries, this process was begun, in good measure owing to the continuing expansion of the Islamic cultural zone. In earlier centuries, for example, Muslim Arab traders established communities on the southern coast of the island and brought with them some flora from across the Indian Ocean, as well as artisanal goods, new technologies, and Islam itself.[26] Later, Muslim communities became established as merchants in the highlands. It is likely, for example, that the coffee tree *(Coffea arabica),* which was to play such an important role during the ecological revolution of the nineteenth century, was first introduced through these Muslim networks of trade. During the centuries from 1500 to 1800, merchants from the subcontinent of India and from coastal Sri Lanka regularly plied the waters between island and subcontinent, carrying principally cloth and dried fish from India, in exchange for a variety of island exports that included, in order of importance, areca nuts (a stimulant chewed with betel leaves), elephants, gems, and cinnamon.[27] Merchants from the mainland and island worlds of Southeast Asia must also have contributed to the exchange of flora within the wet Asian tropics, although this is a topic still largely unexplored by historians.

The Portuguese arrived on the coast of Sri Lanka in 1505 and participated in a new process of the pan-tropical exchange of plants. Through the expansion of the Portuguese and Spaniards into the world of Asian maritime trade and their trading contacts along the western coast of Africa and in the New World, Native American food crops—some with high caloric yields—made their way into the tropics. Cassava, a staple in the wet tropics of Brazil, and the potato, a staple in the highlands of South America, traveled to Sri Lanka along these global circuits, although they may not have arrived until the late seventeenth or early eighteenth centuries.[28] The potato became established on the island, but probably only in the coastal Dry Zone and perhaps in the rainshadow hills. Neither the potato nor cassava seems to have played a major role in the diet of the island populations before the nineteenth century. A pan-tropical exchange of fruits also took place. The pineapple, papaya, cashew nut, guava, and tomato eventually became established in mainland South Asia as well as on the island of Sri Lanka.[29] The chili pepper *(Capsicum annuum)* from Central America was fully integrated, and today it is as essential to the Sri Lankan cuisine as is the tomato to the southern Italian.

The introduction of these plants, however, held little direct economic significance for the Portuguese in South Asia, who concentrated their commercial efforts on the black-pepper trade, along the Malabar (southwestern) coast of India. Also, from the second half of the sixteenth century, the Portuguese export of cinnamon from Sri Lanka became important.[30] In addition to these spices, stimulants played a significant role in trade. The Portuguese introduced tobacco from the New World in 1610,[31] and by the early nineteenth century tobacco had become one of the principal exports from the region of Jaffna, along with arrack, a liquor distilled from the sap of the coconut tree.[32]

The Dutch displaced the Portuguese along the Sri Lankan coast in 1658 and initiated a new era of tropical trade in spices. The Dutch focused their attention on the export of cinnamon bark, harvested from a tree that grew wild in the wet lowlands. They attempted to extend the monopoly trade initiated by the Portuguese, and in this they were largely successful because the peeling of the cinnamon bark was the work of a single caste that could be kept under close supervision and because the Dutch guarded the forests in which cinnamon trees grew and imposed punitive measures on those who dared to defy their monopoly.[33] The export of cinnamon had its economic significance, but in ecological terms, its impact was light. It did not initiate any processes of deforestation, soil erosion, or loss of wildlife habitat. The Dutch did plant some cinnamon groves toward the end of their rule, but these cinnamon gardens were not extensive. The export spice trade rested fundamentally upon the peeling of fragrant bark from naturally occurring trees.

The success of Dutch aspirations to a cinnamon monopoly was something of an anomaly. In 1670, the Dutch East India Company tried to monopolize the trade in all major commodities except rice, although it appears that the Dutch were never able to do so, and large-scale smuggling took place between India and Sri Lanka.[34] In addition to cinnamon, the major exports were elephants, ivory, areca nuts, and chank shells (used for libations, Hindu temple ceremonies, and ornamental wear). The Dutch also specialized in the reexport of cowrie shells, originally from the Maldive Islands, which were bulked in Sri Lankan ports awaiting transshipment toward their eventual market in sub-Saharan Africa.[35]

Both the Portuguese and Dutch also participated inadvertently in the transoceanic diffusion of human disease. They introduced syphilis and yaws to the island populations.[36] These epidemiological influences were likely most acute in the coastal lowlands, where the Portuguese and Dutch troops and administrators were settled. This maritime littoral was also the region where the Portuguese and Dutch focused their commercial interests. There were no roads into the highlands, and this was a matter of Kandyan state policy. Kandyan kings maintained a forest barrier around the kingdom in order to restrict access. Moreover, the difficulty of human porterage along broken footpaths through the forest meant that only items that showed high value relative to bulk could bear the cost of transport, and thus the highlands themselves remained peripheral to the major networks of Asian trade. Until the nineteenth century, despite the introduction of new food plants, spices, and stimulants in the maritime zone, the principal forces for ongoing ecological change were generated within the highlands.

The heartland of the Kandyan state (c.1474–1815) was in the foothills of the Wet Zone, a more difficult ecological zone for human settlement than either the Dry Zone or the Intermediate Zone, where the earlier post-rajarata era Sri Lankan states had taken root. Following the collapse of Kotte, however, the number and density of human settlements in the foothills of the Wet Zone began to increase, and this in turn allowed for the consolidation of the power of the Kandyan state. The ecological impact of this expansion of human settlement was a function of scale. The agro-ecological practices of irrigated rice and dry grain cultivation inscribed larger extents of the wider region with a distinctive ecology. The village template—the presence of an irrigation tank, wet rice fields, and a Buddhist temple—stamped itself across the highland valleys. Rainforests smoldered under the torch and the smoking gaps were planted out in grain, vegetables, and cotton. Most settlements expanded below an elevation of 2,000 feet, and virtually all were below 3,000 feet. Other human activities—including hunting, gathering, pasturing livestock—reached to elevations far above the village wet rice and dry grain fields.

The Highland Mosaic: Grasslands and Forests

At the beginning of the nineteenth century, the middle and upper highlands were a complex ecological mosaic. Perhaps the most striking element of this mosaic was the existence of large extents of open savanna-like areas, known as *patanas*, in the rainforest mountains.[37] In these open areas, grasses were predominant and made up between 75 and 90 percent of the flora. Hardy, fire-resistant trees composed the remainder.[38] Along the ecotones between the forest and the patana, shrubs were sometimes predominant locally, but at other sites the grasses grew right up to the forest edge.[39]

Our ecological understandings of the mountain grasslands have evolved over time. In the 1940s, the distinguished geographer R. A. De Rosayro drew distinctions between the "wet" and "dry" montane patanas, which conformed largely to seasonal patterns of rainfall within the rainface and rainshadow zones, rather than to the total amount of annual rainfall. But the wet patanas were also located at considerable elevation, between 6,000 and 8,000 feet above sea level, above the frost line. Dry patanas fell within 2,000 to 4,500 feet, with an intermediate zone between the two. The vast majority, some 90 percent of the roughly 160,000 acres (250 square miles) of patanas in the highlands, lay in the rainshadow zone, in Uva Province. The total area of the wet patanas was estimated at a mere 14,000 acres.[40] In the 1960s, N. P. Perera developed a tripartite classification system based on elevation (submontane, intermediate montane, and upper montane) that he considered more accurate than De Rosayro's categories of wet and dry patanas, and he made a critical contribution to patana studies, revealing that some but not all of the grasslands were maintained by fire; others were purely natural communities shaped by edaphic endowments; and yet others in the submontane region (including those between elevations of 1,500 and 3,500 feet) remained as grasslands because of soil erosion so severe that native forest species could not recolonize.[41]

The origins of the patana grasslands themselves were thus diverse. Their existence in the up-country contributed immeasurably to the robust density of faunal populations.[42] The patanas were the food supply that nourished the herds of deer (particularly *Cervus unicolor* and *C. axis*), which themselves were the principal food supply for the large carnivorous cats, particularly the leopard (*Panthera pardus*), the dominant meat eater in the food chain.[43] The largest deer, known as the sambhur (*Cervus unicolor*), was far too large for the leopard to tangle with. A prime buck would stand fifty-four inches at the shoulder and weigh six hundred pounds.[44] Other animals such as wild pigs, monkeys, hares, and large rodents were likewise drawn to the patanas, and the extensive edge-habitats at the borders of the rainforests constituted the most biologically productive regions of the highlands.

The patana grasslands also served as the foodlands for the large herbivores—the elephant *(Elephantus maximus)* and the wild buffalo (*Bubalus bubalis*), which ranged throughout the highlands. The elephant was truly enormous, an adult standing roughly eight or nine feet at the shoulder and ranging in size up to 6,600 pounds in the prime of life. The buffalo was also of good size, standing just under five feet at the shoulder and weighing about 2,000 pounds.[45] These animals were well beyond the size of the prey (20–110 lbs.) preferred by the leopard, and lived in safety from attacks from the top carnivore. This was likely true of the gaur (*Bos gaurus*), as well, before its local extinction took place at some time between the late seventeenth and mid-nineteenth century.[46]

The biological productivity of the grasslands was seasonal, in part because the rainfall in the patanas was not distributed evenly throughout the year. Most of the annual precipitation falls during the monsoons, which each last about four months. The patana grasses grow actively at the start of a monsoon season, and then slow as the monsoon draws to an end. These grasses were the main source of food for the highland mammals, either directly for the herbivores or indirectly for the carnivores; underground tubers, foliage, and fruits comprised only a minor part of the herbivorous mammal diet, and thus the patana grasses were of fundamental biological importance. The most common dry patana flora was lemon grass *(Andropogon schoenanthus)*, which grew to a height of from two to eight feet and emitted a powerful lemon smell. The nutritional value of lemon grass, along with other coarse and wiry grasses belonging to other orders, varied considerably at different seasons, and at different stages of growth.[47] The new growth of the lemon grass, in particular, was considered choice pasture for the buffalo. On the wet patanas, the dominant grass species was *Chrysopogon zeylanicus.*[48]

On both wet and dry patanas, the herbage was richest when only an inch or two in height, before much of the food material had been converted into woody culms or fibre generally. This was the logic behind the firing the grasslands.[49] Compared with grasses from the temperate or subtropical regions of the world, however, these patana grasses were poor in nutrition. Even under a regime of regular firing, the natural grasses were too coarse to rear good draft animals. The sward was neither sufficiently close nor compact to assist in soil and water conservation.[50] The poor quality of the indigenous grasses, which were deficient in phosphoric acid and potassium, acted as a serious impediment to the improvement of the highland faunal populations.[51]

The presence of grasslands and the bamboo (giant grass) breaks, even in the higher elevations, allowed for ambulant elephant and buffalo populations. Elephants feed intermittently throughout the day and into the night, spending more than sixteen hours per day, each consuming between 330 and 550 pounds of fresh vegetation. And most of their time—some 89 percent according to contemporary studies—is spent foraging in grasslands. The ecological edges between the forest and patana were their favorite areas, because elephants could graze in safety and move back into the forest quickly if necessary.[52] Elephants and buffalo sheltered in the adjoining forests but could not have survived there without the nutrition from the patana grasses. Elephants and buffalo were capable of negotiating the full forest; indeed they were obliged to do so in order to be able to exploit the separate, fragmented grasslands of the mountains. Thus elephant paths and buffalo paths crisscrossed the highlands and were the principal roads used by the upland hunters. These animal paths were easily distinguishable: the buffalo paths were characterized by few difficult ascents or descents, whereas the elephant paths indicated the large pachyderms' ability to slide and scramble over precipitous declines and inclines. This surprising agility meant that the elephants' range extended to the summits of the highest mountains.[53]

The rainforests of the highlands of Sri Lanka were once part of an extremely heterogeneous band of global rainforests that blanketed the wet tropics. Before the great deforestation of the highlands in the nineteenth century, these high-land forests were complex in their biodiversity and diverse in their overall architecture. Their structure and composition varied dramatically at different elevations and on different soils. They also varied considerably according to rainface or rainshadow orientation. Indeed, as F. D'A. Vincent, the first scientific forester to assay the highlands, noted in the early 1880s, "probably in no other part of the world are the limits of a moist zone, of heavy and light rainfall, so sharply defined by the natural tree vegetation."[54] During the course of the nineteenth century, the forests at elevations between 1,000 and 5,000 feet largely disappeared. What is left today are fragments at higher or lower elevations that are unrepresentative of the great highland forests of the past.[55]

The principal thick forests of the highlands grew on the rainface slopes and were classed as wet evergreen. At elevations above 5,000 feet, the trees grew noticeably smaller and lower, and at the upper attitudes the trees were stunted and much less densely spaced.[56] Within the thick rainforests in the lower and middle highlands, early botanists were able to distinguish communities of flora that were associated with the dominance of two different types of large trees. One community was associated with the dominant presence of the *Dipterocarpus* and another with the *Mesua-Doona*. They had much in common with the forests of the larger Indo-Malayan region, although in general the trees grew to lower heights and were less developed, largely because of the poverty of the island soils. Neither of these community tree associations was able to extend its domain when it encountered burned forest clearings: both patana and chena effectively arrested forest growth. Within these previously burned-over areas, botanists were able to distinguish a variety of secondary forest types. Interestingly, secondary forests were of more mixed composition and occurred over a wider range of soils and sites.[57]

The long early eras in which the great highland forests grew without disturbance from anthropogenic fire allowed for the evolution of forest soils. Their fertility, as reflected in the physical properties of permeability and air capacity, was higher than in the arable or grassland soils.[58] Forest soils and biomass also played an important role in the water balance of the highland region. In years of low-to-average rainfall, the forests acted as gigantic sponges, capturing water vapor in mist and breaking the impact of raindrops upon the surface of the earth. The trees then released this moisture gently into the forest soils, which acted as vast surface-level reservoirs. Water slowly percolated into a multitude of subsurface soil and rock layers, draining into all of the major river systems, releasing water slowly and ensuring year-round stream and river flow. During periods of very high rainfall, however, the forest sponges would become fully saturated and would shed excess water rapidly, much as would be the case if the forest cover were removed. The ecological impact of this inability to absorb excess moisture was considerable. Even before the large-scale removal of forest cover in the nineteenth century, flooding wreaked havoc in both highland and lowland communities.[59]

∼

Thus, as we have seen, over deep time the ecology of the Sri Lankan highlands evolved in response to the waves of floral and faunal immigrants from the South Asian mainland. By the era of early human settlement, the highlands were a distinctive ecological region within the island, and they became increasingly distinctive over historical time in part because they were not inviting to dense human settlement. During the era of the ecological transformation of the Dry Zone, the highlands served as a refuge for fleeing wildlife. Following the collapse of the rajarata civilizations, the highlands themselves began to undergo substantial ecological conversion through a process of highland settlement. Chapter 2 explores the early-nineteenth-century part of these highland historical processes in greater detail.

~ CHAPTER 2 ~

The Highland Ecologies in the Early Nineteenth Century

*B*y the beginning of the nineteenth century, the patterns of human organization in the Kandyan highlands, although deeply rooted in the
rajarata period and traceable even earlier back in time to an ancient
cultural hearth in mainland South Asia, had grown increasingly distinctive
over time. The highland social order, for example, had evolved in idiosyncratic ways. The core South Asian cultural principles that created identity—
the requirement to choose a marriage partner from among those of one's own
social status and the requirement to carry out one type or another of specialized labor appropriate to that status—were still critically important. But in the
highlands of Sri Lanka, the ordering of the hierarchy of social groupings was
markedly different from the general model found on the mainland. In the
highlands, the grouping with the highest ascribed social status was the *goyigama* caste of rice farmers, whereas on the South Asian mainland it was the
priestly caste. Owing to the sheer poverty of the soils, the concomitant
difficulty of growing food, and the high cost of transport, virtually all groups
farmed, in addition to whatever additional specialized labor they might be
called upon to perform. The agricultural surplus was inadequate to support a
large social class beyond the mud of the paddy field. Moreover, the goyigama
caste was also the single largest grouping, comprising perhaps 50 percent of
the total population (although with many gradations of status within the
goyigama caste), and this, too, was in marked contrast to mainland South
Asia, where the priestly caste had always made up a small percentage of a given

social and political formation. In contrast to the more complex social orders found in many of the indigenous states of mainland South Asia, in the highlands no social group inherited as birthright a mantle of priestly responsibility; there were no brahmins.

This, then, was a South Asian social order that had been shaped by Buddhism, in that a priestly caste had been foregone in favor of a self-selecting and celibate monastic order that could not maintain its numbers through natural increase. The absence of a warrior grouping was also striking: all members of the social orders, with the exception of the monks themselves, were eligible to be called up for military service. And because one's birth into a given caste was determined by the merit gained in one's past lives, the social order itself was considered, at least in principle, both just and immutable, which lent it stability. All members of Kandyan society were marked by a deeply engrained tradition of deference to social superiors and of servility before power.

The political order of the Kandyan state had likewise undergone a process of evolution. Seated in the highlands for more than three centuries, the mountain polity had experienced nearly the full spectrum of political disturbance and intrigue that had plagued its predecessors. Yet, although the state had been involved in a number of wars with Kotte and the Portuguese in the sixteenth and seventeenth centuries and had seen its international trade sharply circumscribed by the tightening of Dutch control over the island's oceanic ports in the mid-eighteenth century, the Kandyan kingdom remained remarkably robust. In part, this was because there had been considerable continuity in the succession of rulers. Even when a lineage originally from South India insinuated itself into a position of dominant power in 1739 through marriage with the Kandyan kingly line, this provoked no disturbance. The problem of dynastic succession, which had plagued Kotte and the earlier rajarata states, was checked.

For most of the eighteenth century, the new dynastic South Indian Nayakkar family succeeded in ruling through a dispersed regional hierarchy of political officeholders. Its principal revenues were derived from the collection of land rents in kind. Its legitimacy derived from its willingness to work out a sharing of power with the major Buddhist monastic orders, which also had their administrative seats in the town of Kandy. The sacred and the temporal thus were organized into parallel systems of authority. Yet from the mid-eighteenth century onward, as the Kandyan state was forced to concede control of the littoral and international maritime trade to the Dutch East India Company (known by its Dutch initials, VOC), it became increasingly conservative and inward-looking.

The major shift in political and social norms in this late Kandyan period identified by historians came about when the Nayakkar leadership restricted admission to the Buddhist monkhood, which conferred honor on the initiate's family, to the goyigama caste. This was an attempt to solidify its claim to royal power through the courtship of elite goyigama elements.[1]

The Nayakkar grip on power, nonetheless, loosened in the final years of the eighteenth century. In 1798, only two years after the British occupation of the coastal littoral, the king of Kandy died and the highland kingdom found itself embroiled in a succession dispute. The British attempted to intervene in the political crisis and sent first a British embassy to Kandy to negotiate by treaty the acceptance by the Kandyan king of a British protectorate. The Kandyans rebuffed this initiative. In 1803 the British sent an invasion force, which met with disastrous defeat. But even this Kandyan military victory did not shore up the political position of the unpopular king, who set about unsuccessfully reining in growing disaffection among the Kandyan aristocrats.

The last years of the Kandyan state were marked by a widening political chasm between the Sinhalese aristocrats and the Nayakkar king. Following a gruesome act of political retribution carried out against the family members of an aristocrat accused of treason, the political control of the king collapsed. In the chaos that followed, the British were invited by the chief officer of state to take possession of the Kandyan kingdom, as a short-term measure. In a short forty days in 1815, British troops moved into the highlands without a significant military skirmish and established British possession. The British captured and exiled to southern India the Nayakkar king and his retinue.[2] Hoping to extend their authority in the highlands without bloodshed, the British offered liberal terms to the Kandyan peoples—to suffer British governance carried out with respect for Kandyan law and for Buddhism.[3]

This initial attempt at a *Pax Britannica* was short-lived. It was predicated on the hope that the Kandyan aristocrats would acquiesce in the transition to British rule. But within a year or two, the political calm was revealed as the eye of a storm. In 1817, in the province of Uva, in the rainshadow patana lands, Kandyan chiefs rose in armed rebellion against British rule and attempted to reestablish a Kandyan state. The Great Rebellion spread to many other Kandyan provinces. The British employed drastic counterinsurgency measures and repressed the rebellion with savagery, at great cost to the rebels and to many Kandyans who took no direct part in the uprising.[4] The repression marked a second beginning of rule in the highlands for the British, who now created a governing Kandyan board of revenue commissioners.

Stationing more than seventeen hundred troops in eleven outposts in the highlands,[5] the British determined that effective military control of the highlands could only be accomplished by punching through the forest barrier and rupturing the isolation of the mountain fastnesses.[6] Invoking the labor-service practices of the Kandyan state, the British marshaled corvée labor *(rajakariya)* to build roads. The British managed to open a rough-hewn and indirect route to Kandy (via Kurunagala) in 1821, and this immediately reduced transport costs from the coast to the highlands by 80 percent.[7] The highway from Colombo to Kandy, begun in 1820, was twenty-four feet wide, and by 1823 it allowed for rough cart traffic. The road reached completion in 1825. The British bridged the Mahaweli River, which allowed for easy access to Kandy itself, in 1832. Other new roads branched out from Kandy. The British finished an important thoroughfare to the north and northeast through Matale to Dambulla in 1832. A southern road to Nuwara Eliya in the upper highlands, begun in 1827, was completed ten years later.[8] This new road system continued to undergo expansion into the late nineteenth century. It was one of the keys that opened the door to the economic and ecological revolution that shook the highlands.

The Epidemiological and Epizoological Impacts of Early British Occupation

The British occupation of the maritime provinces, beginning in 1796, facilitated interaction between the ecological systems of the South Asian mainland and the island of Sri Lanka. One ecological impact flowed from the more frequent movement of livestock. The introduction of rinderpest (also known as murrain) from the animal-disease reservoir on the mainland had a devastating effect on the island, resulting in massive die-offs of both domestic and feral quadrupeds. James Cordiner, on the island between 1799 and 1804, reported that one-half of the cattle on the island died in a single epidemic (probably in the year 1800).[9] Its severity moved the government to action. Governor North imported more than three thousand head of cattle and offered a cash premium on every cow fit for breeding that was imported.[10] Another epidemic of rinderpest hit in 1806–7, and yet another in 1815–16. The latter epidemic was most severe in the northern part of the island. Not only cattle and buffalo but elephants, hogs, sambhur, and smaller deer succumbed.[11]

The establishment of British rule over the kingdom of Kandy in turn facilitated exchanges between the ecological systems of the maritime and highland regions. In particular, the repression of the Great Rebellion involved the movement of large numbers of soldiers and carriers from the coast through the Kandyan provinces, which had enormous ecological consequences. This movement appears to have accelerated the advance of the first great epidemic of cholera to occur during the British period, which spread from the subcontinent of India in 1817 to Jaffnapatam and Colombo in Sri Lanka in 1818, and thence to the rest of the island.[12]

Another epidemiological disaster was soon to follow. In July 1819, smallpox broke out in Colombo, and shortly thereafter spread into the Kandyan provinces. The last prior outbreak in the highlands had been some seventeen years earlier, and thus a considerable percentage of the population was fated to a first-time encounter with the disease. The British had attempted to extend Jennerian vaccination to the Kandyan populations beginning in 1816 but had met with considerable resistance.[13] The smallpox outbreak was deadly. In the hospital at Kandy, where only the worst local cases were admitted, the mortality was in excess of 50 percent.[14] The general mortality was undoubtedly much lower, but impossible to estimate. The British counted twelve hundred dead in the Kandyan provinces, but were in no position to measure the damage outside of the military stations.[15]

The inability of the British to enforce quarantine, which had been a standard practice of the Kandyan state during earlier smallpox outbreaks, contributed to the high mortality.[16] Major Thomas Skinner, the pioneer road builder who had a deep knowledge of the interior of the Kandyan provinces, described the chaos that reigned during the 1819–20 outbreak: "Directly persons were attacked, they were banished from their houses. Sometimes a temporary shed was built for them in which they were placed, with a little cooked food, to take their chance of recovery. Many of the poor creatures thus deserted were attacked and torn to pieces by wild animals before life was extinct."[17]

Thus in the wake of the repression of the Great Rebellion came continuing suffering and death. The destruction of food crops and work animals during the conflict caused the collapse of parts of the agricultural economy. In Uva, Wellase, and Bintenne, theaters of some of the most intense resistance and repression, severe damage had been done. The animal stock of the province had been particularly damaged, and in 1819 the British government prohibited the slaughter of any cow, calf, or female buffalo for a period of one year, in an effort to assist the rebuilding of stock.[18] In 1822, the government extended this prohibition to the entirety of the Kandyan provinces for two years.[19]

The lowered nutritional status of the Kandyan population increased its vulnerability to infectious disease and brought about elevated peaks of mortality. It took years to recover from the disaster. As Major Fletcher testified before the Cameron-Colebrooke committee in 1829:

> I came into the Civil Department of the Government about a year after the Rebellion and found the Country Suffering from famine and disease the consequence of the War. The population was much diminished particularly by the smallpox which reduced it at least a third & nearly a half. Without the help of Government the people could not have procured seed grain, which was given to them to be returned in kind without a specified time and it was 4 years before it could be repaid.[20]

Population Density and Settlement Patterns

The earliest highland population figures date from 1821, when Henry Marshall published an enumeration of the Kandyan population. These figures were based on a census "conducted by native chiefs, under the superintendence of the civil servants and accredited agents of Government employed in the respective districts." The total population of the Kandyan provinces, including the areas outside of the highlands, was thus figured at 253,554, although this total included estimates (rather than a count) for Matale and the eastern half of Nuwerakalawiya.[21] In the late 1820s, a second census was taken. It counted a population of 288,486 persons, spread over an area of 14,144 square miles, yielding a population density of about twenty persons per square mile.[22] These early censuses may be considered only approximations, but they convey accurately enough the sense of informed observers that the population densities in the highlands were quite low.

The large majority of people within the Kandyan provinces were settled along river and stream valleys, where there was a ready supply of fresh water for drinking and washing and for irrigation. In the highlands, topography dictated that there were no naturally occurring lakes. Rainfall drained out of the mountains through the major rivers and their multitude of tributaries. On the rainface side of the mountains, there was a generally dependable flow of surface water out of the hills year round, and the highland communities had invested their genius in the creation of intricate hillside terracing for paddy. In some locales, the rice farmers had sculpted the landforms as distinctively as had the Incans in the highlands of Peru. These terraced hillsides were the highland counterpart to the storage tanks of the Dry Zone of an earlier period. Both captured the regional water resources for the service of wet rice production.

Kandyans sited their settlements at elevations well below 3,000 feet because investments of labor at greater altitudes were far riskier. The higher lands were less desirable, in that they were cooler and cloudier, with less solar radiation available for growth of rice. On the rainshadow side of the mountains, in the generally lower-lying province of Uva, some Kandyan communities had constructed catchment tanks. These tanks were destroyed by the British during the repression of the Kandyan rebellion of 1817–18, and thereafter these rainshadow communities came to practice the general style of agriculture of the wetter highlands, although with far greater dependence upon the production of rain-fed grains.

During the early decades of the nineteenth century, cultural evidence suggests that at least in some regions of the highlands there was land hunger. In the area surrounding the town of Kandy, for example, the practice of polyandry was "not infrequent." The sharing of a single wife by two or more men (who might or might not be brothers) was explained to be the result of having inadequate means to support a family, and thus was a more frequent practice among the poor. Others of greater means might also practice polyandry for the purpose of preventing an impoverishing division of inheritable land.[23]

Further evidence concerning a socially enforced imbalance between population and land resources may be deduced from the strikingly skewed sex ratio of the Kandyan population, in which males greatly outnumbered females. This seems to have been the direct consequence of widespread female infanticide. As Marshall observed:

> The small proportion of females to males (84 to 100) is a very remarkable circumstance. Many motives exist among the people which might induce the males to evade enumeration; no cause is, however, known that could occasion an omission of females. In England, the proportion of females to males is 98.8 to 100. To what, then, are we to attribute the great difference in this respect between the Kandyan provinces and Great Britain? It may be feared that the disproportion is in part owing to the occasional murder of female infants. The father of the new-born babe either carries or sends the little innocent to the jungle, and there abandons it; in general, the poor infant soon dies from cold, or it is devoured by wild beasts. This practice is known to obtain in some parts of the country, particularly in those districts where want, indigence, and disease greatly prevail. In these insalubrious and uncultivated tracts, the poverty of the inhabitants is often extreme; and this

circumstance is sometimes assigned as an excuse for female infanticide. It has been observed, in the districts where this practice prevails, that more than one female child is rarely to be found in a family. The chances of the life of each infant being foretold at birth, it becomes the interest of the fortune-teller to ascertain the views of the male parent (for the mother is rarely consulted) in regard to the preservation of the offspring. Infants whose lot in life is predicted to be unlucky, are generally neglected, and often exposed. According to the information I have been able to collect on this subject, it appears that male infants are rarely considered to have an irretrievably bad fortune, neither are the first-born infants of a family. The female infants that follow are said to be often considered unfortunate, and sometimes suffer the immediate consequences of such a prediction. The people talk of the exposure of infants as not an uncommon circumstance, and without appearing to attach the slightest shade of culpability to the unnatural act. Still, however, it is done with some degree of privacy, and individuals seem unwilling to admit that they have thus treated their own infants. Under the native government, the exposure of infants was prohibited: the king's mandate, however, had little influence in restraining the practice, particularly in the districts distant from Kandy. To what extent infant murder now obtains, it is impossible to conjecture; but it is to be hoped Government will endeavor to put a stop to such a horrid practice.[24]

This practice of female infanticide "particularly in districts distant from Kandy" must have been a significant constraint on population growth.

The Economy of the Kandyan State

All early-nineteenth-century observers agreed that agriculture was the economic foundation of the Kandyan kingdom. Early British administrators were convinced that the Sinhalese agricultural system was "feudal" and that this system constrained inordinately the possibilities for the improvement of agriculture. The key to economic growth thus appeared to be in liberating the farmers from excessive taxation and in allowing them to produce for the market. The British located the core problem in the system of land tenure. This system gave local headmen substantial control over arable lands, which were worked by social inferiors; it artificially restricted access to freehold and thus constrained production. As J. Burnand said in his 1809 memoir written to assist A. Johnston in his efforts to promulgate suggestions for the improvement of agriculture on the island:

The Native chiefs of the interior are, generally speaking the greatest obstacle to the establishment of Agriculture, because it is more or less adverse to their interests. They and their families, are in possession of the best fields, which their dependents cultivate for them at a low rate, it is for their interest that grain should be dear, and consequently that the whole of the lands shou'd not be cultivated, nor so well as they might be.[25]

Burnand's observation echoed that of the British sailor Robert Knox, who was detained as a prisoner in the Kandyan kingdom for nineteen years in the second half of the seventeenth century. Knox, too, was critical of Kandyan agriculture, and like Burnand this earlier writer placed the blame for its low productivity squarely on the Kandyan political system. He noted that the Sinhalese farmers would do "only what their necessities force them to do, that is, to get food and raiment. Yet in this I must a little vindicate them, for what indeed should they do with more than food and raiment, seeing as their estates increase so do their taxes! And although the people be generally covetous, spending but little, scraping together what they can, yet such is the Government they are under, that they are afraid to be known to have anything les [*sic*] it be taken away from them."[26]

Other writers stressed the fact that the Kandyan economy was constrained by the lack of an adequate transportation network. As George Turnour, revenue commissioner for the Kandyan provinces, testified in the 1820s: "There are very few markets in the Country, and in general it may be said, that nine tenths of the produce is consumed where it is grown. If there is a succession of favourable seasons, and the surplus on hand should become great, cultivation is checked, on account of the difficulty of disposing of the grain."[27]

It is clear, nonetheless, that although both internal and external trade were quite limited, villagers regularly produced grain in excess of what could be consumed by the household. Villagers held their lands on grant from the ruling authority, and in obligation to the local headman or to the local Buddhist temple, and farmers labored to harvest an agricultural surplus in order to pay their taxes in kind. The extent of the tax obligation varied between one-tenth and one-half of the harvest, a range of variation that seems to have been of long standing.[28] The Kandyan taxation and land tenure system itself, however, was not static. It evolved. By the end of the eighteenth century, service taxes began to be paid by individuals for the whole of the land that they used, rather than by each class of land. Litigation increased sharply, even between members of the same family, with regard to land that was put to the production of dry grains.[29]

The Kandyan economy was also at least partly monetized, although the currency that did circulate was not of Kandyan provenance. The entire island had long been familiar with the wider currency zones of the Indian Ocean world. Currencies from India (in particular, the silver rupee), from the Dutch East Indies, and elsewhere made up a complex zone of money and exchange. At least from the early Dutch period (1658–1796), the extension of trade credit within Sri Lanka had been handled by merchant bankers from South India.[30] In the highlands, the Kandyan state kept a stock of money, but currency was not used for most transactions. Most Kandyans of goyigama caste paid tribute in grain or in labor to their social betters or to the Buddhist monastic orders who oversaw the maintenance of the temples. Similarly, most Kandyans of lower caste paid their obligations in kind, and these might include the artisanal crafts appropriate to their caste.

On the other hand, the payments of fines to the chiefs were discharged in currency, and funds for this purpose (and others) could be borrowed, usually upon the mortgage of land. It was, however, mostly individuals in considerable distress who were reduced to mortgaging land, and the rates of interest ran high. If the principal was not repaid within the year, the usual rate of interest charged to the mortgagee was 100 percent in the town of Kandy, although additional interest did not accumulate thereafter; in the countryside the rate was 50 percent. Traders were also able to borrow money within the Kandyan kingdom, and for merchants the interest was generally figured on a monthly basis, at roughly 20 percent per annum, although in the last years of the independent Kandyan state, the state sanctions against higher interest rates did not hold.

Although the rate of transactional money use was low, it was general practice for many cultivators to borrow paddy or other seed grain in order to be able to plant. These extensions of agricultural credit in kind were quite expensive. The established rate of interest was 50 percent per annum, with the entire debt in seed corn required to be paid at the time of harvest. If the cultivator, after handing over the interest and principal payment in seed at harvest time, found himself in need of another extension of seed corn, the same creditor would consider the grain as a new loan, chargeable at 50 percent per annum.[31]

In sum, at least in core areas, the Kandyan political system placed constraints upon the expansion of the highland agricultural economy. The political system focused upon the extraction of agricultural surplus and tethered farmer to social superior through the regular extension of credit on usurious terms. Under these conditions, the various layers of elite society, including the king and his retinue, the temples and their doyens, and the village headmen could exercise considerable influence over simple economic growth, through their control of access to cultivable land. Yet, taking the longer view, it is apparent that this control was unstable and imperfect. Complex and idiosyncratic land-tenure arrangements (including access to chena lands) evolved over the centuries before British rule. This complexity had its roots in these historical processes of agricultural expansion.

Paddy Rice

Within the Kandyan village communities, farmers invested most of their agricultural labor hours in the cultivation of rice, and rice was the principal agricultural product. An early estimate of the produce of the Central Province in 1835, for example, listed 1,575,000 bushels of paddy (787,500 bushels of clean rice) and only 186,775 bushels of fine (dry) grains; 130,000 bushels of coffee; 100,000 bushels of cotton, and much smaller amounts of gram, pepper, maize (Indian corn), sesame (known by the trade name "gingelly"), and mustard.[32] This concentration of human energy on the production of rice had a very long history, dating back to the era of the great irrigation works, and the cultivation of rice was highly valorized. But in the Dry Zone itself, following the collapse of the rajarata civilization, rain-fed grains had become the dietary staple, and the tradition of rice farming had moved up into the hills even though the cultivation of rice was extremely labor-intensive and was recognized as onerous by the peasantry.[33] So strong was the bias toward rice cultivation that the lesser grains—principally kurakkan and maize—were stigmatized as less nutritious than rice, although it is now known that this is not the case.[34] Simply put, the cultural preference for rice was a reflection of the social order. To live in a village, near a temple and a tank with a cultivated home garden nearby, suggested greater merit than to live at great distance from the rice fields, in the temporary shelters of the chena fields, where crops other than rice were grown. The social order shimmered in the brilliant mirror of the tank.

In the highlands, the cultivation of rice was a hazardous affair. The diversity of the microclimates precludes any simple gloss of the agronomic systems, but some general features can be outlined. The monsoons governed the schedule of plantings. Over many centuries, Sri Lankan rice farmers had developed a broad array of rice varieties, selected for their varying rates of maturation. Some could be harvested at 60 days, others at 90 or even 120 days. Rice farmers planted in two major seasons. In the *maha* (great) season the fields were prepared and sown between July and August and were reaped in January and February. During the *yala* (small) season, the fields were prepared between 10 March and 10 May and reaped between July and September. Two successive crops of paddy (yala or maha) were rarely taken out of the same field.[35] Even this broad organizational schema must be somewhat qualified because, within each season, the planting of the individual rice fields was staggered in time, as well as planted with differently maturing varieties. One of the principal benefits of this staggered planting regime was to reduce the labor shortages that could occur at critical moments during the agricultural season. Some tasks—for example, those of field preparation and harvesting—demanded group labor, and Kandyan rice farmers took turns working on each others' fields. The staggered planting schedules also reduced the risk of crop shortfalls owing to short-term drought or flood.

Yet for all of the labor invested and for all of its cultural valorization, rice cultivation was hard won. Nineteenth-century writers were nearly unanimous in their observations about the low returns to seed in the rice fields. Estimates of an average return ranged from fourfold up to fifteenfold, in marked contrast to the average returns of twenty- to fiftyfold that were said to obtain in the best Asian rice paddies. This was true in the low country as well as in the highlands.[36] In addition, quite apart from the maturation requirements of the rice varieties, the other segments of the tillage-to-harvest cycle were daunting—forty days to till; sixteen days for reaping; and thirty days for winnowing.[37] Attempts to measure the gross production of rice over time founder on the flexible nature of the Kandyan agronomic categories. The Kandyans (and low-country Sinhalese, too) had no standard measure of surface area. The unit known as the *amunam* represented the amount of land that could be sown with a unit measure of seed, also known as the amunam; the surface area sown by an amunam of seed varied greatly by local topography and soil type. Variations in local weather also had a significant influence on yield. A minidrought in the midst of a critical few weeks of rice growth could spell disaster for the field. An excess of rainfall could do the same.[38] In addition, rice diseases could utterly destroy the crop.[39]

Because of the staggered schedule of planting, some section or another of villagers' paddy fields was generally vulnerable to insects and wild animals, and thus rice farmers developed elaborate ceremonial rituals to ward off these plagues. Villagers built bamboo lookout huts roofed with rice straw, or more occasionally with fronds from coconut palms near the fields. Watchers perched in the elevated huts, armed with double-stringed bows that were capable of launching either arrows or rocks, depending upon the size of the predator to be chased off the paddy. Some fields were also outfitted with systems of alarm rattles that could be shaken by means of coir ropes attached to the hut.[40] Others used stick scarecrow figures or flags attached to sticks, to be animated by the wind, as a defense against birds. This was serious business, and hard-won crops could be lost quickly through a lack of vigilance.

Other losses might be incurred in the postharvest period. And indeed, because of the high level of rainfall in the Wet Zone, the highland rices required storage techniques different than those in the lowlands. The style of Dry Zone rice storage huts in the household compound were found to be less secure against rot and fungus and had to be abandoned in favor of storage inside the cultivator's mud-brick-walled family house, thatched with rice straw. There a room could be set aside for separate storage, or at the least a large woven basket (a meter in diameter and one and one-third meters in height) could be installed in the cooking corner to hold the paddy against hunger.

The recycling of the by-products of rice cultivation was deeply integrated into the ecological system of the farming communities. At the end of the threshing period, the domesticated water buffalo or the few cattle owned by the villagers would be turned out to graze on the rice stubble, and the manure dropped on the fields would be well worked into the mud in the field preparations for the coming rice season. The rice straw from which the paddy grain had been removed would be gathered and burned or a portion allotted to fodder for the cattle and water buffalo.[41] The ash would be spread over the fields as fertilizer. Even so, the mud flats and irrigated terraces were depleted of essential fertilizing minerals and generally could not be worked two seasons in a row. The fields thus fallowed would be colonized by invasive grasses, which would fix, although in a highly inefficient manner, some nitrogen from the air in the soil, and permit a future cropping of paddy.

Not all wet rice fields, however, were laid out on the carved flats of the valleys. Some farmers depended upon terraced hill paddy; others banked first upon the irrigated mudflats and had recourse to the hills only in the event of failure there. Everywhere in the settled highlands, control of water was of the essence. Farmers could and did divert water to the service of paddy cultivation not only from the major rivers but from mountain streams. By the end of the century, demographic pressure had pushed settlements well away from the river courses. Some waterworks involved considerable engineering feats, stretching for miles to move the precious resource away from its natural flow pattern. Some aqueducts were built above ground, of stone or bamboo or mud; others were subterranean.[42]

Chena Lands

The chena lands were those on which the villagers grew dry grains, including rain-fed rice and cotton, and they were neither irrigated nor terraced. Initially, the villagers charred their chena fields from the surrounding forests by selectively lopping the high and middle canopies of the rain forests, allowing them to dry, and burning the shattered trunks, foliage, and understory. If any trees with economic use were present in the forest, the highland farmers spared them the ax and the firestick. These trees could later be used as watchhuts.

After the fire, the villagers allowed the blackened, smoking earth, out of which stumps jutted, to cool, and then spread out the ashes. There was no need to rip out the roots of the burned plants and trees because the introduced cultigens had shallow roots that were not in competition with the deeper root systems of the trees and shrubs. This conversion by fire of the biomass into organic ash allowed for the broadcast sowing of dry rice, kurakkan, or maize. These cultivations, like those of the irrigated lands, were subject to the random variations in weather, and the crops grown in these slashed-and-burned fields at times utterly failed.

Growing any crop at all on chena lands, without the benefit of controlled irrigation (which introduced fresh nutrients through sediment transport) and without the benefit of livestock manure, exhausted the productive potential of the soil after one or two harvests. The chena land would then be abandoned to a process of natural colonization by opportunistic flora. Depending on the properties of the soils, the degree of demographic pressure from the neighboring villagers, and the success of the irrigated paddy flats, chena land could be let fallow for anywhere from five to thirty years. The historical record will not permit exact quantification, but most early nineteenth-century writers on chena indicated that a period from seven to fifteen years was usual. Villagers used floral indicators to judge whether abandoned land was ready to be burned again. One positive indicator was if the secondary growth trees had attained the girth of a man's arm. Another was if the undergrowth had attained a height and density to shield an elephant from view. A negative indicator was the presence of *Gloriosa superba* (Sinhala: *hiyangala*) flowers, which indicated that the soil had become "bitter." Another was colonization by *Calotrepis gigantes* (Sinhala: *wara*), which meant that the soil was too poor to bother to recultivate.[43]

The significance of chena in Sri Lanka was large because it was a general practice. By contrast, in early-nineteenth-century South India, slash-and-burn techniques were principally the province of itinerant cultivators in the mountainous regions.[44] Chena lands were more commonly cultivated by lower caste (non-goyigama) groups, for whom caste restrictions sometimes prevented their owning the rice fields in which they labored. The role of chena cultivation in the highlands was rather the reverse of what it was in the Dry Zone.[45] At least for the goyigama caste, which made up roughly half of the Kandyan population, chena cultivation was a necessary adjunct to the village agricultural endeavor, rather than the principal crux. There was, however, considerable variation by subregion. In Narlandé, for example, about thirty miles from Kandy in the mid-nineteenth century the communities lived for the most part on kurakkan, rather than rice.[46] Thus, the role of chena cultivation varied. In some regions, it was neither of marginal importance nor only a hedge against famine; it was the core agronomic practice.[47]

Chena lands had a larger significance than simply being the source of rain-fed grain. These burned-over fields were also essential to the cultivation of vegetables and yams, which were a core element in the Kandyan diet. And the importance of chena extended beyond food production. Cotton was exclusively a dry-field crop, and chena cultivation was essential for the production of common cloth.[48]

The extent of chena cultivation at the beginning of the nineteenth century was considerable, but like so many other matters Sri Lankan and agricultural, it defies exact quantification. It is clear that over the course of the nineteenth century, chena cultivation increased enormously in extent and was one of the two principal forces that brought about the deforestation of the highlands. There were significant variations by subregion. Most of the chena expansion took place below elevations of 3,000 feet, although chena was found as high as 6,000 feet toward the end of the nineteenth century. In the upper highland district of Nuwara Eliya, for example, roughly 2,000 acres were cleared annually for chena, in comparison with roughly 7,300 acres of wet paddy. Because the chena fields were cleared only once every several years, however, the extent of the chena lands would have been considerably greater than those of paddy, and indeed was probably a low multiple of them.[49]

In most villages, the chena fields, often numerous and only sometimes contiguous, were generally at various stages of succession toward scrub jungle.

These burned-over fields were not of such size as to create a problem with soil erosion. The reversion to scrub was relatively rapid, and a dense and tangled growth soon protected the bare and depleted soils from the percussive impact of rainfall. Chena practices caused some soil erosion, but by and large, the chena soils of the highlands maintained their structural integrity, although the soils' fertility declined after their use and remained degraded for an extended period.[50]

Kurakkan *(Eleusine coracana)*, or finger millet, grew acceptably well in the highlands, and it could be cultivated up to an elevation of 4,000 feet. It enjoyed a number of extremely positive attributes. It is a highly nutritive grain; in fact it is higher in protein, fat, and minerals than rice or maize. And the straw of this dry grain also made valuable fodder for cattle and buffalo. It stored well for extended periods without undergoing damage from pests and diseases.[51] Kurakkan also required less water—only twenty to thirty-five inches of rain per season—than did rice, and thus in the highlands it was generally planted in the mountains' rainshadow and in the intermonsoonal periods. Its cultivation could be ruined by too much rainfall. Kurakkan, like rice, was subject to a fungal blast *(Pyricularia oryzae)*, but this was the only important disease that plagued this dry grain, and even into the early twenty-first century this blast had not become sufficiently serious to warrant direct curative treatment. Yet in the hierarchy of foodstuffs, kurakkan did not enjoy an exalted position.[52] Somewhat remarkably, this attitude reigned despite the fact that returns to seed were on the order of sixtyfold to ninetyfold.[53]

Kurakkan was not the only important dry grain grown in the highlands. Maize was also cultivated, particularly in the drier Uva region. Maize, like kurakkan, enjoyed a pestological advantage over rice. The destructive diseases that plague maize cultivation in the Western world (particularly the United States) were absent in Sri Lanka.[54] Particularly in wet years, this afforded the cultivators of these dry grains a decreased vulnerability in comparison with either dry or wet rice cultivators.

In some areas, the extent of chena cultivation was a function of the success of the irrigated rice crop. When the rice yields were lower than expected, a compensatory investment in labor could be made in the chena fields, to make up for the shortfall. This point comes out clearly in, for example, a consideration of the annual agricultural production of the Badulla district at mid-century. In 1855, the rice crop was poor. Just under 182,000 bushels of rice were harvested, and farmers went to work in their chena fields, bringing in a little more than 90,000 bushels of dry grain. By contrast, in 1858, the rice crop was a fine one.

More than 280,000 bushels were reaped, and farmers left their chena fields in fallow; fewer than 16,600 bushels of dry grain were realized.[55]

The Forest or Home Garden

The highland village complexes, close by the paddy mud flats, extended from the valleys up into the surrounding hills, where both terraced rice fields and chena fields ate into the natural forest. The Kandyan villagers exploited the natural abundance of the highland forests for medicinal plants and for wild fruits, nuts, leaves, and spices. They had regular recourse to the forest and chena edges for a wide variety of medicinal plants. These were the base of the ayurvedic system of medicine practiced in the highlands. The forest also provided a wealth of lower-quality edibles, which served as a safety net during times of duress. These were "famine foods" that could sustain life until the normal patterns of cultivation were reestablished after drought or flooding or political disruption. In the Kandyan period, high-status individuals had the right to gather honey in nearby forests; these practices continued in the British period. Another general pattern that carried over into the late nineteenth century was the collection of firewood and fencing sticks, which had been a general right of villagers in most of the Kandyan royal forests.

Over the course of the nineteenth century, as the middle and upper highland forests were cleared for plantation agriculture and for expanded chena cultivation, many villagers found their access to the natural abundance of the forests circumscribed.[56] In the face of increasing demographic pressure, highland villagers began to give greater attention to the cultivation, rather than gathering, of fruits, nuts, vegetables, and spices on plots that adjoined their compounds, in the "forest gardens" or "home gardens" (Sinhala: *géwatte*).[57] The forest garden came to involve the mixed cropping of trees yielding timber and fuelwood, as well as food, fruits, nuts, and medicines. These gardens typically were located in the lower and middle highlands, at elevations between 600 and 2,400 feet. Little sunlight penetrated the multistory canopy of the forest garden, and thus it was not possible to grow grass or fodder crops for large animals, although chickens could be kept and fed on household refuse.[58] These areas came to provide an ideal environment for birds. They were the avicultural complement to the biologically-diverse habitats that were formed where the chena and paddy fields met the forest edge. These forest gardens, moreover, had an impact on the surrounding ecologies. They were centers from which the seeds of the selected trees and shrubs could be disseminated by birds and wild animals. Even within the forest gardens there were specialized microecologies. Some of the wetter spots near the rice fields were suitable for tuber crops such as cassava *(Manihot esculenta)*, sweet potato *(Ipomoea batatas)*, taro *(Colocasia spp.)*, and yams *(Dioscorea spp.)*, all of which had been introduced from abroad in earlier centuries and whose cultivation had become established in the highlands.

Particularly prominent in the forest gardens were *jack* trees *(Artocarpus heterophyllus)*. Although jack also grew naturally in the rainforest, farmers prized them for their fruit and planted them in their gardens. They served as a buffer against want. In the event of grain-crop failures, villagers fell back on the jack fruit as a staple. Indeed, so common were the tall jack trees that they served as arboreal markers, allowing travelers to identify the presence of human settlements from a considerable distance. Yet, missing from the garden of the early nineteenth century were many of the plants commonly found in contemporary forest gardens. The clove tree, the nutmeg tree, the cardamon plant, and other staples were borne to the highlands on the winds of the nineteenth-century ecological revolution.

Animal Husbandry

The highland village systems depended in some good measure on draft power from two animals. The most important was the water buffalo *(Bubalus bubalis)*, an animal slightly lighter in color and perhaps less hairy than its wild cousin, which ranged freely in the island wildernesses, like the elephant, although the wild buffalo seems to have preferred the Dry Zone to the Wet Zone.[59]

The buffalo had several prime virtues. First, it required only pasture for its sustenance. The buffalo could simply be turned out into the fallowed chena and paddy fields or be allowed to forage more widely in the patanas. Second, the water buffalo was highly competent for agricultural tasks. It was capable of negotiating the mud flats by virtue of the structure of its foot, which could expand to provide traction. It could thereby pull the Sinhalese plow and the flat board that, after plowing, smoothed the surface of the muddy field so that the irrigation waters flooded a level terrain (this was done to prevent water from pooling in the low spots, which was wasteful and could damage the growth of paddy). Third, the buffalo was a competent producer of milk; indeed, buffalo curd was one of the principal animal foods known in the highlands. Fourth, the buffalo bred well, the cow producing a calf every year and giving milk for seven months.

Buffalo husbandry was not without its problems, however. The buffalo was never domesticated as fully as the livestock of more temperate zones. The buffalo ranged widely for pasture and bred freely with its wild cousin. The net result was that buffalo remained a volatile presence, particularly to humans unknown to them. Powerful animals, they were known to charge and trample their victims underfoot, and then to use their black, thick horns (which pointed backwards) to gore. In addition, buffalo calves had delicate constitutions and were readily subject to disease.[60]

The other draft animal was the *Bos indicus* (Sinhala: *harakah*), or Indian humped cow. It, too, was capable of living solely off pasturage, but it was unsuited to field work because it could manoeuver neither in the paddy fields nor on the steep hills. It was also smaller and less strong than the buffalo. Additionally, it was a poor producer of milk. Since its principal use was for cartage, there were few in the highlands. This cow had been originally introduced from India, and nineteenth-century observers distinguished two varieties. The Lankan animal was small, compact, hardy, and black in color. It may have been a specialized variety of the generic *Bos indicus,* which had adapted itself to the poor nutrition afforded by the island's grasses by becoming smaller in form. It was thought to be inferior to the Indian variety, which came either from the Bengal (northeastern) or the Coromandel (southeastern) coasts.[61] The Sri Lankan animal was of very small size; it grew and matured slowly; its bones were light and poorly developed; and its horns were small and stunted. In its favor was the qualified recommendation that the cart oxen (the castrated bulls) had good muscular development for their size.[62]

One direct result of the poor quality of the indigenous grasses was that the pattern of human exploitation of buffalo and oxen in the highlands (and elsewhere) in Sri Lanka was exactly the opposite of the patterns in India. As Sir H. Marcus Fernando noted:

> Dealing with animals destined for agriculture the most remarkable feature is that out of about one and one half million animals less than a third are buffalos; and these are practically the only animals that are used for plowing and mudding the rice fields. Oxen are seldom used for such purposes. On the other hand oxen are used for cart transport and buffalos are seldom seen as drought animals. This practice is almost the reverse of what takes place in India. All throughout that great country the farm animals par excellence are oxen. They are used for the plow on

Fig. 2.1
From R. K. de Silva, Early Prints of Ceylon *(Sri Lanka) 1800–1900 (London, 1985):*
Samuel Daniell's "The Water Carrier"
"The cattle of Ceylon generally used for this purpose (carrying water), are of a very di-
minutive size, with short horns, and a large hump across the shoulders. The most
predominant color is black. They are in fact, the common horned cattle of the continent
of India, from whence they are frequently imported into the island, especially after an
epidemic of distemper, peculiar to them, has thinned their numbers."

rice fields as well as on high land and for the drawing of water from wells for irrigation. One scarcely sees a single buffalo working on the fields, but the latter are
the chief animals in the transport of heavy goods all over Northern India. Enormous buffalos as docile as cart horses in England may be seen yoked to large sized
carts all over Bengal, Punjab and as far south as Ahmedabad.

The reasons for this difference in use between India and Ceylon are obvious. In
Ceylon the average village bred bull is so small and so weak that it is useless for even
the primitive plow of the rice field. On the other hand the buffalos as bred in the
rural districts are semi-wild, and are so unruly that they cannot be used for the cart.[63]

Somewhat surprisingly, perhaps, small ruminants were not introduced
widely into the highland farming systems. The sheep might have been well
suited to the up-country, except for the fact that the spacing of the hair follicles

in its coat made the animal particularly susceptible to the highland leech. This in itself was an insuperable impediment to sheep culture. The leech bites attracted flies and became infected; the sores were incurable. Nor was the goat ever integrated into the highland farming systems. Like the sheep, it would have required full-time supervision by a herder and would have needed to graze beyond the paddy and chena fields, in the open patanas. There the small ruminants would have been vulnerable to predation by wild cats and jackals. The same concern about predation may well have inhibited the production of poultry. Some Kandyan farmers did raise poultry, but this was far from a common practice. Such poultry raising that did take place was carried out principally by the Muslim communities of the highlands.[64]

Human–Wild Animal Interactions

The chena and paddy fields, cut and burned from the surrounding forests, were edge habitats par excellence and duly attracted a wide range of fauna interested in eating paddy and dry grain before the villagers could get to it. These edge habitats, including the forest gardens, were rich in bird life and attracted wild pigs, deer, rats, and insect life. Villagers responded with a variety of inventive methods to scare away the birds and larger animals, and to keep the insects at bay they resorted to smoke and ayurvedic medicinal preparations. These efforts were not, of course, fully effective, and villagers fought an ongoing battle against the predators that thrived in the edge habitats. The villagers also hunted the animal predators for food. Hares and deer were fairly easy to bag because they could be hunted with bow and arrow, and they made good eating. The wild pig was also said to be esteemed as a foodstuff; but hunting the wild pig involved considerable danger and seems to have been more of an exploit than the routine harvesting of small game.

Well into the middle third of the nineteenth century, the extensive forest and patana lands above 3,000 feet remained a natural reserve for many wild animal species. The Kandyan villagers did not establish permanent communities in the middle and upper highlands because the decreased solar radiation at these elevations made wet rice and dry grain cultivation too difficult. This in turn provided natural protection to the wild fauna. Villagers did occasionally hunt at higher elevations, but the Kandyan hunting expeditions into the middle and upper highlands were small and their exploits were episodic, principally for the gathering of honey and the shooting of small game.[65]

The Kandyans, although Buddhist, were not averse to killing game for the table. Wild deer and wild pig, if not dietary staples, were not unknown to most Kandyan households. Indeed, as Robert Knox, writing in the second half of the seventeenth century, observed, hunting was common practice in the Kandyan kingdom. Knox's observation is interesting because it provides a baseline against which to measure change in the eighteenth and nineteenth centuries. It is clear that at least official attitudes toward hunting were changed in the years following the accession of the South Indian Nayakkar lineage to power. In an effort to legitimize their rule, from the mid-eighteenth century they supported a revival of Buddhism in the Kandyan kingdom. There, the newly empowered Buddhist orders flexed their political muscle, at least in the highlands, where their religious orders were seated near the Dalada Maligawa, the temple said to hold the tooth of Lord Buddha. As the first British official to carry the title of resident, Sir John D'Oyly, noted, the rules of the Kandyan state that governed hunting had been tightened up considerably in the mid-eighteenth century:

> Hunting and Killing of Animals. This practice was declared unlawful in the Upper Districts within the last 50 or 60 Years on the Ground of being contrary to the Precepts of Religion, and in some Instances was punished by Whipping through the streets of Kandy, and Imprisonment in a Distant Village. In other Cases, which came under the Cognizance of the Chiefs, the Transgressors escaped with slighter Corporal Punishment, or Imprisonment, and Fine.
>
> The Practice however continued in Secret and was in fact connived at by the Kandyan Chiefs, to whom a portion of the slain Animal was usually Presented, and it was Chiefly when the necessary Precaution was Neglected that the Hunter subjected himself to the Penalty.[66]

It is not possible to come to a judgment concerning the impact of the mid-eighteenth-century prohibition or, indeed, to quantify any aspects of Kandyan game hunting. Highland game hunting was neither highly organized nor large-scale, however, and there is no evidence in the historical record that suggests the pressure was sufficiently heavy as to reduce appreciably the populations of the game species.

A rather different set of considerations governed relations between the larger animals and the villagers because of the large animals' powers of destruction. The leopard represented a potential threat to domesticated cattle and buffalo and even to small children, but it took its prey almost exclusively among the wild fauna of the forest and patana; in fact, the leopard was rarely seen by human eyes. The sloth bear, too, kept largely to its own isolated habitats, although an occasional incursion into a remote village was not unknown. And the bear was herbivorous and thus did not kill to eat. For the villager, by far the most problematic large animal was the highland elephant. These elephants did not live solely from the grassland pasture or forestland browse. Throughout the highlands, elephants made incursions into the rice fields of the villagers. They raided mostly at night, and it was not a simple matter of the elephants' being short of food: the pachyderms were drawn to the village ponds and irrigation tanks. But more importantly, the raids took place because the cultivated crops were more palatable, nutritious, and concentrated in one place than were their wild counterparts.[67]

Here the villagers' agronomic strategy to stagger the planting of a variety of rices carried a decided vulnerability. It ensured that confrontations with elephants would be ongoing. And because the rices matured and had to be harvested at different times, farmers were often unable to combine their efforts at crop protection, and consequently were less effective.[68] Elephants are particularly attracted to paddy both when it flowers and when it ripens. And under the Kandyan farming system, one set of rice fields or another might be in bloom or ready for harvest for much of the maha and yala seasons. This meant that when elephant herds came into the orbit of a settled community, they had little incentive to move on. Herds often remained in the forests nearby to enjoy extended periods of night raiding.

What was true for the paddy fields was true also for the chena lands. Elephants were drawn to the nutritious kurakkan and hill paddy, and marauding elephants could do extraordinary damage in a short period of time. Farmers built lookouts and huts adjoining their chena fields, but because the fields were often somewhat isolated, the farmers' efforts at protection of rain-fed crops were principally effective only against deer and smaller ruminants. There was little a solitary farmer could do against a herd of elephants, particularly if he lacked a rifle.

Against rogue elephants that seemed bent upon large-scale destruction, it was possible for the villagers to organize a determined hunt to the death. But these hunts were uncommon. In the lowlands, by contrast, it was well-established practice to hunt down rogue elephants, and indeed the lay of the land could also afford the hunters the ability to sweep large areas and to drive the disoriented elephants toward an enclosure, or kraal. In the highlands, though, the possibility of organizing large-scale hunting of elephants was all but foreclosed by the topography of the rough terrain. The giant, grey pachyderms were capable of fleeing up and over and down mountainous inclines where trailing human hunters exposed themselves to great risk. The elephants had the superior ability to scale difficult slopes.

Kandyan Perceptions of Highland Ecologies

The highland villagers described the flora of their ecological world in a nuanced folk language.[69] There were three great classifications of flora—trees, creepers, and herbs. And native Sinhala-speakers drew many sorts of distinctions within these classifications that provided close floral definition. Distinctions were drawn between plants that were indigenous and those that were exotic. In addition, the locale of growth might often be expressed by prefixes, and in this manner plants could be described, to cite a few examples, as growing on land, in water, by the seacoast, or in valleys. Sinhala-speakers also employed terms for size and color, fruit and flower, as well as an array of adjectives to describe the plant physiology—scaly, milky, thorny, angular, dentate, and so forth. Other terms could describe other properties of a plant—oily, bitter, astringent, fibrous—or could associate plants with spiritual forces (e.g., a devil) or with the animal world (e.g., serpent, elephant, or pig).[70] Parallel to this descriptive language was the specialized knowledge of the practitioners of ayurvedic medicine, which was based upon a profound understanding of the medicinal qualities of the island flora. But it is also clear that villagers grouped some plants together under a single descriptor, and that the system of nomenclature lacked the rigor of nineteenth-century botanical science. Local knowledge of the highland flora was strongest on the flora in proximity to human settlements. Highland villagers were unfamiliar with some of the upper highland flora. For example, many trees grew in remote areas where there were no villages and had no real names. And considerable confusion was introduced in the nineteenth century when low-country carpenters gave low-country names to the newly discovered, upcountry trees.[71]

But even the remoter highland forests were not perceived as a hostile or threatening environment. In a broad sense, they were regarded as part of a spiritual garden reservoir found throughout the island that lay beyond the ken of human communities. As W. A. de Silva, a nineteenth-century writer on Sinhalese plant lore, noted:

In different parts of the Island, where there are unexplored jungles, there is a common belief in the existence of what I may call a "god's orchard." The god is said to be Saman, and "Saman Deviyannagé Uyana" is said to exist in the heart of the jungles where no man is able to penetrate. These gardens are said to be replete with all varieties of delicious fruit, which hang on the trees in abundance. It is also said that if a person loses his way in the jungle and wanders about, he generally comes across the orchard, where he can eat any quantity of the fruits, but is not able to take away anything from it; for if he happens to take any fruit with him he will not be able to find his way out of the garden until he throws it away.[72]

The forests that surrounded the villages were part of the living landscape of the highlands, and Kandyans used two key terms to describe them.[73] These ecological terms were not entirely discrete but differed in nuance. *Kelle* was a generic term for the full forests of the highlands, which could be combined with adjectives to describe height, as for example in *mahakelle* (high forest). The term kelle did not, however, suggest an undisturbed natural forest; indeed many, and perhaps most, such full forests supported a variety of hunting and gathering activities by neighboring settled communities. Kelle did, however, suggest the absence of any large-scale human habitation within the forest itself. By partial contrast, the term *wanay* described a full forest more remote from settled human habitation, but even these wanay forests could be hunting grounds for the Veddyas, the forest peoples of the island.

There was also a separate lexicon of terms that was used to describe forests that had been designated by the political authorities. The broadest term was that for the king's forest (Sinhala: *rajasantaka*), considered to be royal property. Some of these royal forests were further designated as prohibited forests (Sinhala: *tahansikelle*), set aside by the king for royal use.[74] In designated forests close by the royal residences, the prohibitions on use by villagers were strict. This was true in *Udavattekelle* (literally, "upper garden forest"), near the royal palace in Kandy. In cases where vital natural resources could be found, prohibitions were likewise enforced. One "prohibited forest" near the Galata Oya (stream), for example, was used for the production of charcoal for the royal armory.[75] But elsewhere, although the forests might be considered in a broad sense to belong to the king, the prohibitions were unenforced, and in such designated forests certain villagers might hunt game and gather firewood, timber, and honey, although the villagers were not allowed to clear these forests for chena.[76]

Another important political designation was that of the forest barrier

(Sinhala: *wanadurga*), which was used to describe the forest belt that the Kandyan kings had established by edict to surround the kingdom and to impede easy communication with the lowlands. There was no term to describe forests into which people had never ventured, and indeed it is likely that there were no such forests on the island, although the idea of such forests existed in the popular imagination. The Kandyan kings had been concerned to maintain strictly a forest barrier encircling the highland kingdom. It had proved its strategic worth many times over the early centuries of European rule in the lowlands. A succession of Portuguese armies and Dutch armies had come to ruin, either in their approach to Kandy or upon their retreat from the highlands. Up and down the forested mountains there were only paths, too narrow to allow for more than single-file foot traffic and that all but excluded the movement of cannon. The single-file of soldiers and carriers could be handily ambushed from the lateral depths of the forests, and for the European soldiers retaliatory pursuit of their harassers into the dark recesses of the woods was virtually out of the question. Furthermore, the Kandyan policy of barring the paths at the tops and bottoms of mountain passes with thorn gates, which themselves could be easily defended, meant an additional degree of military vulnerability for the European troops aligned in single file, unable to advance until the gates were taken. For European armies, guerilla warfare inside the forest belt was a nightmare from which they were lucky to escape.

Other terms for forests concerned secondary growth. Chena cultivation was an important agronomic practice in the highlands, and Kandyans had terms to describe the variety of growth that followed on the abandonment of these forest patches. *Landu* was the basic term for scrub or secondary-growth forest, although it may have been more commonly used in the lowlands. It could be used in combination with *kelle (landukelle)* to indicate land that had partially regenerated. *Mukulana* described forest that had regrown after chena cultivation, although, interestingly, it also could carry the connotation of royal forest land that was reserved for the use of the king.

British Perceptions of the Highland Forests

Early nineteenth-century British writers in Sri Lanka, stationed on a tropical Asian island with a biota so different from that of their native land, were understandably struck by the differences between the tropical vegetation of Sri Lanka and that of the British Isles. These writers were strongly impressed by the sheer density of the foliage on the island, and when they wrote about the vegetation in the western maritime zone, near their British settlements at Colombo and Galle, they generally described it as luxuriant and tropical.

The full forests of the island interior, on the other hand, were something else. They did not appear welcoming, and were often described as gloomy and foreboding.[77] To be sure, this was owing, at least in part, to the sufferings that European troops had encountered when passing through the forests on their way to Kandy. But there was yet another, even more fundamental, reason that forests were threatening: the interior forests were thought to be reservoirs of disease. The principal threat to health was fever, and the generic culprit that caused fever was "marsh miasma" or "vegeto-animal effluvium" that rose out of the forest depths to cause death and disease.[78] As Anthony Bertolacci, a Frenchman who served sixteen years in the British civil service on the island and who authored Ceylon's first economic history, described in 1817 the problem of the interior forests:

> That part of the island which was in the possession of the King of Candy, and which the hand of the cultivator has not cleared from the thickest forests, is certainly unhealthy. If any portion, however, of the Candian territory has been more particularly neglected, it is that which lies contiguous to our old provinces; for the timid and suspicious policy of that Government viewed a broad belt of wild and thick jungle as the strongest barrier that they could oppose to the attacks of an European Power established around them upon the whole sea-coast of the island; and, truly, they owed, for many centuries, the preservation of their independence, solely, to the unhealthy atmosphere exhaled from those uncultivated grounds, where the vegetation of very wild or hurtful plant is most vigorous, and where the constant luxurience [*sic*] of foliage, impeding the penetration of the sun's rays, promotes a vegetable corruption upon the surface of the soil. The consequence is, a deadly fever, well known by the name of the Candian Fever, which generally proves fatal to persons who are not born in that climate.[79]

In addition to this perception of the unhealthiness of the interior forests, the British viewed the great tracts of forests and "jungles" that were not put into agricultural production as an economic waste. The obvious solution to the problem of disease and lack of economic activity was to cut the forests down and to introduce new cultivation. After the construction of roads into the highlands, this became increasingly practical. As the highland pioneer Samuel Baker waxed optimistically:

The felling and clearing of the jungle, which cultivation would render necessary, would tend in a great measure to dispel the fevers and malaria always produced by a want of free circulation of air. In a jungle-covered country like Ceylon, diseases of the most malignant character are harboured in those dense and un-disturbed tracts, which year after year reap a pestilential harvest from the thinly-scattered population. Cholera, dysentery, fever, and small-pox all appear in their turn, and annually sweep whole villages away.[80]

Europeans likewise suffered increased mortality in the highlands, owing to their encounters with malaria, smallpox, and beriberi, and they attributed the origins of these diseases to an unhealthy forest environment. The rain-forests certainly did present a dangerous epidemiological environment, par-ticularly for the Europeans who, without knowledge of ayurvedic medicine and living before the great revolution in Western medicine that began in the second half of the nineteenth century, suffered elevated mortality rates on the island.[81] The lands that biologists and ecologists would appreciate today as a storehouse of the world's tropical biodiversity appeared to the British of the early and mid-nineteenth century as a well of human suffering and neglect.

~

By the early nineteenth century, human communities had expanded into those highlands that were generally below an elevation of 2,000 feet. In the vil-lages, rooted in the mountain valleys, the villagers practiced a refined and di-versified economy, based on wet rice cultivation in irrigated fields, dry grain cultivation and horticulture in the chena fields, and fruit, vegetable, and me-dicinal cultivation in the forest gardens. Over time, these highland communi-ties had expanded in idiosyncratic ways, and new communities had been formed. But at the beginning of the nineteenth century, the highland political system worked as a significant brake upon the rate of economic expansion and thus on ecological change.

In the aftermath of the Great Rebellion of 1817–18, the highland political system began to crack apart. The vast disparities in cultural appreciations of the highland ecologies and the introduction of new pathogens into the high-lands during the early decades of the nineteenth century presaged the even greater transformations that began in the 1830s.

CHAPTER 3

Early-nineteenth-century Processes of Change

*E*uropeans who were posted to unfamiliar colonial environments tried to establish a sense of normalcy, and they paid particular attention to the "regularization" of their diet. They worked to accomplish this by transporting plants and animals from their home countries and establishing them in the colonies. In many colonial contexts, including those far outside of South Asia, a Europeanized diet—in addition to being a psychological comfort to those far from home—has been a significant marker of political and ethnic status. In the New World, for example, from the sixteenth century onward the Spaniards planted wheat and introduced Iberian sheep, and this food frontier moved inland from the Caribbean to the mainland in the wake of military conquest. In Spanish America, this became one of the signal indicators of social identity: those who ate wheat and mutton were of higher status (and often of European descent) than those who ate maize and beans.[1] In the case of the eighteenth-century colonial Russian empire in North America, Russian fur traders sustained an enormous effort in order to assure that they would not be reduced to eating the fare of the Native Americans with whom they traded. To this end, Russians carried their own grain supplies thousands of miles.[2] In the colonization of Australia, the importation of familiar fruits and vegetables was also important, and there it was to supplement what the British perceived as a paucity of natural foods available in the wild.[3]

In many colonial tropical circumstances, efforts at the naturalization of European flora and fauna were fraught with difficulties and were only partly successful. On the island of Sri Lanka, from the early sixteenth century, first Portuguese, then Dutch, and then British colonial forces attempted to enhance the local fare in order to provide a more familiar cuisine. This was frustrated in some important respects. The Portuguese, in possession of parts of the maritime districts from 1505 to 1658, found the climate of the maritime provinces, and in particular the environs of Colombo, simply too wet to grow wheat or olives, and the poor quality of the pasture grasses, even in the low country, meant that the introduced sheep produced an extraordinarily tough mutton that was less than appetizing. The Portuguese also introduced the potato and some European vegetables—plants that enjoyed greater success in the highlands than in the maritime provinces. The wet lowland tropics simply were not a suitable environment for the European-grown grains and vegetables. They could be sown, but the seed quality degenerated seriously after a generation or two or three. Far more successful were the introductions from elsewhere in the tropics. The outstanding example was the Portuguese introduction of chili peppers from the New World, which diffused throughout the island and chili became a standard condiment.

The Dutch, in power in the maritime districts from 1658 to 1796, likewise realized that in the wet tropics it would not be possible to naturalize most European fruits and vegetables, but the cultural dietary imperative pushed them to set up gardens nonetheless and continuously to import fresh seed. In this manner they persevered with efforts to produce a regular supply of familiar fruits and vegetables. For the Dutch, this generally meant fruits and vegetables from the West Indies and European fruits and vegetables that had been previously naturalized in the Cape Colony in southern Africa (which enjoyed a Mediterranean-style climate) and where successive generations of planting and harvesting did not result in a degeneration of seed quality. These colonial gardens, tended principally in order to serve the tables of the governor and the chief administrative and military officers, became the sites where ornamental plants from other tropical regions (as well as from the temperate world) were also introduced. The horticultural imperative was integrated with a larger colonial agenda of learning about the unfamiliar natural flora beyond Europe.[4] The early Dutch botanical garden blossomed from the humble needs of the colonial table.[5]

For the British based in the maritime provinces, it was not possible to adhere fully to a British-style diet. The maritime districts were too wet to grow wheat, barley, or oats, and thus there was little choice but to have a rice-based diet. It was likewise not possible to make beer, because hops and malt could not survive in the wet lowland tropics. The British—a community of several thousand civilians and military—were able to distinguish themselves from the Sri Lankan population by their commitment to eating red meat, and to this end they imported cattle and sheep;[6] they adapted, however, to drinking arrack, the alcohol distilled from toddy, or sap, from the coconut palm (*Cocos nucifera*) and the kitul palm (*Caryota urens*). But if the British had to reconcile themselves to locally produced alcohol and a rice-based diet, they made efforts, like the Dutch before them, to assure that some portion of their vegetables and fruits would be familiar to them.

Just before their capitulation to the British, the Dutch had failed for two successive seasons to procure their usual supply of vegetable seeds from the Cape Colony, and in the first years of British occupation, European vegetables were in very short supply.[7] The British chose not to attempt to rejuvenate a Dutch-era garden, apparently located somewhere in Slave Island (Colombo) in the 1790s,[8] but instead to establish their own. This horticultural project of growing fruits and vegetables was a concern of the leading administrative and military figures. Indeed, there were well-founded reasons for improving the military as well as the civilian diet. British troops during the earliest years of the nineteenth century suffered greatly from nutritional deficiencies. Thomas Christie, the superintendent of hospitals, writing in 1803 of the Fifty-first Regiment's mission to the highlands, judged that "the diet of the men at Candy consisted almost solely of beef and rice, without any admixture of fresh vegetables, and but little addition of spice, or other condiment. This is by no means a healthy diet, and will readily be conceived to predispose to many diseases, particularly to Beri-berry, which has, at different times, been so extremely fatal to the troops in Ceylon, and to which complaint it will be found that the greater number of deaths that occurred in Candy are to be attributed."[9]

The Creation of the Royal Botanic Gardens

In the early years of British colonial rule in the maritime provinces, two of the leading colonial authorities undertook botanical initiatives. The first British governor, Frederick North, set up his own private fruit and vegetable garden at Peliyagoda, near Colombo,[10] and General MacDowell, the senior military officer, established a private garden for exotic flora. Until he left Colombo in February 1804, MacDowell imported plants from the East India Company's botanical garden at Calcutta; his garden included flora from the West Indies and China, as well as from Europe.[11] But these efforts were modest in extent: Governor North's garden produced fruits and vegetables for the official table, and General MacDowell's enthusiasm for exotic plants was for him a fascinating sideline.

These early initiatives were soon to be nurtured under an opening umbrella of imperial botany. In 1810, Sir Joseph Banks (1743–1820), the director of the Royal Botanic Gardens at Kew, near London, who guided its course for nearly one-half century, advanced his suggestions to the British government for "the establishment of a Royal Botanic garden and Minor gardens in Ceylon."[12] Banks argued that a botanic garden was essential for a multitude of political and scientific reasons, including the necessity to bolster British prestige among the practitioners of ayurvedic medicine.[13] Banks's choice for the post of chief gardener, William Kerr, who had held the post of botanic collector to the royal gardens at Kew and who had been successful in this capacity in Canton and Macau, accepted the appointment, and the Royal Botanic Gardens of Ceylon were launched on 11 August 1812.[14]

Kerr died in 1814, without having had much time to develop the Royal Botanic Gardens, either in Colombo or at the newly opened site at Kalutara, farther down the southwestern coast.[15] And then in the months following the British accession to power in the Kandyan provinces in 1815, the military opened up a garden in the highlands and began to report the hopeful horticultural results. Captain L. De Bussche wrote in 1817 that in Kandy "all European vegetables thrive in the highest perfection, and in such abundance throughout the whole year, that green peas, potatoes, cabbages, turnips, carrots, &c. &c. are sent daily to Colombo, where such vegetables were seldom seen before, and never in the market."[16]

Kerr's successor, Alexander Moon, another gardener from Kew, arrived on the island in 1817.[17] Moon was initially optimistic that the garden at Kalutara would enjoy great success in growing European fruits and vegetables if a regular supply of fresh seeds from England and the Cape of Good Hope could be secured, and he was sanguine that vegetable production in the highlands might become independent of extraneous aid.[18] The problem of exotic European seed supply, however, remained troublesome. European vegetable seeds were not always fresh when they reached the garden at Kalutara and they sometimes arrived in the wrong season. Moon reassessed the situation in 1820:

> The Horticulture of the maritime province cannot be expected to be much improved untill fresh and regular supplies of seeds are secured, for never or seldom

any sort of European vegetables can be brought to such perfection on the sea coast as to produce seeds, and in my humble opinion a Garden in Kandy under the liberal views of Government offers the only source from which such supplies may be expected, and would in the end lessen the present expence in as much as it would in a few years render the charge of bringing such seeds from England unnecessary, and as far as I am enabled to judge labourers may be obtained in Kandy for nearly half the hire at Colombo.[19]

In the same year, upon the instructions of Governor Brownrigg, the Royal Botanic Garden began to expand its botanical portfolio. In 1820, the garden received 113 live plants that had been sent, gratis, from the Royal Botanic Garden at Calcutta, and more plants from the British East India Company were said to be on the way. Moon entered into a correspondence that would allow him to furnish plants from Sri Lanka to Calcutta.[20] This marked the beginning of the island's official engagement with the great intertropical exchange of flora between imperial botanic gardens.

Horticulture and the Highland Garden

By early 1822, Moon had secured land in Peradeniya for the up-country garden.[21] Governor Edward Barnes (whose own agronomic experiments are described below) ordered the garden at Peradeniya to generate as much revenue as possible from horticulture to finance the production of coffee.[22] But alas, agronomic reality interceded. European fruits and vegetables grown at Peradeniya produced degenerated seed.[23] After years of experiment and effort by successive superintendents, in 1835 J. G. Watson of the Royal Botanic Gardens at Peradeniya finally admitted the failure of sustainable horticulture. He suggested, hopefully, that a garden at a higher altitude, at a location intermediate between Peradeniya and Nuwara Eliya, at Pussellawa, would be far superior.[24] To this initiative, the government turned a deaf ear.

Into the 1840s, the orientation of the garden remained so strongly focussed on the production of European fruits and vegetables that scant attention could be paid to the cultivation of indigenous plants or to other exotics. As Superintendent Normansell described the garden to W. T. Hooker, the director of the Royal Botanic Garden at Kew, in 1842, "if the planting here of the few Palms that we possess, were removed the vegetation, to an unexperienced observer would appear similar to that of Europe."[25] And that was exactly the

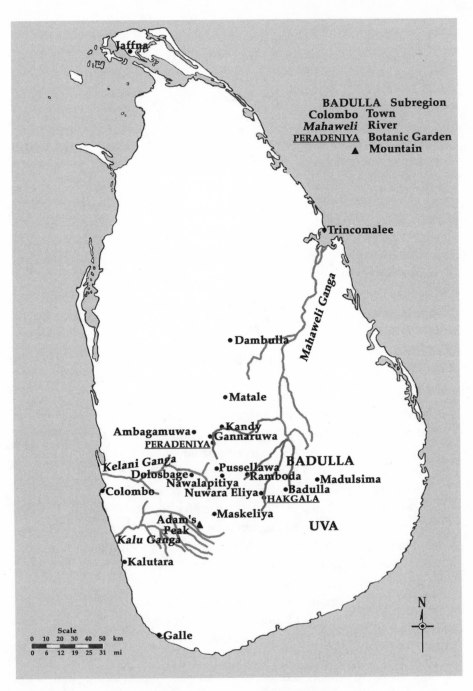

BADULLA Subregion
Colombo Town
Mahaweli River
PERADENIYA Botanic Garden
▲ Mountain

Jaffna

Trincomalee

Mahaweli Ganga

Dambulla

Matale

Ambagamuwa• •Kandy
•Gannaruwa
PERADENIYA

Kelani Ganga **BADULLA**
Dolosbage• •Pussellawa
•Ramboda •Madulsima
Nawalapitiya
•Colombo Nuwara Eliya• •Badulla
HAKGALA

•Maskeliya **UVA**

Adam's▲
Peak
Kalu Ganga

•Kalutara

Scale
0 10 20 30 40 50 km
0 6 12 19 25 31 mi

N

•Galle

Map 4. *Towns, Rivers, and Subregions*

emphasis demanded by the government. As the colonial secretary wrote to Normansell in 1842, "It is hardly necessary to remind you that if it does not afford supplies of seeds and plants for the public's benefit, your establishment will be almost useless."[26]

In 1844, George Gardner, the newly appointed superintendent of the Peradeniya garden and the first professional botanist to hold the position, arranged for the regular quarterly shipment of seeds for resale. This was to allow the Royal Botanic Garden to act as a retailer of seeds, and eventually to extricate itself from vegetable and fruit gardening. The core difficulty was that seeds from Europe, shipped around the Cape of Good Hope or carried across the overland route, could arrive late and/or damaged by the salt air.[27] Nonetheless, the Peradeniya garden succeeded in relinquishing its horticultural obligation, but before doing so it had popularized many "European" vegetables and fruits to the point that they found acceptance in the Kandyan diet.

The superintendents of the Royal Botanic Garden at Peradeniya were not alone in introducing exotic foodstuffs to the highlands. Indeed, immediately after the British accession in 1815, the first attempts to grow wheat took place in both Kandy and at Badulla, and both enjoyed success. The market for wheat was, however, limited to the European community and thus the acreage under wheat cultivation was very limited. Then in the years following the suppression of the Great Rebellion in 1817–18, other initiatives were undertaken to "improve" the agriculture of the highlands. In 1823, the Ceylon Literary and Agricultural Society financed potato cultivation in the Kandyan provinces, apparently with considerable success. George Turnour, revenue commissioner for the Kandyan provinces, gave evidence in 1829 that potato cultivation had increased rapidly, although at that time the market for the potato, like that for wheat, was principally among the European population; it, too, however, was undoubtedly making inroads into the Kandyan diet.[28] Yet other initiatives were undertaken by individual planters. J. W. Bennett, an immigrant planter from Mauritius, claimed to have introduced the white and variegated mulberry plant to the island in the 1820s, as well as manioc, the Brazil cherry, the poppy, Portugal fig, Bengal sholl, and nutmeg.[29] In later years, other initiatives with tropical exotic foodstuffs were launched from the Royal Botanic Garden itself. The first major effort took place in 1843, when acting superintendent W. C. Ondaatje cultivated a large quantity of West Indian yam *(Dioscoraceae),* which could be propagated by seed buds, and distributed it liberally to Kandyan farmers.[30]

Early British Experiments with Coffee, Sugar, and Tea

The coffee tree *(Coffea arabica)* was an exotic, probably first introduced by Arab merchants from the Arabian peninsula in the first half of the second millennium C.E. and then reintroduced by the Dutch from their plantations in Java during the late seventeenth or early eighteenth century. At some point—the timing and the agency are not known—the coffee tree was introduced into the highlands, where it became naturalized. By the early nineteenth century, it grew wild in the forest, sprung from the droppings of birds and quadruped browsers who ate the cherry-red fruit. These wild seedings were in addition to the trees tended in home gardens and dense plantings on temple lands that provided white seasonal blossoms for Buddhist services.[31] The Dutch had set out their coffee trees in Sri Lanka on chena land. Coffee had not performed particularly well for the Dutch, but early in the British period, Governor North used government monies in an attempt to resuscitate the old Dutch coffee plantations, and in 1812 a British civil servant set up a private plantation. Both initiatives seem to have ended in failure.[32]

The hopes for successful coffee (and sugar) plantations, however, were not so easily extinguished, powered perhaps by the long experience with coffee in the West Indies. At the Royal Botanic Garden at Peradeniya, the superintendents had no prior experience with coffee planting, and beginning with Superintendent Moon in the mid-1820s, they experimented by mixing both Sinhalese and European agronomic techniques. The superintendents had the coffee fields plowed, but with elephant rather than buffalo traction. They tried this in the (unirrigated) paddy lands and on flat lands near the garden.[33] By the late 1820s there were more than a hundred acres under cultivation, with coffee trees planted at ten-foot intervals.[34]

Elsewhere, a few British capitalists likewise tried their hand. George Bird, celebrated as the first highland coffee planter, in 1824 began to plant coffee on 200 acres of his holding of 1,086 acres in Gampola. His techniques were similar to those used at the Royal Botanic Garden. The European practice of deep plowing was at its heart:

> Small low jungle is plowed up with the Elephant Plough. The Bushes being cut down the roots are plowed up. But in strong jungles it takes 40 Native workmen with the assistance of the plough to clear an acre in one month: It is necessary to root it entirely out, as in a single year it will grow to be impassable. The Natives are not in the habit of working these high grounds so as to root out the jungle or

turn up the deeper soils and are consequently obliged to nip over the shoots from the stumps that have been left which would otherwise choke their crops.[35]

Bird's initial results were encouraging, but he found that the first yields could not be reproduced. His plantation went on to prove itself unprofitable, and he was forced to abandon the property by 1833 and move on to other coffee lands, which he farmed without much financial success over a period of thirty-three years.[36] Thus, although George Bird's first coffee plantation at Gampola is often cited as the harbinger of the coffee revolution that began in earnest in the late 1830s, it might as well be considered an exemplar of the deep confusions initially experienced by the British in their encounters with the highland ecology.

Other plantations drew their inspiration from a Kandyan ecological model. At Governor Barnes's coffee plantation at Gannaruwa, for example, some of the coffee was planted in the shade of jack trees, in what amounted to a spatially extended modification of the forest garden. There the plants grew luxuriantly. The idea was to replace, through fertilization by jack-leaf fall, the nutrients absorbed by the coffee plant. But whatever the virtues of coffee-under-jack, the coffee yields there were low, a direct result of the decreased solar radiation. Other coffee plants were set under coconut palms, and their poor performance bore out the soundness of the Kandyan farmers' advice that coffee and coconut were incompatible.[37]

Similarly, although the details are not recoverable, it is clear that the later experiments at the Peradeniya garden itself did not yield a profitable model of coffee production. In part, the production and maintenance of the coffee fields were crimped by fiscal constraints that prevented the superintendents from raising the workers' pay to levels sufficient to attract the requisite number of laborers. And the practice of both deep plowing and planting on relatively flat gradients ensured that the plants would suffer from inadequate drainage.[38] In the years for which records of the harvest survive, coffee-berry production was modest in the extreme. In 1833 and 1834, the harvests were approximately thirty-three hundredweight.[39] In 1838, sixty-five acres were in coffee, interspersed with coconut, jack, cinnamon, and various forest trees. The coffee trees were, however, in a "very unhealthy state, comparatively unproductive and irrecoverable."[40] The scant crops were simply picked, sun-dried, packed into bags, put into bandy carts, and sent to Colombo for sale.

The garden had rather more success as a government-sponsored nursery for young coffee plants. At least by 1840, the garden was in the business of distributing coffee seedlings to the burgeoning European agricultural community. Again, the records are discontinuous and fragmented. But in the planting season of 1840, five planters bought 123,000 coffee plants from the garden nursery.[41] In the second half of 1843, the garden sold 57,200 coffee seedlings.[42] This nursery role was to be short-lived, however, as planters found that they could as easily grow coffee seedlings in their own gardens or purchase plants from neighboring Kandyan farmers.[43] Nonetheless, this support from the garden played a role in the early years of the European coffee boom.

Sugar

Sugar, like coffee, had been a successful plantation crop in the West Indies and Mascarene Islands. During the 1830s, British planters set up a number of plantations in the Sri Lankan lowlands. Some seemed initially promising; but all failed. The historical sources are largely silent on just what was responsible for the failure, but it is likely that the poor soils were the fundamental problem. A similar process unfolded in the highlands, where sugar was first grown at Dumbera, in the environs of Kandy, and then extensive cane fields were opened up at Peradeniya, outside of the Royal Botanic Garden. The highland plantations produced a bright yellow sugar that tended to absorb moisture. Enthusiasts were initially hopeful that highland sugar could be carried inexpensively via river transport down to the coast and that highland sugar would find a market abroad. But these hopes would be proved unrealistic.[44]

The Peradeniya garden also experimented with sugarcane. Gardner planted out a sugarcane field in 1844/45 that yielded a better-than-average West Indian first crop. The second crop, however, was poor, and Gardner attributed this to the deficiency of the soil.[45] Elsewhere in the highlands, the soils were likewise found to be largely unsuitable for sugar cultivation, and most of the plantations failed. By the mid-1850s, there was only one profitable sugarcane venture on the island, at Peradeniya, outside the garden (likely on the bands of alluvial soils near the Mahawelli River), and its success was attributable to the existence of a local demand, which obviated the difficulty of expensive water or overland transport.[46] The success was, however, short-lived; it is likely that the local market was limited to the European community since the Kandyans ate jaggery sugar, which they produced from the kitul palm trees in the forests surrounding their fields and in their forest gardens.

Tea

Tea *(Camellia sinensis)*, originally from China, was recorded in Sri Lanka as early as 1824, when Superintendent Moon noted the presence of "China tea" in the colony, perhaps in the Royal Botanical Garden itself.[47] It is possible that this introduction was made by William Kerr, the royal gardener who came from his station as plant collector in Canton directly to Colombo in 1812.[48] The date of the transfer of China tea into the highlands, however, is uncertain. The first mention of "Assam tea," dates to 1833, when J. G. Watson, superintendent of the RBG at Peradeniya, requested permission from the government to re-move from Kalutara to Peradeniya three tea seedlings, although no evidence survives as to whether or not this transfer took place or was successful.[49]

In 1839, Governor J. A. S. Mackenzie bought some land near Nuwara Eliya for experimental tea planting. J. G. Lear, the acting superintendent of the RBG at Peradeniya, reported to Mackenzie that he was not particularly impressed with the soil or slope of the land, but Lear went ahead and planted tea seeds there. The seeds did not germinate.[50] Normansell, the successor to Lear at the RBG, renewed the initiative and, in 1840, established a nursery of Assam tea plants at Nuwara Eliya. Normansell looked to a future role for the garden in the upper highlands:

> Having been engaged during the last fortnight in establishing at Nuwra Ellia a nursery of Tea Plants lately received from Assam, it has occurred to me, that something more is required to promote the object of doing so—and also for its ultimate success, than I had previously contemplated. . . .
>
> I am decidedly of opinion that Tea Cultivation in Nuwra Ellia will at no distant period open a new and profitable speculation and form a valuable source of reve-nue to the Government of this Colony. It is therefore desirable that the Tea plan-tation as now in progress should be made subservient on the Control of the Office which I hold and established a connecting branch of the Royal Botanic Garden, as a guarantee I should hope of its receiving very necessary attention.[51]

Governor Mackenzie, however, had no interest in the project.[52] On the ex-perimental tea plot itself, bad weather doomed the initiative. No rain fell for six weeks after planting, and the tea seedlings largely failed. Of the original 140 plants put in the ground in April 1840, only 36 survived until November of that year.[53]

This failure, however, did not extinguish Normansell's interest. He received another shipment of Assam tea plants from Calcutta in 1842, and he again requested permission, this time from the new governor, Colin Campbell, to set up a tea station in Nuwara Eliya.[54] In October 1842, some of the Assam tea plants were sent to a planter in Nuwara Eliya, and at about the same time, some China tea was planted on coffee plantations at Pussellawa, Ramboda, and Dolosbage.[55] Within a few years, the Pussellawa effort appeared to hold the promise of establishing a new branch of export commerce.[56]

But just as tea cultivation was enjoying small successes as a sideline on the highland coffee plantations, a new professional botanist came to take the helm at the Peradeniya garden. George Gardner had his own views on tea and did not believe that its cultivation would succeed in Ceylon. As he stated in a letter to the colonial secretary in 1847: "I have good reason for believing that Tea Cultivation will never Succeed in Ceylon, I should be very sorry to see the Garden put to so much expense for an Article that will not benefit it. Through the kindness of a friend, I already possess two Tea Plants which are quite enough for Botanical purposes."[57] Without government support, tea cultivation in the highlands would remain the hobby of experimental planters into the last third of the nineteenth century.

Horticulture in the Upper Highlands: The "New Scotland"

In the early 1830s, Sir Edward Barnes began a program of experimentation with exotic fruits, vegetables, and grain in Nuwara Eliya. The climate was susceptible to frost, which wrought damage on the potato plants and some of the other vegetables and fruits, but the potential of the grains (oats, wheat, barley, and hops) appeared very promising.[58] In the 1840s, a small group of British settlers led by Samuel Baker arrived in an attempt to transplant fully the British farming model to the upper highlands, to import both British flora and fauna, and to naturalize them in a climate deemed similar to that of Scotland. The altitude and cool temperatures of the upper highlands suggested to the British that the old and familiar might be transplanted with success to regions above 5,000 feet. Surely, barley and European vegetables and fruits would thrive in the region of Nuwara Eliya ("City of Light"), which was proclaimed a "New Scotland."[59]

Samuel Baker's entourage suffered numerous accidents on the route to the upper highlands, but undeterred he set himself to his work of ecological transformation. He hired about 150 native workers and undertook the tedious process of exterminating jungle and forest, not felling, but regularly digging out every tree and root, then piling and burning the mass, and levelling the cleared land in a state to receive the plough. This was very expensive work, amounting to about 30£ per acre. The root of a large tree would frequently oc-cupy three men a couple of days in its extraction, which at the rate of wages, at one shilling per diem, was very costly. The land thus cleared was a light sandy loam about eighteen inches in depth, with a gravel subsoil, and was considered far superior to the patina (or natural grass land) soil, which was in appearance black loam on the higher ground, and of a peaty nature in the swamps.[60]

Baker also reworked the patanas, burning off the grass, then scraping the turf off and putting it in long rows to be reburned. This done, the ground was plowed and harrowed and then planted.

These efforts were overwhelmed by a spate of unanticipated ecological problems. The scale of the agricultural initiatives had inadvertently created new ecotones and new ecological opportunities for other species. Sambhur deer and hogs almost wholly destroyed the first crop of oats. Grubs totally de-voured the potato crop. A rinderpest epidemic swept away the cattle and horses. As Baker lamented, "everything seemed to be going into the next world as fast as possible."[61] What finally brought the agricultural experiment to a close was the realization that the upper highland soils were poor and that neither grain nor even fodder grasses would grow without fertilizer.

Vegetable production, however, was another matter altogether. The new immigrants found that intensive gardening could be sustained where farming could not. Conducted on a much smaller scale, gardeners could produce good crops of peas, beans, turnips, carrots, cabbages, and even potatoes. Moreover, the gardeners found a market for their produce among the European commu-nity at Kandy and among the Europeans who came to the upper highlands to convalesce.[62] But these horticultural initiatives likewise were bonanzas for the animal and insect populations at their edges. These new edge habitats at-tracted a plethora of birds. Deer for the most part did not interfere with the new horticulture, and neither did elephants. But the new crops created a niche for a burgeoning population of pig rats, or bandicoots (*Bandicota indica in-dica*), that became established at Nuwara Eliya and attacked grain crops, po-tatoes, and peas, as well as dovecotes and poultry yards.[63] The adaptation of farm animals was likewise fraught with possibilities and perils. Domesticated cattle from the lowlands found that they could subsist on the coarse grasses of the upper highlands, low though they were in nutrition, and even some sheep were established for a time. But these livestock, and domesticated dogs, were a magnet for leopards and cheetahs from the surrounding forests.[64]

The New Scotland in the upper highlands soon found itself in competition with the horticultural initiatives of the Kandyan farmers in Uva Province, in the eastern rainshadow highlands, who had adopted the cultivation of the potato in the aftermath of the Great Rebellion of 1817–18. There, too, over time, specialized production systems had developed. As the assistant government agent in Uva noted in 1848, this process had become quite advanced:

> There is not much fine grain cultivated in this division. People grow Potatoes and Cabbages to a considerable extent and they are very partial to them. A constant trade is carried on with Nuwera Ellia and Kandy by the people of Yattipalata. The people are always taking onions. Plantains. Potatoes. Rice and Paddy to Nuwera Ellia. this trade with Kandy is principally in Potatoes and Onions. they do not grow rice sufficient for their Consumption. but as the price obtained in Nuwera Ellia Bazaar is very high they take it there for sale. & they eat Potatoes and Cabbages in stead. they are in the habit of going to Bintenne, [?]allapanny [first letter uncertain], and Kandapalle for dry grain. they barter with the people of those divisions for fine grain with onions and Salt which they obtain from the Tavalam people in exchange for Potatoes and onions. the people are in very comfortable circumstances and healthy.[65]

Thus by the late 1840s, horticulture with European fruits and vegetables had been successfully transferred both to the upper highlands and to Uva. The highland road network allowed for the long-distance transport of even relatively low value-to-bulk foodstuffs, and new centers of production and patterns of trade developed.[66]

Burning Off the Forest Barrier

While the experiments in the lower highlands with sugar and coffee and those in the upper highlands and Uva with European vegetables and fruits were unfolding, the Kandyan farming communities launched a different kind of ecological initiative. The expansion of the Kandyan chena farming systems into the forest left little documentation in its wake, but its effects were broad. It consumed the entire forest belt surrounding what had been the Kandyan kingdom. By the 1880s, foresters would be unable to discern even the traces of what had been a formidable barrier.

The forest barrier around the highlands had been a preeminent symbol of Kandyan independence, and following the crushing of the Great Rebellion, the British were just as concerned to carve through the forest barrier in order to allow easy access to the highlands as the Kandyan monarchy had been to restrict it. The political and military dimension of the open road was obvious. But it also heralded the dramatic expansion of economic opportunities, because in the Kandyan period, high transport costs had drastically limited the extent of trade. After the completion of the Colombo-to-Kandy road, the highlanders began to export goods to the maritime provinces. Paddy rice, along with coffee, jaggery, and areca nuts led the way. Salt, salted fish, and cotton cloth made the return journey to the mountains.[67]

The new road, however, made its way through dense forest, from which wild animals attacked the cart traffic. One of the first concerns of John D'Oyly, the first British administrator in the highlands, was to issue a permit to Kandyan cultivators to cut down the forests within one mile of the mountain roads, to eliminate the habitat that provided cover for dangerous wild animals (particularly elephants, leopards, and cheetah). This signaled a fundamental shift in the rules governing the forest belt, and Kandyans moved to avail themselves of the new opportunities. In part of a long essay on this question, the government agent for the Central Province reflected:

> When the British took possession [of] the Kandyan Provinces the first object to which the authorities turned their attention was the improvement of the means of communication by opening up the country. It was with this view that Sir John D'Oyly issued a general permit for the clearing of the forests which bordered the main roads and afforded cover to elephants and other wild animals.
>
> The Kandyans were not slow to take advantage of this license, which was, as might have been expected, considerably abused, for not content with felling the forests in the vicinity of the roads they cut down and cleared the jungle for miles around their villages. Often when traveling through the district extensive tracts of chena land have been pointed out to me to which were said to have been covered with impenetrable forests at the time that we took possession of the country.[68]

Before the expansion of British capital into the highlands in the 1830s, the colonial administrators had been largely unconcerned by the rapid expansion of chena agriculture. They did not consider highland terrain particularly valuable, except to the extent that there were tree species suitable for construction and carpentry that were at reasonable proximity to the colonial outposts. Toward this end, the colonial administrators acted to conserve forest resources within a small radius of the major towns and along the rivers and the main road to Colombo. They wanted to ensure that economically valuable timber was not lost in the expansion of chena lands. In August 1821, the Board of Revenue Commissioners published an official notice that prohibited the cutting of chenas in government forests or in any new high ground without a license from government.[69] This was followed by Regulation No. 2 of 1822, which was likewise designed to protect timber valuable for building purposes, and to realize revenue on the cutting of jack on private lands. The regulation was explicit that it did not extend to palmyra wood, coconut, areca trees, firewood, bamboos, or other wood not usually understood as timber fit for building or carpenters' or joiners' use.[70] But these regulations did little to stem the burning off of the forest barrier. Year after year, thousands of new acres of forest were put to the torch.

Why did Kandyan farmers move so aggressively to expand their chena holdings? There were undoubtedly a multitude of reasons, some imbedded in the economic logic of the Kandyan production systems and some created by government policy decisions. The reasons located within the Kandyan farming systems can only be imputed, but they are persuasive nonetheless. It is likely, for example, that the demographic disaster of the Great Rebellion and the increased incidence of disease that followed played a significant role. In the decade or two following the loss of human population from warfare and epidemic, the destruction of domesticated animal populations, and the smashing of irrigation works in the Great Rebellion, numerous individuals within the devastated farming communities undoubtedly decided to divert scarce labor from paddy cultivation to chena cultivation, which had lower labor requirements, or put differently, had higher caloric returns per labor hour. (These Kandyan chena practices did not necessitate either the cutting down of all the forest trees or the uprooting of the lopped-off trees.)

In addition, as the precolonial order of the Kandyan state lost legitimacy in the aftermath of the Great Rebellion, a vacuum of political power was created. Kandyan farmers, if they transferred their labor from paddy field to chena field, not only released themselves from the obligation to pay grain taxes (which obtained only on paddy production) but also partially escaped from the orbit of the politically appointed headmen. They gained more control over their own labor, just as a world of new economic possibilities emerged. Opening new chena lands meant creating new wealth, and the simple technologies of slashing and burning offered the possibility of securing simple title to land in an era of rising land prices. There were also substantial financial incentives. The expansion of chena into the forest belt was directly responsible for the rapid expansion of coffee exports, which were grown, harvested, and in some cases shipped by Kandyan farmers directly to markets in Britain. And indeed, this was true in the patanas of Uva as well as the forest belt.[71]

New colonial economic policies also triggered the ecological transformation of the highlands. Some of these policies were owing to Sir Edward Barnes's quest for a viable economic foundation for the island and his personal enthusiasm for coffee-production prospects. Barnes, as governor of Ceylon (1824–31), played a pivotal role in advancing the prospects for coffee producers. The British conquest of Kandy in 1815 had emboldened some Kandyan farmers to develop new coffee fields and chena lands. The lag time between the clearing and burning of the forest, the planting out of a new seedling, and the mature tree's readiness to bear fruit was four to five years, and the coffee exports doubled between 1820 and 1824. Significant political support for the production of coffee was extended by the British administration. This process began in 1820, when Barnes, as lieutenant-governor, abolished the 5 percent export duty on Sri Lankan–grown coffee. In 1824, Barnes exempted coffee lands from a land tax of one-tenth of the produce. These decisions reverberated throughout the Kandyan highlands, and Sinhalese farmers increased their production of coffee for export more than 100 percent between 1820 and 1824, and then nearly doubled their exports again from 1826 to 1833. In 1829, the governor released all Sri Lankans engaged in growing coffee (or any related manufacture) from their obligation to perform annual labor service for the government.[72] In 1832, even more labor time was freed up by the British abolition of the institution of *rajakariya*, under which Kandyans had seen their labor obligations to the Kandyan state transferred to the British colonial government.

At various points throughout the highlands, in the aftermath of the British accession to power in 1815, Kandyan farmers commenced or intensified their coffee production. Some of this was within the home garden, but much was not. The Kandyan method of coffee growing was far from the British conception of "scientific agriculture," and it earned the scorn of most British competitors. In the home garden, the coffee was picked green, to avoid the depredations of animal and birds. This produced a coffee judged inferior by the consumer, but it reduced to near zero the labor expense of warding off pests. In 1835, Jeronis de Soysa, a low-country Sinhalese, bought up a large tract of forested mountain near Hangurankette, which had been a nucleus of coffee production for the Buddhist temple there. He paid to the government the minumum legal price at auction (the "upset" price) of five shillings per acre, and later realized a fortune from his investments.[73] He grew coffee on a hybrid model, allowing the coffee trees to grow wild, but investing in pulpers, cisterns, platforms for drying, and stores for bulking. De Soysa probably took the additional trouble to sort the ripe from the unripe, because his coffee brought "first prices."[74]

The expansion of coffee planting was a large-scale phenomenon. The volume of "native" coffee harvested was such that it could not possibly have been grown in home gardens. And because newly opened chena land could be used for either dry grain, upland rice, or coffee production, it is not possible to estimate with precision the amount of forest land that was cleared by Kandyan farmers before the European-led coffee boom of the 1840s. But the production of coffee alone would have necessitated the clearance of approximately 50,000 to 60,000 acres in the highlands. And indeed, this explains why it was Kandyan farmers who produced the bulk of coffee exported from the highlands into the late 1840s.

Table 3.1: Estimate of Extent of Forest Land Newly Opened by Kandyan Farmers for Coffee Production, 1812–1845

1812–16	500 acres
1816–20	2,000 acres
1821–25	3,600 acres
1826–30	4,500 acres
1831–35	10,000 acres
1836–40	24,300 acres
1841–45	60,400 acres

Source: Coffee export data drawn from I. H. Vanden Dreisen, "Coffee Cultivation in Ceylon (1)," Ceylon Historical Journal 3 (1953): 31–61.

Note: These figures are derived from figures for coffee exports and are thus only roughly approximate. The volume of coffee exports has been converted to acreage in production at a conversion rate of five hundredweight of coffee harvested per acre per year, which may well be too high, because it is derived from the European-style coffee production systems of the 1840s. If so, the figures for Kandyan farmers' coffee land in production would underestimate the actual acreage. The figures also impute a lag period of five years to account for land clearance and growth of coffee seedlings to age of bearing.

The decade of the 1830s thus marked a departure from the earlier model of growing coffee in home gardens or on chena lands. The earlier belief that chena lands were the more suitable, underwritten by the fact that they were certainly less expensive to develop, gave way in the face of practical experience. The soils under full forest were indeed richer, and by the late 1830s, both the Kandyans and the early British planters began to move toward larger-scale forest clearance. By the late 1830s, their commitment to forest clearance matched that of the Brazilian coffee planters, who never experimented with previously cleared forest.[75]

In the mid-1830s, the expansion of chena agriculture into the forest barrier and other highland forests near the colonial administrative outposts became a cause for British administrators' serious concern. At this time, the forested highlands began to take on greater monetary value as a result of the luminous prospects of the new coffee-dominated export economy, and Kandyan farmers emerged as competitors with the British colonial elite. Many of these administrators had direct personal financial interests in opening up forest lands, and their judgments about the chena issue reflected these conflicts of interest and must be interpreted with caution. What is clear is that the administrators began to stigmatize chena as a destructive agronomic practice that ruined land that might otherwise bring in colonial revenues. Prime forested land that had once been the domain of the Kandyan king was put on the auction block, at the same time that other lands, far from the newly carved roads, fell to the Kandyan ax. George Turnour, government agent for the Central Province, was concerned that Kandyans might acquire government forests through a down payment of only 10 percent, cut the valuable timber and convert the land to chena, and then refuse the pay the remainder. The converted land would be less valuable for coffee planting. As early as 1837, Turnour advocated for restricting the sale of government land except on the stipulation that the purchaser grow coffee or another cash crop.[76] Between 1836 and 1843, more than 250,000 acres of Crown land (land held by the British government) in the highlands were sold.

Other land issues became clarified in the crucible of rough experience. A dispute over the ownership of highland forest land in 1836 pitted members of the British colonial elite who had purchased land from some Kandyan nobles and from the government against some other Kandyan nobles who claimed rights to harvest game and honey from an extensive region. This dispute threw into bold relief the core land-tenure issue elevated to prominence by the opening up of the highlands: how could secure title to land be assured, in the face of competing claims and absent a tradition of written title?

The government promulgated a land-tenure ordinance in 1840, revising it the same year to produce the notoriously illiberal and confusingly worded

Table 3.2. Acreage of Crown Land Sold, 1833–1886

Year	Acreage of Crown Land Sold	Year	Acreage of Crown Land Sold
1833	146	1860	33,600
1834	337	1861	28,329
1835	434	1862	25,302
1836	3,920	1863	32,567
1837	3,662	1864	34,122
1838	10,401	1865	41,150
1839	9,570	1866	45,546
1840	42,582	1867	44,019
1841	78,686	1868	24,492
1842	48,534	1869	35,823
1843	59,800	1870	29,556
1844		1871	25,227
1845		1872	19,829
1846		1873	21,656
1847	4,508	1874	32,089
1848	2,761	1875	17,609
1849	786	1876	25,632
1850	1,862	1877	28,543
1851	939	1878	30,975
1852	1,848	1879	26,738
1853	2,200	1880	31,619
1854	5,392	1881	26,818
1855	7,286	1882	22,446
1856	11,656	1883	25,099
1857	19,795	1884	21,943
1858	15,752	1885	22,085
1859	23,447	1886	20,460

Source: I. Vanden Driesen, "Plantation Agriculture & Land Sales Policy in Ceylon—The First Phase, 1836-1886: Part I," *University of Ceylon Review* 14 (1956), 6–25.

"Waste Lands" Ordinance No. 12 of 1840.[77] It declared that all highland forests belonged to the British Crown. With a flourish of the pen, the ordinance imposed, in principle at least, a complete restriction on the expansion of chena. It also threw into question the Kandyan farmers' right of possession of virtually all of their chena lands, regardless of when they had first been cut, except under rare circumstances where the owners could produce preaccession grants from a Kandyan king. The goal of the British administrators was to liberate some of what they perceived to be potentially-prime coffee lands that had been put into chena in the twenty-odd years since the suppression of the

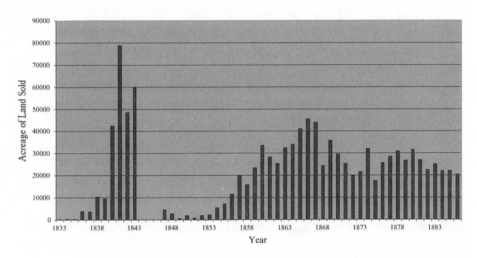

Table 3.2 Graph. *Acreage of Crown Land Sold, 1833–1886*

1817–18 Great Rebellion. In their view, if the Kandyans who had recently opened new lands for the harvesting of timber or for chena were allowed to retain possession, they would be able to sell their lands to European coffee speculators and the revenues would be lost to the Crown.[78]

The prohibition against the expansion of chena was, however, one that existed largely on paper.[79] The fact on the ground was that, throughout the highlands, Kandyans continued to expand their chena holdings in the nineteenth century. This was a sprawling and discontinuous process that, in principle, came under the purview of colonial government agents. But much of the chena clearances took place in remote areas, and the interest of the government agents in enforcing the regulation was sporadic. Nevertheless, during the great era of highland deforestation, government agents did invoke Ordinance No. 12 of 1840 many times, and some Kandyans did indeed lose their claims to chena lands that they insisted were theirs by right of clearance. In other cases, Kandyan litigants contested with success government efforts to invoke Ordinance No. 12.[80]

Transformation in Currency Use

The transformation of the agricultural systems of the highlands was accompanied by a transformation in currency use. The Colombo-Kandy road opened a world of new opportunities to Kandyan chiefs and farmers. Exchange of highland produce meant that not only low-country commodities but Indian Ocean currencies flowed into the highlands. The official British administrative correspondence from these early decades suggests a preference among the Kandyans for gold, rather than silver. The tendency to hoard all currency against duress, rather than to use it for a broadening range of transactions, was, however, deeply engrained, and by 1839, the British introduced fiat money (paper currency) into the highlands to address what they perceived as a maddening scarcity of specie.[81] Before the opening of the European coffee estates, this increase in the money stock was owing largely to the engagement of Kandyan farmers with the new commercial possibilities of the larger world market. Credit and currencies that facilitated this engagement were in the hands of merchant bankers from South India, and the Sri Lankan market was just one small part of their larger Pan-Asian (South and Southeast Asia) operations.[82] Later, an even greater volume of money would flow into the highlands, paid in specie to laborers.[83]

The new access to currency by Kandyan coffee producers facilitated the transformation of the government system of agricultural taxation, which involved the commutation of grain taxes (in kind) to money-tax payment.[84] At least by the 1840s, money use was becoming common even in small transactions, which in an earlier period would have been accomplished only in kind.[85] And the inflow of currency to the highlands generated a welter of economic opportunities for Kandyan laborers. As the Governor Sir J. Emerson Tennent observed in 1848:

> Vast numbers [of natives] have been engaged, both as superintendents and labourers, in the felling of forests, and the planting of coffee and sugar; the construction of roads, the building of bridges, the erection of houses and stores, and the carriage of supplies from the coast to the interior, and of produce from the interior to the coast. Artisans and mechanics have found abundant occupation and extravagant wages, without which it was difficult to overcome their dislike to exertion. Great numbers are employed in the cleaning and preparation of coffee for shipment, as well as in the general business of the merchants; and in the principal towns and villages, a new impulse has been given to the retail trades of the bazaars, by the unusual demand for food, tools, and stores of all kinds for the use of the new estates. Above all, many of the higher class of natives have at length been kindled into something like enterprise by the example of the European settlers, and have begun to clear their forests, plant their estates, and enter into competition with the English merchants in the production of coffee, cinnamon, and the other products of the island.[86]

These new economic initiatives, begun in earnest in the 1830s and 1840s, would launch the ecological transformation of the entire highland region.

∼

During the first decades of the nineteenth century, British colonists brought grains, fruits, and vegetables that grew successfully in the British Isles in an attempt to "regularize" their diet in Sri Lanka. Along the coast, the British failed in these efforts at naturalization, and in the early 1820s they opened up a new botanic garden in the lower highlands to pursue a program in sustainable horticulture. The Royal Botanic Garden at Peradeniya, however, likewise proved unable to produce undegenerated seed. Some colonists advanced the initiative to higher altitudes, and in the upper highlands at Nuwara Eliya in the 1840s, European-style horticulture finally took root. Other British initiatives were inspired by their imperial experiences in the Caribbean and Mascarene islands. They tried to establish coffee, sugar, and tea plantations in the highlands.

Beginning in the 1820s, coincident with the early era of road construction into the highlands, Kandyan farmers in the lower highlands began to expand aggressively their chena lands and their plantings of coffee. They concentrated their ecological work in the great forest belt that surrounded the former kingdom of Kandy. The economic activity of Kandyan coffee producers foreshadowed the dramatic entrance of British capitalists, who launched the ecological transformation of the middle highlands.

~ CHAPTER 4 ~

The Transformation of the Middle Highlands

Before the 1840s, the principal centers of tropical plantation agriculture within the British Empire were in the West Indies and the Mascarene Islands. The labor forces for these plantations were enslaved workers of African descent. When slavery in these British colonies was abolished in 1834, the repercussions were felt immediately. The abolition of slavery raised the cost of labor on the sugar and coffee plantations, and by the late 1830s, agricultural production in these sectors had begun to decline precipitously. Many of the men and women once held in slavery tried their hands at creating a new economy and were unwilling to work on the plantations.[1]

At the same time that the abolition of slavery sounded the death knell of the slave system of British tropical agriculture, the prospects for opening up new plantation lands in the East Indies improved substantially. In 1835, British imperial coffee tariffs were equalized. Prior to 1835, "East Indian" coffee had paid a tariff 50 percent higher than coffee grown on British plantations in the West Indies or the Mascarene Islands. The equalization of tariffs reverberated throughout the imperial tropics.[2] Both coffee drinking and tea drinking were coming into vogue in Britain, replacing an earlier preference for imported wine.[3] This increased demand nearly tripled the price realized per unit of Sri Lankan coffee in the period 1835–42, and the volume of coffee exports increased nearly eightfold. This expansion was underwritten by another set of imperial duties that initially protected British-grown coffee from competition with coffee grown outside the formal bounds of the British Empire.[4]

The Rush for the Forest Estate

The disruption of plantation activities in the British West Indies brought about by the abolition of slavery forced planters there to reconsider their options. Some chose to uproot their fortunes and to replant them abroad. The highlands of Sri Lanka were a major attraction, because densely forested tropical lands were available and the costs of opening up a coffee plantation were thought to be lower than in the West Indies.[5] Capital from the West Indies began to flow to Sri Lanka. By 1843, this capital inflow accounted for more than one hundred coffee and sugar plantations, and the average outlay on each was estimated at £1,000.[6] This increase in circulating capital, in turn, helped to inflate radically the sale prices of forest lands in Sri Lanka and to launch a land rush into the highlands. This rush was, in turn, intercepted by shrewd land speculators on the island, many of whom were in the employ of government and who profited handsomely by their intervention.

Some West Indian planters arrived in person, but others engaged British agents to work on their behalf.[7] Speculators bought and sold in splendid ignorance. In Ambagamuwa, excessive rain and clayey soils brought financial disaster to those who ventured their capital.[8] Elsewhere, patana lands initially appeared attractive investments, offering their purchasers the prospect of foregoing the expensive process of forest clearance. New patana owners soon found to their chagrin that beneath the grasses were not only poor soils but an environment conducive to a variety of grubs, which could feed on the coffee plants.[9] Prospective planters of all abilities soon learned to concentrate their efforts on the dense forests under which lay the richer forest soils. Indeed, an early general belief among planters, and one that propelled the "coffee mania" forward during the early boom years, was that the forest soils were so rich that it would be possible to keep the coffee trees at maximum fruitfulness without the application of manure. This, of course, was a far cry indeed from the underlying ecological reality of the highlands.

Clearing the Highlands

The first step in preparing the forest estate for production was to fell the forest and to prepare the biomass to be burned off. This was a major undertaking. British superintendents and estate owners relied upon Sinhalese ax men, often hired from highland villages, who had had extensive experience with forest

clearance for chena.[10] It was impractical to fell a few trees at a time because after
their falls they would render it virtually impossible for the workmen to reach
the adjoining giants. Thus the highland technique was wholesale and labor-
saving: Workers hacked their way into the forest and slashed down the seedlings and underbrush; they then began again at the bottom of an intended
clearing, chopping an incision on both the lower and upper sides of the trees,
the one on the upper side about six inches higher than the one on the lower
side. When the trees were large in girth at their base, they often narrowed considerably at a height of eight feet or so, and thus the ax men chopped away at the
narrowed girth while standing on small stages, axing their way up the mountainside for many days. At the top, the largest trees would be cut clear through
and allowed to shatter their way down the mountain, toppling and uprooting
incised trees of majestic height. The upper and middle stories of the rainforest
would collapse upon themselves; then the workers lopped off the largest
branches from the shattered giants and left the tangled and toppled biomass to
dry for a matter of months. The trunks of the forest trees were simply too large
to repay the effort to cut them into lengths convenient for burning, and thus the
giants remained where they crashed, near their standing stumps, with brush
and branch loppings clumped close by.[11]

There was little selection for valuable timber, either before or after the felling. The mountain streams that rushed through the hills were choked with
boulders. The satinwoods and ebonies and jacks, which would have brought
remunerative returns in the low country or in close proximity to the Mahaweli
River at Peradeniya, were generally too distant from river transport to justify
the costs of overland haulage and thus were put to the torch.[12] The most
forward-looking superintendents built saw-pits for producing beams and
planks that would later be needed for building purposes on their estates, but
this was an uncommon practice. Some owners of forest parcels intended to re-
sell the plots after clearing and planting, but most seem to have assumed that
they could later harvest wood from the surrounding forests.

The felled forest was then left to desiccate partially, during the drier months
of the year. This was to maximize the possibility of a full, clean, and controlled
first burn that was of the first order of importance.[13] If unachieved, the charred
and half-burned trunks had to be laboriously gathered together and gone at
again. This was a prodigious task that was best avoided, if at all possible. One
could also err on the side of a fire that was overly intense, that would leave the
humus scorched and its fertility compromised. The hoped-for ideal was a burn
where all the small branches, understory plants, and debris were incinerated,

the wood ashes leaving the soil in some places white, in others black. Where the ground appeared red, this indicated a burn that was too hot.[14] Conflagrations of searing intensity, of course, could also prove difficult to control, and as increasing numbers of European estates were carved out of the highland forest, the possibility for unintentional destruction increased. Indeed, even as early as 1842, the proprietors Major Parke and Henry Wright at their property at Hantenne lost seventy or eighty acres to fire, set off inadvertently by a contractor burning a newly cleared forest across a nearby valley.[15]

The Evolution of Estate Agronomic Practices

In the early years, many planters carved out small fields in the forest blocks and left narrow forest belts between the fields to protect against wind.[16] This was practicable when the land for coffee plantations was truly extensive and prospectors could secure land within reasonable proximity of one of the few roads through the highlands that was negotiable by cart.[17] But soon, the increased demand for land meant that these limited land-use practices were trampled in the scramble for land within range of the highland roads. Shelterbelts shuddered under the ax.

The European planters found to their dismay that the cumulative effects of deforestation in a district could be quite unanticipated. Some properties with steep faces and quartz ridges exposed to wind lost their productive potential after a few years.[18] The clearing of surrounding ridges to facilitate the opening of new coffee estates could radically increase wind across the older plantations. This, in turn, would produce stress in the coffee trees, ripping the leaves off and chafing the stem bark at ground level, and thereby increasing the vulnerability to infection.[19] Some sites proved simply too windy for coffee cultivation, and the plantations failed as a result.[20] C. R. Riggs, who failed as a coffee planter, wrote an essay on the experience in the early 1850s and counseled that smaller plots be put into cultivation.[21]

In any case, over time most planters found these wind blocks to be more trouble than they were worth. The increased edge habitat of the shelterbelts was a haven for rodents, particularly rats, which launched destructive incursions into the coffee fields.[22] One solution to the problem of wind burn and chafing was to prune the coffee trees back into shrubs. The tree of five feet could be transformed into a bush of two feet or even eighteen inches as a prophylactic measure. A bush this size hugged the side of the mountain and benefited from every swale, rock-outcropping, and other microvariation in landform capable of deflecting the monsoon gales.

Closely allied to the issue of shelterbelts was the controversy over the value of shade trees. In the early years, coffee planters were divided into two camps, one favoring the planting and retention of selected trees to shade the coffee shrubs and the other favoring the complete removal of all arboreal cover actually within the coffee field. The matter reached a fair degree of resolution when R. B. Tytler, an energetic planter who had spent three years in the West Indies, cut down all the shade trees on his property and thereafter enjoyed increased yields. The benefits of the shadeless coffee field proved convincing to other planters, and over time the "West Indian" model came to be generally adopted.[23] Other influences, too, flowed in from the Caribbean. Coffee beans from Jamaica, Berbice, and Cuba were imported for use on the estates, and by the late 1840s the Cuban beans were said to be the most successful.[24]

The West Indian planters also brought with them their predilections for standardized agronomic practices such as pruning, manuring, and weeding that had enjoyed at least short-term success in the Caribbean.[25] This "scientific" model of agronomic practices for the coffee planter was also available in a late-eighteenth-century text by P. J. Laborie.[26] But to a surprising extent, many of the agronomic practices that took root in the highlands of Sri Lanka were the result of experimentation on the island's own forested slopes. For example, coffee plants were generally planted on a diamond pattern at five foot intervals, instead of at ten or twelve feet, the common practice in Java and the West Indies. This resulted in greater soil disturbance, because the usual planting practice was to dig holes eighteen inches wide and eighteen inches deep and to fill them, around the seedling, with topsoil from the surrounding surface, avoiding the gravelly or clayey subsoils. The necessity for "holing" lay in the fact that the burned-over forest soils were a tangled mass of forest roots and stones in which the taproot of the coffee plant, unaided, would have little chance.[27]

Similar experimentation took place in the domain of pruning. Some superintendents did not appreciate that suckers would not be as productive as primary branches, and they pruned without a system, reducing their yields, or pruned not at all, to the same effect.[28] Harvesting likewise was often haphazard. Workers picked the fruit green or ripe, and the unripe was thrown away. In sum, in the early years, for many novice planters there was little absolutely systematic about the coffee plantation, and tried-and-true practices evolved only out of years of experimentation. Moreover, the variations in soil, rainfall, lay of the land, and other variables meant that coffee planting successes would remain idiosyncratic. Few, if any, general rules could supersede intelligent experimentation in situ.[29]

Ecological Impact on Soil Resources

The felling of the biologically diverse forest cover and its replacement with a monocrop, tropical plantation culture focused intense pressures on the soil resources of the highlands. The steep slopes exacerbated the problem; indeed, it was not uncommon to find the upper portion of a three-hundred-acre coffee estate at 1,800 or 2,000 feet above the lower portion.[30] The removal of the forest cover exposed the topsoils to the direct, percussive impact of rainfall and began the erosion of the soil, a process that was most exacerbated on the relatively steep gradients of the highland slopes. A second wave of pressure was exerted by the burning-off of the biomass. This reduced the acidity of the forest soils to levels more amenable to plantation cultivation, which, as in the case of chena, could be used to enrich the soils for a season or two of cultivation. But this was true only if the ash could be spread and worked into the soil before the onset of heavy rains, and the sheer scale and intensity of the fires meant that this was often difficult to achieve. Tytler described vividly the effect of a rainstorm after a burn: "The potash, magnesia, and soda, which the forest trees had elaborated during succeeding generations, lie exposed on the bare, charred surface of the hill side. A thunderstorm, following the fire carries them roaring off in torrents to the sea. When walking subsequently over the burned and washed surface our feet will tread among the lixiviated ashes, crisp and metallic, like frozen snow; but these are the insoluble silicates and carbonates of lime, as valueless as the charcoal among which they lie."[31]

In the absence of leaching rainfall, an enrichment of the soil could be achieved, as the nutrients from the biomass were placed into the soil. But this enrichment was only temporary. As in the case of chena, cultivated plants drew down the nutrient account in the highland soil bank. Planters were in short order disabused of the notion that the forest soils were so rich that they could be worked without fertilizer. The breaking-up of the soil by mamoty, a broad-bladed, mattock-like tool, in order to plant coffee seedlings meant that accelerated soil erosion would necessarily continue for years, until the coffee plants formed a dense growth capable of breaking the force of the rains. Planters did, however, endorse the diamond pattern of planting on the slopes (in contrast to the linear pattern in Brazil), and at maturity this pattern may have mitigated the full extent of erosion.

The search for fertilizers to replenish the nutrients extracted by the coffee plants and to arrest the increasing acidity of the soil caused by wash was an ongoing concern of the estate superintendent. One relatively inexpensive solution was to burn dolomite (dolomitic limestone) which could be found scattered throughout the Central Province, often mixed with lime phosphate. The general prescription was to burn the dolomite in a kiln with a good quantity of wood, and later to mix the wood ashes with the burnt lime, allowing the mixture to be exposed to air under shelter for several days, and then spreading it over the estate at about one hundredweight per acre. If the land was relatively flat, the mixture could be broadcast, but otherwise the workers placed it in ridges cut horizontally across the face of the slope.[32]

One solution to the problem of manure supply that seemed natural to those familiar with cattle and the mixed farming systems of the middle latitudes proved impractical on most estates. Here the problem was the poor quality of the indigenous patana grasslands. To provide cattle fodder, some estate managers brought in the higher-quality exotic guinea grass (*Panicum maximum*), but this crop demanded considerable attention. It had to be planted in rows, kept free of weeds, thinned out, and manured every two or three years.[33] Guinea grass grew continuously, and under cultivation could produce six or eight crops during the course of the year.[34] Large extents of the estate, under a highly labor-intensive system of cultivation approximating that of coffee itself, were necessary to produce sufficient cattle manure. Three acres of guinea grass could provide fodder for six cattle for one year; the manure from these six cattle could fertilize four acres of coffee; if mixed with bone dust and other nutrients, the same quantity of cattle manure could be stretched to cover twelve acres. Under an ideal system, fields of coffee might even alternate with fields of cultivated grasses, and indeed, in principle, somewhere between 20 and 40 percent of an estate might usefully be put into cultivated fodder grass, although this was rarely achieved. The fact that the patana grasses were deficient in nutrients meant that most estates kept few cattle and were unable to produce adequate quantities of manure. It also meant that the managers of the estates were dependent upon Muslim cartmen ("Moormen") to get their produce to market.[35]

One alternative to cattle manure was to utilize pig offal, and some planters recommended imported breeds of pig for this purpose. Pigs had the advantage that they could eat coarser grass and "jungle stuff,"[36] but when the pigs were wide-ranging, their manure was difficult to collect; at all events, pig culture never became deeply ensconced in the functioning of the estates. Another option for planters was to import humus from the neighboring forest. This was thought to be most effective when the coffee fields were so denuded of soils that the roots of the shrubs lay exposed to the air. This, however, was an expensive undertaking, estimated at twenty-five rupees per acre. Planters also experimented with exotic manures. Guano was imported from islands in the South Pacific and from South America, but the cost proved prohibitive.[37] Cattle manure was generally held to be one of the best, apart from the difficulty of its supply, but it, too, had its unintended ecological consequences. Grubs were attracted to the manure, and these in turn attacked the coffee trees.[38]

The cost of transport, the availability of grass cover on the patanas, and access to dolomite were important determinants of the types and quantities of fertilizers used. If the grasslands would not support cattle, one solution was to blend the refuse of the pulping house with whatever vegetable matter was on hand, as well as with lime and burned clay. R. B. Tytler extolled the virtues of his preparation of mineral salts.[39] Others experimented, although with little success, with human excrement gathered from the Indian coolie labor force.[40]

As the planters struggled to ensure the continued productivity of the coffee soils, they had also to struggle against an array of unwanted competitors for the soil resources. Early in the coffee era, planters found to their chagrin that it was necessary to weed the burned-over plantations every month and to commit a large number of laborers to rooting out with mamoties the grasses that invaded the scorched earth. Weeding was the bane of the early plantation work. There were two methods. The deep cut could, at least in principle, sever the roots well below the surface, allow for the weeds to be taken out by hand, and for the soil to be shaken off. If done properly, and the weeds were pulled out by hand, soil loss was minimized. The shallow cut severed the roots closer to the surface and did not always kill the weed. Some planters, however, were impressed by the smooth surface that the shallow cut left behind and thought that it reduced soil loss through erosion. These methods were practicable only if the weed infestation was limited in extent, however. Few planters succeeded in maintaining this fundamental economy.

Once weeds became established, weed scrapers—iron hoops that cut away the top inch of the topsoil—were called out, and this scraping had to be repeated every month or so. If even this proved ineffective, labor gangs with mamoties were sent in to break up the soil and to root out the invaders.[41] This was somewhat specialized work, and contracts were let out to "weeding contractors,"

who engaged to provide their services on a monthly basis. Some of the colonizing weeds were indigenous, such as the misnamed Spanish needle *(Bidens pi-*
losa). But most of the aggressive colonizing grasses were exotics that had escaped
from the gardens at Peradeniya.[42] Among the worst were sow-thistle *(Sonchus*
arvensis); goat-weed, also known as white-weed or wind-weed *(Ageratum co-*
nyzoides); and mile-a-minute *(Mikania scandens)*, the term for which in Sinhala
translates literally as "world-ruin." Unwanted grasses competed with coffee
shrubs for nutrients. Estates that were infested by weeds suffered sickly crops,
and once established the colonizing grasses were extremely difficult to evict.
Manuring the estate under these conditions just made matters worse.[43]

The practices of clean weeding that evolved in the Sri Lankan highlands were
far from standard in the wider region. In fact, they stand in stark contrast to the
practices employed on the British coffee estates on the mountains of southern
India. There, "weeds" were used as ground cover, protecting the soil from washing away and serving as a manure when they were dug into the soil. The conviction of the British planter in Sri Lanka was that the soil was too poor to support
both weeds and cash crops, and thus weeds would have to go.[44] There were other
problems associated with clean weeding in addition to soil erosion. Clean weeding removed all protection from the soil, and thereby increased heat radiation
and evaporation. This in turn encouraged coarse grasses, rather than succulents,
to grow and reduced the potential of the green manures.[45] The soil-damaging
practice of clean weeding was also linked to the larger economic patterns. With
the abandonment of estates during a financial crisis in the late 1840s, the colonization by exotic flora took place with astounding rapidity. In particular, the
seemingly ubiquitous prickly lantana shrub *(Lantana aculeata)*, introduced into
the island as an ornamental plant in the mid-1820s, overpowered the abandoned
"shuck" estates, growing in luxuriance across the expanses of the estates at
heights from five to eight feet.[46] Similarly, weeds became well-established on
the coffee estates during later financial downturns in the 1850s, 1860s, and 1870s,
when maintenance expenditures were cut to survive lean times.[47]

If the environmental problems visible above ground were vexing for the
coffee growers, the same was true below. The taproot of the coffee shrub could
be killed off by excessive dampness, or poor drainage, and thus one of the major concerns on the estates was drainage of wet lands. On slopes, this was effected by building drains to evacuate the excess water. These drains ran
vertically down the slopes. This was apparently reasonably effective in evacu-
ating the rainwater, but the trade-off was that the rushing water stripped the
surface soils off rapidly.[48] Some areas were simply too wet to plant coffee and

were too flat to drain. There it was possible to plant, at elevations up to 3,000 feet, the exotic, succulent water grass *(Panicum barbinode)*, introduced from tropical America about 1850, which produced a good fodder.[49]

Ecological Impacts on Fauna and Flora

During the early years of the estate coffee industry, the ecological impact was in some respects similar to that of the chena cultivators, albeit on a larger scale. On the edges of the burned areas, there was a dramatic increase in the duration and intensity of sunlight, which undoubtedly changed the composition of the flora.[50] Carving out estate lands from immense forest blocks created extensive ecotones, which increased the productive habitat for elephants, deer, hogs, and small game, and improved the hunting prospects of the large cats. Thus it is no surprise that, in many respects, the estates suffered the same problems from wild-animal incursions as did the Kandyan villages. Rogue elephants, for example, were known to terrorize coolies on the plantations.[51] These rich ecotones also meant that the high density of the faunal populations, including hares, made for easy hunting for the stewpot.[52] And from these edge habitats came bewildering attacks upon the coffee shrubs. In 1847, the coffee rat *(Golundus ellioti)* experienced an extraordinary population explosion, apparently as a result of the extensive ripening of coffee shrubs and perhaps the failure of the rat's usual food source, the *nelu* plant *(Strobilanthes)*.[53] The rodents wreaked havoc. As E. F. Kelaart noted:

> Whole plantations, are sometimes deprived of buds and blossoms by these rats. They are found in all the higher parts of the Kandian provinces. The attention of Europeans, has only been drawn to them since coffee planting commenced in the Island. They appear to be migratory; and are not always seen in Coffee estates: when they do visit the cultivated parts, their numbers are so great, that in one day more than 1,000 have been known to be killed on one estate alone. In clearing forests, the nests of these rats are met with under the roots of trees. We have not been so fortunate as to see many fresh specimens; only one was brought to us from Kaduganava: a premium is set by some coffee planters on the heads of these rodents. The Malabar coolies are very fond of eating them roasted, or fried in oil.[54]

In addition, some estates sat astride the migration routes of small animals that ran up and down the mountainsides in quest of food supplies. The nelu plant, in bloom, attracted honeybees, and when the nelu seed ripened, thousands of jungle fowl *(Gallus lafayetti)* from the low country wandered to the upper highlands in search of it.[55] Some estates became open hunting grounds on the jungle fowl, and pressure on the small game was likely considerable.

The fauna drawn to the edge habitats provided their own ecological dynamics, and propelled the coffee estates outward. Birds, squirrels, monkeys, and other animals fed upon the coffee shrubs, digested the sweet pulp of the coffee berry, and evacuated the beans whole. They deposited their droppings in the nearby forests, where large stocks of coffee plants grew up independently of the planters' volition. These plants were generally scraggly and had to be radically pruned ("stumped") before planting on the open estate; there, however, these stumps usually proved robust.[56]

The coffee plantations themselves, however, were quite vulnerable ecologically. Their uniformity and extent represented an enormous supply of food for parasitic insects, much as was the case with wet rice fields and, indeed, with monocultures in general. The continuing growth pattern of the coffee plant reinforced this vulnerability. Unlike a farm crop that is harvested at short intervals, coffee grew on-site year after year, and this allowed for pests or disease to build up over a long period of time.[57]

Very early in the coffee era, insect infestations became sufficiently serious to attract the attention of both the planting community and the colonial administration in Colombo. In 1843, "bug" began to appear on a few coffee estates on the western boundary of the central mountain range, and over time the bug spread east. The infestations were partial, and they could intensify over time or be short-lived.[58] "Bug" could appear unpredictably and disappear just as unpredictably. It left a soot-like covering on the coffee leaves.[59] *Bug,* of course, was an umbrella term that covered a wide range of pests, and sometimes distinctions were made between black bug, brown bug, and white bug. The major pest in the 1840s was the brown bug, and indeed the death of the coffee enterprise was confidently predicted on this account as early as 1847.[60] The extent of the damage done by the brown bug was a function of the length of its infestation. An average loss of crop was estimated at two-thirds of the yield from healthy trees. The female bugs did not have wings, but walked from one tree to the next and gave birth to large numbers of minute young, which were all but undetectable by the naked eye. "Bug" was thus easily transmitted by coolie laborers going from one estate to another, as well as by birds and large insects. And then, quite unexpectedly, in 1848 the "bug" began to disappear in many areas and moved from being a daunting threat to the entire industry to a major, if sporadic and localized, blight.[61]

Planters looked in vain for an effective antidote to "bug," but the solutions proposed were futile and/or impracticable (as, for example, dipping the leaves of the affected coffee shrub in hot water). Help came from the ecological knowledge of the Kandyan farmers. They introduced red ants to destroy "bug," as well as caterpillars. The efficacity of the red ant against the bug was reported at the general meeting of the Ceylon Branch of the Royal Asiatic Society in 1854, but so, too, was the aversion of the coolie population to its introduction because of the red ant's bite. At all events, during the course of the 1850s, "bug" became downgraded to a periodic menace to the fortunes of the owners of afflicted estates.[62]

"Grub" were another matter altogether. Grub presented a chronic problem: they preferred the edge habitats bordering the coffee estates and thrived on the coffee plants. It was necessary to kill the winged grub by hand, after it settled on the leaves of shrubs or trees at night, because during the day it burrowed an inch or so below the soil surface. Planters tried everything. Burning did not work because the grub that were above ground simply flew away and those in the soil remained unaffected. As with "bug," there were ecological allies from the natural world to be called upon. Wild pigs, birds, spiders, and lizards fed upon the big cockchafers, or beetles, and their larvae, and pigs in particular were able to grub a field of coffee thoroughly. But the scale of infestation overwhelmed the capacity of the local fauna.[63] Once the infestation in the soil became severe, there was no alternative to "grubbing them out" with a mamoty. The result, of course, was extensive soil surface breakage with a concomitant increase in soil erosion.

Conflicts over Water and Pasture

The expansion of coffee estates involved both competition with Kandyan villagers over access to resources and conflicts about land use.[64] In the period 1840 to 1860, the expansion of the estates took place principally on lands at elevations above 1,500 and below 3,500 feet; Kandyan villages were almost always sited below 2,000 feet, although the villagers' chena and hunting lands extended to higher elevations. The patterns of competition and conflict resulted from the estates' absorbing some lands in which villagers claimed rights. It is not possible to reconstruct a detailed geography of Kandyan settlement, land rights, and land use in the highlands in the early nineteenth century, and thus it is not possible to assess quantitatively the extent to which the estates directly impinged upon the villagers' resources.[65] The broad patterns of competition and conflict, however, are clear.

A series of contentious water-use issues arose first during the early coffee era, as a result of forest clearance and because the coffee estates were generally upstream from the rice cultivators. Early in the coffee era, when planters learned that there were larger profits to be made by pulping the coffee berries on their estates and drying them out before paying cartage fees to Colombo, they invested in pulping mills, generally powered by mountain streamflow. Even a moderately sized coffee estate could produce from one hundred to several hundred tons or more of pulp, which at least in principle could be allowed to rot and could be enhanced with other organic compost. But planters found that the fertilizing quality of the pulp was low, and they thus sloughed it off into the mountain streams. Unfortunately, when dumped into the streams, the pulp slime tended to cling to the rocks and stones in the stream beds and reduced the water quality of those dependent upon that source who lived downstream.[66]

This dumping occurred at a time when the patterns of river and stream flow in the highlands were changing. The removal of the forest cover not only increased soil erosion but reduced the infiltration of rainfall into the denuded soils. When the great absorptive sponges of the forest floors were chopped up, the mountain streams ran more rapidly after heavy rainfalls and carried increased loads of sediment. This could mean the silting of downstream paddy fields—a problem that became more severe in the late nineteenth and early twentieth centuries. Another problem was the disappearance of springs as a result of deforestation. As early as 1841, at least one assistant government agent raised the issue of requiring purchasers of lands to protect watercourses in order to prevent injury to downstream paddy lands, and his suggestions were forwarded by the government agent for the Central Province.[67] But the incidence of complaint was apparently low, and government did not move on this issue until much later in the century, when corridors were prescribed to be left undisturbed along the banks of the highland watercourses (corridors that, in the event, proved to be largely inefficacious). Evidence from the mid-1860s suggests that the principal conflict between upstream coffee planters and downstream rice cultivators was over the upstream diversion of water, rather than from coffee-pulp pollution or siltation.[68] The extent of these ecological problems was, of course, in ratio to the size of the plantation sector, which began to grow rapidly from the late 1860s.

Another set of issues concerned access to forest pasture. As the extent of the coffee plantations grew, particularly in the rainshadow zone, increasing pressure was focused on the forest pasture available to villagers. This was particularly significant during dry spells. In the era before coffee estates, when the patanas became parched, villagers had been able to drive their cattle into the forests to allow them to forage for themselves. The loss of forest cover thus compounded the difficulties of the Kandyan villagers during droughts.[69] The shortage and poor quality of pastureland generated conflict between villagers and plantation managers over the grazing of cattle and buffalo. Villagers' cattle made incursions onto the coffee estates, in search of grazing grasses. And buffalo not only ate grass; they also trod down the young coffee plants and butted at the mature shrubs with their horns in order to scratch themselves.[70]

Additional pressure on the scarce forest pasture came later in the century as more forest land was converted to other uses. The significance of the reduction in forest pasture available to the Kandyan farming communities is difficult to judge. At a minimum, the reduced forest pasture probably constrained natural growth in the buffalo and cattle populations at least in some areas, and it may have been the case that some highland farmers were forced to dispense with animal husbandry altogether.[71] Although highland livestock farming itself was under increasing constraint, across the island as a whole there was a substantial increase in animal husbandry over the period 1815–80, estimated to be on the order of sixfold. The principal constraint to livestock farming in the highlands may well have been the poor quality of the natural pasturage on the patanas,[72] rather than a shortage of forest pasture per se.

South Indian Migrant Labor and South Indian Rice

In the early years of experimentation with coffee, highland planters had relied principally upon the labor of Kandyan and low-country Sinhalese farmers to fell the forests, burn off the biomass, and establish the nurseries and seedling plantations. It soon became apparent, however, that there were not enough Kandyan Sinhalese who were willing to sign up for regular work on the plantations or enough low-country Sinhalese seeking employment on the estates to meet the needs of the burgeoning coffee industry. For most Sinhalese near the lower highlands forest belt, the better prospect was to establish tenure by opening up new lands through chena agriculture. The returns from the firestick and plow trumped the meager cash wages paid to plantation laborers.

Across the Gulf of Mannar, in South India, however, there were large numbers of lower-caste Tamil men from impoverished communities who were willing to risk ocean travel in the small boat known as the dhoney and then undertake the long walk overland into the highlands. The coffee estates paid wages that were sufficient to draw these men by the prospect of improving their economic status through wage labor, even in the face of great hardship, poor working conditions, and high mortality. These migrant wage workers, known as coolies (Tamil: wage), became the primary labor force for the highland export economy. The demand for this migrant labor was seasonal and varied according to the rainface or rainshadow orientation of the estate.[73] The rhythms of highland coffee production dictated that the peak demand for labor was during the four months of the coffee harvest, followed by the drying, packing, and shipping of the beans. This agronomic calendar for coffee lagged the agricultural cycle in South India, however, and this allowed many of the Tamil men to return to their villages to carry on agricultural labor there. Tamil laborers from South India arrived on the island in considerable numbers, increasing from a few thousand per year in the early 1840s to tens of thousands per year by the late 1840s and continuing to increase throughout the coffee period. Most returned annually, but many stayed on the plantations.

Table 4.1. Average Annual Arrivals of South Indian Laborers in Sri Lanka, by Decade, 1840–1887

1840–49	35,490
1850–59	56,114
1860–69	67,209
1870–79	104,474
1880–87	39,574

Source: These annual arrival averages have been calculated from data published in Ian H. Vanden Driesen, *The Long Walk: Indian Plantation Labor in Sri Lanka in the Nineteenth Century* (New Delhi, 1997). This text also includes data on departures and on mortality. Not all workers returned to South India on an annual basis.

The second fundamental linkage of the highland estate sector with South India was in the supply of food. The productivities of the rice systems on the island of Sri Lanka were low by regional standards. The result was that the Indian coolie laborers were unable to be supplied with food from within the highland ecological systems, or for that matter from elsewhere on the island. Estate managers purchased food supplies from South India and had the sacks transported to the highlands by bullock cart. Imported workers ate imported rice.

The supply functions of labor and rice were volatile and linked, although in ways that were not readily predictable. During periods of drought and extreme

Table 4.2. Rice Imports in Bushels, 1837–1899

Year	Rice Imports in Bushels	Year	Rice Imports in Bushels
1837	650,042	1869	4,406,216
1838	860,012	1870	4,735,832
1839	884,628	1871	4,278,708
1840	1,043,064	1872	5,367,302
1841	1,106,152	1873	5,708,142
1842	1,102,192	1874	5,717,775
1843	1,594,114	1875	5,527,620
1844	1,700,136	1876	5,855,645
1845	2,167,334	1877	6,938,160
1846	2,162,206	1878	6,668,969
1847	2,121,022	1879	5,954,934
1848	1,910,585	1880	6,094,999
1849	1,985,752	1881	6,030,820
1850	2,355,763	1882	5,757,025
1851	2,221,466	1883	5,746,184
1852	2,331,796	1884	5,490,768
1853	2,574,580	1885	5,734,129
1854	2,161,706	1886	5,567,100
1855	2,852,178	1887	5,870,632
1856	3,157,385	1888	6,744,145
1857	3,254,623	1889	6,677,920
1858	2,856,124	1890	6,499,697
1859	3,511,768	1891	7,162,024
1860	3,182,204	1892	7,364,346
1861	4,181,096	1893	7,456,366
1862	4,218,601	1894	7,556,505
1863	4,415,821	1895	8,722,823
1864	3,943,896	1896	7,594,413
1865	4,851,414	1897	8,723,750
1866	3,777,320	1898	9,023,598
1867	4,543,327	1899	9,097,238
1868	4,455,315		

Sources: John Ferguson, *Ceylon in the Jubilee Year* (London, 1887), app. 7, 268.

John Ferguson, *Ferguson's Ceylon Handbook and Directory for 1900-1* (Columbo, 1901), 611.

Note that a small percent (less than 3 percent as a maximum) was reexported.

For rice imports in the period 1816–1833, see Ameer Ali, "Peasant Agriculture in Ceylon, 1833–1893," 12.

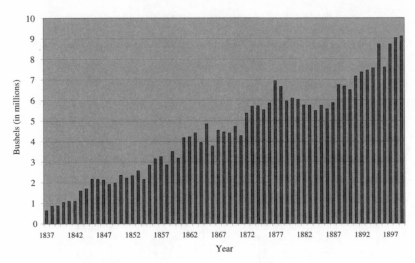

Table 4.2 Graph. *Rice Imports in Bushels, 1837–1899*

hardship in South India, the supply of available laborers increased. But droughts were sometimes extremely localized, sometimes more widespread, and the same was true for bumper crops. The highland plantations as importers of both labor and food thus were dependent upon the vagaries of South Indian economic and ecological processes. This instability itself was a wild card for the highland planters, who were never sure if the next year's supply of Indian laborers would be sufficient to work the estates; this in turn meant they were unable to forecast the price of rice.

The coolies from South India were extremely poor. The trip overland to the Indian coast and the sea travel by dhoney were arduous, and many arrived on the island in a weakened condition, sometimes fully emaciated. Some were suffering from contagious disease. Others suffered from malarial infections. They then undertook the long trek from the coast into the highlands, suffering fearsome mortality along the way. They undoubtedly brought smallpox and cholera with them. Government agents logged the peaks of mortality in their districts and often assigned causation to the arrival of the Indian migrant workers. Indeed, it is likely that the annual flow of coolie laborers was at least in part responsible for the annual outbreaks of cholera in the highlands. Cholera alone occurred either in sporadic or epidemic form during every year save one of the entire era of the coffee boom (1842–78) for which records exist. The historical data are incomplete, but they do permit a glimpse of the ravages of this disease. In 1845, for example, an outbreak of cholera claimed one-fifth of the population of Kandy.[74]

On the coffee estates themselves, the coolies had encounters with other deadly diseases. The edge habitats around the coffee plantations, like those around chena fields, harbored mite vectors, which carried the deadly scrub typhus.[75] Worker mortality, however, is impossible to calculate, because so many died on the road or, when seriously ill, were cruelly driven off the plantations into the surrounding woods to die. It does seem to be the case, however, that the first fifteen years of the coffee industry were the worst and that a series of policies aimed at the amelioration of the immigrant workers' circumstances slowly brought about a wholesale improvement.[76]

Cattle Disease

The new roads from the coast into the highlands also opened the way for the transmission of animal disease from South India, where the cattle populations had long suffered from the ravages of rinderpest. This disease reservoir in southern India was itself part of a larger zone of chronic infection that can be traced back to the steppes of central Asia, where the disease became established among the herds of pastoral peoples. The infectious disease was spread from diseased to healthy animals through running sores on the mouth and nose that drained into the watering points and feeding troughs and adhered to pasture grasses. Moreover, rinderpest was an epizootic that could infect other ruminant populations besides cattle and buffalo. Sambhur deer and wild pigs were particularly susceptible.

Because of the long history of interactions between South India and Sri Lanka, it is possible that rinderpest may well have been introduced on numerous occasions before the nineteenth century. If so, the disease would have wreaked destruction upon the afflicted animals and then disappeared since the cattle herds in the maritime provinces were not numerous enough to have sustained the infection. By contrast, cattle within India itself were sufficiently numerous and widespread as to prevent the disease from running a terminal course, and India remained a regional reservoir of the disease. The endemic nature of the disease within continental South Asia also meant that it was less virulent in outbreak. At all events, the greater commercial intercourse between India and Sri Lanka encouraged by British rule brought about a major outbreak of rinderpest at the beginning of the nineteenth century, probably in the year 1800. James Cordiner, writing in the early years of the nineteenth century, reported that one-half of the cattle and buffalo could be swept away by an "epidemic of distemper" in a matter of months.[77]

In nineteenth-century Sri Lanka, rinderpest was an epizootic infection that produced high mortality among both infected cattle and buffalo. The signal presenting symptom of the most virulent form of the infection was a swollen inflammation of the throat, which marked a stage of the infection that was swiftly followed by death. The fact that villagers were generally unaware that an animal was ill until shortly before the animal's death meant that it was not possible to separate the sick and dying from the uninfected. This, of course, contributed to extension of the disease.

Dying cattle and buffalo could wander away to die or drop dead near the villages. The carcasses generally were not buried by the villagers and this led to a multiplication of the disease vectors. Buffalo and cattle often died in or near pools of water, and sambhur deer contracted the disease by drinking at the contaminated sites. Wild pigs fed on the carcasses of dead cattle and in this manner spread the infection from one district to another, wandering for miles before succumbing to the disease. Villagers and estate workers were also known to have carried away diseased carcasses for food, and although human beings were not subject to rinderpest, it is possible that the infection was carried to villages and plantations in this manner.[78]

After the devastation of the epizootic of 1800, outbreaks of rinderpest recurred during the first four decades of the nineteenth century. The details of these outbreaks are not recoverable, but the eruptions seem to have been caused by the importation of diseased "coast" cattle from South India. The possibilities for enhanced disease transmission improved with the extension of roads into the highlands and the consequent increase in *tavalam* (caravan of carriage bulls) traffic from the coastal regions into the highlands. Indeed, very early in the coffee era, in 1841, a general epidemic broke out both around Colombo and in the Kandyan provinces. This outbreak was severe, at least in part because it was exacerbated by a simultaneous eruption of hoof-and-mouth disease. According to a report in the *Colombo Observer and Commercial Advertiser* of that year:

> The first symptom of the complaint is a gummy leaden appearance of the eyes and nose, and a disrelish for all sorts of food. The throat speedily becomes affected, and is swollen and very hard, giving acute pain when handled. Ulceration of the tongue, gums, and entire inside of the mouth follows, with much rapidity, and the flow of saliva is considerable—whilst the bullock stands in a cramped

posture, with the head depressed, and, seemingly, suffering great pain. The mouth when looked into is much inflamed—the teeth are loose—the skin that covers the gums and lines the lips cracks, and becomes detached on the slightest touch, laying bare an inflamed and discoloured surface; the tongue loses its fur, and, with great heat in the mouth, there seems to be the general destruction of the papillae that cover the inside,—At an after stage of the complaint, and immediately following these symptoms there is a discharge from the nose, and an ulceration takes place in the feet. The horny part of the hoof in some cases falls off, and, in others the thick skin that is between the mouth and the nose goes also—leaving an ugly raw sore that hinders the bullock from feeding, and affords an opportunity for grubs to get into the feet. The illness is now at its height, and the sufferer laboring in severe fever, under which it frequently sinks and dies. The Singhalese, amongst whose cattle in some parts of the country, the disease has been eminently fatal, say that its recurrence maybe looked for periodically—at the expiration of an uncertain number of years, which may be three, or four, or seven, or ten, or more,—but generally about this season of the year, when the rains set in after the dry months. They say that it is caused by the sudden wetting and cooling of the earth, that, for some months previous, had been baked by the sun, and hot and dry—and that buffaloes, and sheep, and hogs, and deer, as well domesticated as in a state of nature in the jungle, are alike subject to the visitation. It is on record amongst them that this Epidemic prevailed amongst the working and breeding stock some four years before that, but not in a very devastating degree either time. It was not so, however, on another occasion, some forty years ago, when amazing numbers of domestic animals were carried off, and the whole jungle of the Island almost totally denuded of wild animals, from the same cause.[79]

The disease was particularly difficult to contain because the period between infection and presentation of symptoms was two to fourteen days, and this provided ample opportunity for infected working animals to make their way into the highlands from the coast. In both the highlands and the maritime provinces, rinderpest had devastating effects on the highland black cattle and buffalo populations. The epizootic, which had been principally confined to the maritime districts, began its full-fledged career in the highlands in 1840–41 and broke out with frequency thereafter. The 1841 epizootic produced severe economic distress in the export sector. A large proportion of the coffee crop remained on the estates owing to the high cost of transport.[80]

In the early years, transport costs from the highlands to the coast were highly variable, depending upon proximity of the estates to the major roads

Table 4.3. Volume and Value of Cattle Imports, 1837–1886

Year	Number	Value (Pounds Sterling)	Year	Number	Value (Pounds Sterling)
1837		1,801	1862	4,490	12,095
1838		820	1863	14,085	46,883
1839		1,156	1864	7,607	23,509
1840		1,270	1865	8,326	22,785
1841		1,727	1866	9,059	43,079
1842		5,131	1867	8,912	50,190
1843		7,596	1868	7,392	39,469
1844		22,885	1869	6,799	40,338
1845		25,557	1870	7,605	53,018
1846	47,237	23,745	1871	10,058	64,897
1847	61,594	28,914	1872	14,198	84,596
1848	47,265	26,425	1873	14,749	82,550
1849	8,895	17,884	1874	12,541	70,148
1850	8,507	17,120	1875	15,392	84,628
1851	8,994	17,698	1876	17,831	91,661
1852	7,951	16,363	1877	28,958	102,522
1853	9,295	18,886	1878	17,492	55,929
1854	12,524	25,268	1879	27,483	108,796
1855	16,534	33,280	1880	11,872	73,943
1856	11,317	23,515	1881	8,683	38,776
1857	10,575	21,635	1882	9,537	36,100
1858	11,228	25,119	1883	11,980	60,693
1859	10,776	26,608	1884	13,461	68,517
1860	10,514	24,471	1885	10,081	50,283
1861	9,753	23,730	1886	47,108	37,796

Source: John Ferguson, *Ceylon in the Jubilee Year* (London, 1887), 269. Before 1846, cattle imports were described as livestock and the quantity imported was not specified in the customs returns.

that were negotiable by bullock carts. Early producers of coffee had the beans head-loaded by coolies and carried down to the carriage roads, but the costs proved prohibitive. The best early alternative was to have coffee beans from the estate pack-loaded on the backs of the native draft cattle. In a further effort to reduce costs, a variety of solutions to the problem of transport were floated, and some were tried out. Some planters favored importing donkeys from Muscat as beasts of burden, and indeed a group of planters in Kandy in 1841 raised money by subscription for this purpose,[81] although for reasons that have escaped the historical record, this experiment never enjoyed success. There was also interest in importing donkeys from South India, but experience showed that they slipped on wet or uneven ground and they suffered

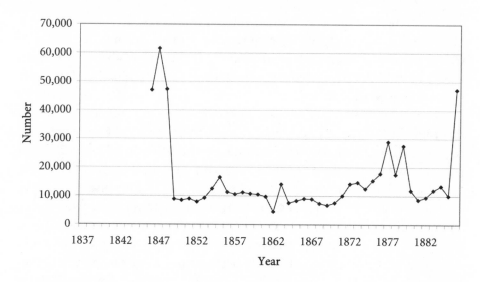

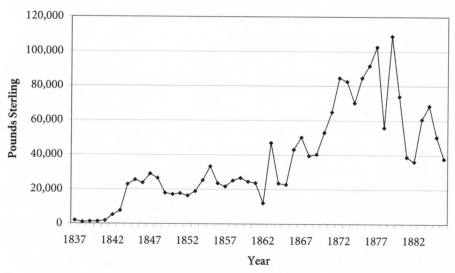

Above: **Table 4.3, Graph a.** *Volume*
Below: **Table 4.3, Graph b.** *Value*

greatly from leach bites. The superior option proved to be the importation of the coast cattle. The imported cattle were larger, ate more, and had to be shod once a month because their soles were soft; but they could carry greater weight than the local black cattle and were sturdy on their feet.[82] On the carriage roads, the native bullocks were capable of pulling only twelve to fifteen hundredweight for twenty miles per day, compared with twenty to thirty-five hundredweight by the coast cattle.[83] By the mid-1850s, the small, compact, hardy, native black cattle were being rapidly replaced by imported bullocks, and by the 1860s, transport to and from the highlands was being carried on wholly by bullock carts pulled by the large coast cattle. The native black cattle were on their way to extinction.[84]

The extension of roads into new highland terrains difficult of access meant that rinderpest outbreaks were highly idiosyncratic, varying by settlement and region. The tavalam drivers made their way up and down the hills, arriving with rice and leaving with their carts filled with coffee beans; along their path, they introduced rinderpest.[85] In some villages, the eruption of the disease might be contained to a very few animals; in others the eruption might be widespread. This produced a patchwork of variation. The coffee estates in general suffered much less than the villages. The estates were generally at higher elevations; some had no herds; those with cattle herds used the animals principally for traction and manure and depended upon Sri Lankan drivers of bullock carts for transport of their coffee; and no coffee estates kept buffalo on their premises.

The most widespread and persistent outbreaks were found in the rain-shadow patana lands of Uva. Six years after the early 1840s outbreak, the buffalo population of one district in Uva had still not reestablished itself, and villagers were obliged to rent buffalo to plow their fields.[86] In 1852, the entire Central Province suffered a loss of more than one-quarter of its cattle population, more than twenty-five thousand head. Mortality was high: three-quarters of the animals that contracted the disease died.[87] Similarly, in 1857 Northwestern Province lost one-quarter of its cattle.[88] In the highland district of Bintenne, the cattle population was hit hard by the epizootic in the 1860s, decreasing from 8,000 in 1862 to 2,500 in 1868.[89] At an ecotone where the moist highlands shade into the dry zone, in northern Matale, some seven hundred or eight hundred head of cattle out of a population of four thousand were lost between 1865 and 1868.[90] The high incidence of rinderpest resulted in a decrease in the cattle and buffalo populations over the short to medium term. This in turn produced a considerable increase in the price of both cattle and buffalo, enriching those whose herds had escaped the infection. The loss of cattle and buffalo in some areas meant that fields were left uncultivated; in other areas it meant that villagers were required to rent field animals, and thus there was a net shift in resources from those who had lost their cattle to those who had not. The increased value of traction animals varied by region and by year; but in 1868, the Cattle Disease Commission reported increases in the cost of traction animals on the order of two to ten times over earlier years.[91] The integration of the highlands into the larger disease reservoir of mainland South Asia thus was a ragged and chaotic process. At the extreme, spasms of disease could turn prosperous communities to poverty in a matter of days.

Hunting with Rifles: New Pressures on Highland Game Species

The burning-off of the dense forest and the opening up of the highlands dramatically reduced wildlife habitat. And beginning in the 1830s, Europeans and Kandyans—both with firearms—began to exert new pressures on the wild animal populations in the highlands. Europeans began to hunt for sport, to bag trophies. Kandyans began to hunt to support a commerce in hides and horns or to rid their districts of wild animals that posed threats to the human communities there. The carnage began on a large scale and continued throughout the century.

During the Kandyan period, Kandyan farmers had hunted small game as well as the medium-sized elk and wild pig.[92] They had entrapped with snare and killed with arrow, rather than musket.[93] The big game—in particular, the elephant—had been hunted with drums and torches, under the aegis of the Kandyan king. Large-scale parties had fanned out across the landscape and driven the fleeing giant pachyderms before them into stockaded corrals, where specialists broke the elephants for domestic work. Some of the captured elephants were bound into royal service for the Kandyan state, but most seem to have been shipped abroad. During the last centuries of the Kandyan state, the elephant had been by value one of the principal Sri Lankan export goods, destined for India or Southeast Asia.[94]

After the annexation of the Kandyan highlands, the British brought different attitudes to bear on the question of wild game. In 1831, the colonial governor, Sir R. Wilmot-Horton, gave permission for and even encouragement to the destruction of elephants. No longer were wild herds only to be driven into logged stockades and tamed. It was now thought right simply to kill the elephants in order to remove the threat that they posed to farming communities. There is no doubt that this open-door hunting policy both exacted a toll and conveyed its benefit. Writing in 1840, Major J. Forbes was certain that the destruction of the elephant herds was an important element in what he perceived to be an increased prosperity enjoyed by the Sinhalese villagers.[95] This pressure on the elephant populations was intensified by the fact that the villagers were able to acquire firearms, in part through their increasing access to currency, which permitted them more easily to repulse marauding elephants.[96] Farmers now had a means to kill or maim the pachyderms, when previously the best that they could hope for was to drive them off. British hunters had the more devastating impact. The scale of destruction possible by an individual was impressive. The mid-nineteenth-century colonial figure Major Thomas Rogers is said to have himself killed more than 1,500 elephants, and Captain Gallaway and Major Skinner are reputed to have shot about half that number each. Other sportsmen shot between 250 and 300 each.[97]

The pressure on the elephant herds was not restricted to hunting for sport and protection of crop fields. The export of elephants continued to be important into the late nineteenth century. Between 1858 and 1862, some 1,600 elephants entered the export trade.[98] Elephant exports continued until the end of the century, but the volume declined markedly at the end of the 1860s. Most of these elephants would have been captured in the maritime regions, rather than in the highlands. It is not possible to arrive at definitive elephant population figures, neither for before nor after the great ecological upheaval. Jayantha Jayawardena's recent estimate of perhaps twelve to twenty thousand on the island before the 1840s and perhaps two thousand at the end of the nineteenth century is an informed assessment of the magnitude of the decline.[99]

Hunters carried out an onslaught against wild animals throughout the nineteenth century. As a greater number of rifles made their way into the hands of the Kandyan hunters, the larger threat to the remaining highland animals was no longer from trophy hunting but from the commercial exploitation of the wild fauna for meat, horns, and hides. Efforts to mitigate the damage began only in the last few decades of the century. A law to control the shooting of game was promulgated in 1872, but it did little to stop the carnage. In 1889, a committee "appointed to consider and report on the existing laws relating to the protection of game, elephants, and buffaloes" reported that the 1872 "Game Law" had been ineffectual and noted significant decline in the abundance of animals. The general possession of firearms had spawned groups of "hunters and gipsies" who hunted year-round.[100]

The impacts on wild animal populations of this new mode of hunting, in conjunction with the destruction of habitat, varied. Leopard populations decreased markedly, from thousands in the early nineteenth century to mere hundreds in the late twentieth century. The fact that the leopard, as the top carnivore in the terrestrial ecosystem, hunted alone and had hunting grounds of perhaps twenty square kilometers, meant that this animal was particularly

Table 4.4. Volume and Value of Elephant Exports, 1863–1899

Year	Number	Value in Rs
1863	173	28,690
1864	194	45,920
1865	271	72,660
1866	203	63,250
1867	148	23,280
1868	167	47,,450
1869	199	46500
1870	38	8,050
1871	74	17,600
1872	53	22,270
1873	83	28,900
1874	77	41,230
1875	7	3,500
1876	3	1,000
1877	1	500
1878	1	500
1879	1	1,100
1880	12	11,200
1881	8	7,470
1882	25	10,105
1883	86	40,010
1884	51	28,100
1885	17	9,700
1886	50	19,100
1887	58	26,000
1888	57	33,550
1889		
1890	42	31,050
1891	48	34,350
1892	24	26,750
1893	21	18,400
1894	36	36,000
1895	12	10,800
1896	29	24700,
1897	9	9,500
1898	3	4,800
1899	9	17,750

Source: J. Ferguson, *Ferguson's Ceylon Handbook and Directory for 1900-1* (Colombo, 1901), 651-52.

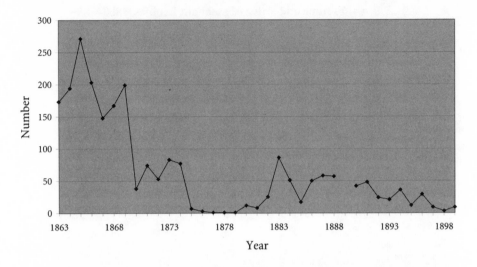

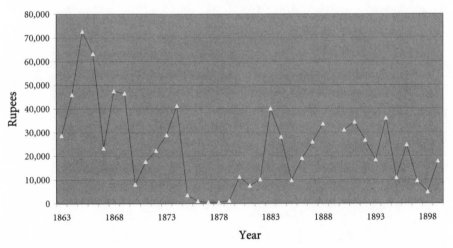

Above: **Table 4.4, Graph a.** *Volume*
Below: **Table 4.4, Graph b.** *Value*

vulnerable to the destruction of forest and patana habitat. The clearing of forests produced increasingly isolated subpopulations of leopards, who came to hunt cattle, dogs, and even poultry within the cultivated areas.[101] The herds of sambhur deer, hunted for their horns and hides, became fewer in number and more isolated, found only in the most remote, steep, or coldest highlands that had little economic value to planters. Monkeys, wild pigs, sloth bears, wild buffalo, and the smaller deer were also subject to human predation, and their numbers shrank dramatically under the pressures of hunting and habitat destruction.

Contemporary Perspectives on the Nineteenth-century Ecological Revolution

The progressive deforestation of the lower and middle highlands in the period 1840–70 brought about by the expansion of the coffee estates wrought widespread ecological change. This was not lost on contemporary observers. As early as the 1840s, some government officials had expressed concerns about the possible ecological repercussions of deforestation, particularly with regard to the desiccation of stream courses. A legislative ordinance had been passed—ordinance no. 24 of 1848—that at least on paper reserved to government the jungle or forest in which the streams were situated. But it had not proved practicable to enforce this ordinance, and both the plantation and the chena sectors continued their rapid and uninhibited expansions.

The failure to enforce the ordinance may in part be understood as owing to insufficient means to do so; but there was also a lack of political commitment. The simple fact was that many in government and in the planting communities did not consider the preservation of watercourses to be important. Consider for example the comments of Clements Markham, who was so influential in the great cinchona experiment, and who added his voice on the issue of deforestation and the desiccation of water courses in an 1866 sessional paper. As he wrote of the Rothschild estate at Pussellawa:

> Excepting a clump of Jacks high up on the eastern side, and some palms near the houses, every tree has been felled as far as the eye can reach, and rows of coffee plants entirely occupy the site of the primeval forest. No regard whatever has been paid to forest conservancy, belts of verdure are neither left along the water-courses nor on the hill tops, and planters have to send many miles for their firewood, yet there has been no sensible diminution of the water supply, and cascades and torrents dash over masses of rock through this coffee covered valley.[102]

In fact, the actual utility of narrow protective belts along the stream banks may well have been fairly low. In principle, a protective streambelt would filter the water coming off the estates and chena fields, and thus reduce the siltation in the lower-lying paddy fields. But the subsoil configurations of the highlands were exceptionally stable. As a result, the highlands of Sri Lanka, even with a massive topsoil loss owing to plantation agriculture and chena—estimated at one-third of an inch per year on estates[103]—did not suffer from rain scour. There were no erosion ravines. The rainwaters ran clean off the plantations after the topsoils were lost.[104]

Some members of the professional botanical community sounded cautions that would reverberate with increasing intensity in the twentieth and twenty-first centuries. George Gardner, the superintendent of the Royal Botanic Gardens at Peradeniya, as early as 1843 raised an alarm over the threat of species extinction. He was aware of the results of large-scale deforestation in the Mascarene Islands and in the West Indies and sought to avoid this fate for the highlands:

> Of late large tracts of the country have been cleared of the virgin forest by which they were covered, from the rapid spread of cultivation; and as this is likely to go on to a great extent, there can be no doubt that many of those trees which are peculiar to the Island, and local in the range, will ere long become extinct; and the Botanists of future times will look in vain for many of those species which their predecessors had recorded in the annals of science as natives of the Island. This is no idle speculation, such having already occurred in other countries.

Gardner, writing during the initial (European) coffee boom and the rapid expansion of chena cultivation, saw no solution other than to shelter specimens of what we could call today "endangered species" at the Royal Botanic Gardens. He recommended the creation of an arboretum.[105] Gardner began to plant indigenous trees in the garden at Peradeniya, and his successor G. H. K. Thwaites, who directed RBG-Peradeniya from 1849 until 1880, also moved aggressively to set out endangered plants in the protection of the Peradeniya garden as well as in the satellite gardens developed during his tenure.[106]

For the European planting community, the principal concern was the impact of deforestation on human health. There were diverse opinions. Some contemporary observers were sanguine. According to the marsh theory of malarial vapors, the burning off of the forest cover was certain to improve the health of the population. This was the view of Edmund Hull, who authored a well-known book about coffee planting in the highlands: "It is also satisfactory to know, that the clearing away of forest necessitated by coffee culture, has had the effect of rendering the climate in many districts much more healthful than formerly. A curious proof of this is found in the case of an estate not far from Kandy, which many years ago acquired the ominous appellation of the 'white man's grave,' that part of the country being now almost as free from malaria as the town of Kandy itself."[107]

The burning off of the forest cover and the tearing apart of the great forest soil cover meant an increased velocity of run-off after rainfalls. Many planters did note the drying up of streams on their properties, but took this as a sign of improving ecological health. In this view, as the "miasmas" disappeared so would fever, and the highlands would be a safer place to live.[108]

Others asserted a nearly opposite opinion. Henry Dickman advanced counterexamples in a handbook on Ceylon published in the late 1860s. He asserted a causal chain that could be traced back to the woodsman's ax: deforestation had brought about climate change and climate change had resulted in an increase in human morbidity. The remedy was the creation of forest reserves:

> On a limited scale, we observe the effect of the destruction of the forests in and around the Coffee districts in the interior. The unhealthiness of a "new clearing" is an admitted fact. Districts that have been noted for their salubrious climate have changed their character since the commencement of the Coffee enterprize. In days gone by, Doombera was noted for a healthy and vigorous population. Fever is now devastating the country, and Rajawella has become the hot-bed of miasm. Kaduganawa and Allagalla have become very unhealthy, and people now begin to look upon Happootella as a feverish district, whilst a few years back all were loud in praise of its "dry healthy climate" as well as its fertile and productive soil. These violent changes in the character of the climate of different places in the interior, are, in my humble opinion, greatly due to the destruction of their noble forests, and "Forest Conservancy" is a subject that must shortly force itself on the attention of the authorities.[109]

Interestingly, even with the benefits of hindsight and a wealth of contemporary scientific malariological studies, the direct relationship between forest clearance and human health in the nineteenth-century highlands cannot be specified. This is true in part because malaria, although considered a global disease (in the sense that it is widely found throughout the tropics and subtropics), depends upon confluences of idiosyncratic ecological dynamics that are not generalizable. In this sense, malaria may be understood as a local disease. In Sri Lanka, the Dry Zone has long been a region of hyperendemicity, and the Wet Zone a region susceptible to epidemic. The principal triggering mechanism is the failure of the southwest monsoon, which dramatically reduces river and streamflow and causes the riverine waters in some cases to pool, providing ideal conditions for breeding mosquitos. Although it is possible that the highland deforestation of the nineteenth century triggered epidemics of malaria there, no compelling evidence has yet come to light. It would seem that malaria did not flare up with truly ferocious mortality in Sri Lanka until the 1930s.[110]

The Sri Lankan perspectives on the mid-nineteenth-century ecological transformation are largely lost to the historical record. There can be no doubt that there was great bitterness among the Kandyan villagers who lost their access to chena lands through Crown sales and additional festering injury for those who lived beside streams polluted by coffee refuse. Yet what is conspicuously absent from the historical record is any resistance—village-based, caste-based, or ethnicity-based—to the expansion of British plantations in the middle highlands. Some elements of the Kandyan populace rose in rebellion against newly imposed measures of British taxation in 1848, but the 1848 rebellion was not broadly based, and although the rebels had a spate of grievances in addition to taxation, they did not focus on the plantations as the source of their complaints. The colonial government suppressed the rebellion militarily and lifted some of the tax measures that had given such offense.[111]

There are probably several reasons why the British plantations did not occasion more corporate resistance. At least some Kandyan villagers perceived the changing economic conditions of the mid-nineteenth century as opportunities. Some villagers, although relatively few in number and seemingly of low caste status, accepted employment on the coffee estates, because these jobs offered an improvement in their life circumstances. Some villagers with access to capital participated in and came to control the burgeoning system of transport. Yet others improved their economic status by opening up new chena lands and by planting coffee for export. As a whole, Kandyan villagers did not experience the extenuating provocations that might have galvanized them into opposition to the colonial plantations.

~

In this chapter we have seen how from the late 1830s, coffee mania swept through the middle highlands. British capitalists and their superintendents hired Sinhalese ax men to cut and burn rainforest plots and (mostly) Tamil laborers from South India to plant, weed, and harvest coffee. The agronomic practices on the coffee estates produced some deleterious environmental effects, both on the plantation itself and downstream. This degradation took place in the larger context of the integration of coastal and highland ecozones with South India. The increase in transport introduced rinderpest into the highlands to devastating effect. Indian labor migrants in their turn introduced successive waves of contagious disease that killed large numbers. Beginning in the 1860s, the transformation of the middle highlands would be followed by a dramatic series of economic opportunities and ecological crises that would remake the upper highlands.

CHAPTER 5

Into the Upper Highlands

D uring the 1860s, highland road construction initiatives received a new round of support from government, and some of the isolated mountainsides and valleys began to enter the network of cheaper transport.[1] This process of expansion accelerated in 1867, when workers completed a railroad line from Colombo to Kandy. Overnight it became possible to move coffee from the railhead in the highlands to the coast in a matter of a few hours at a fraction of its former cost,[2] and as a result it became economically feasible to open up coffee fields in ever more remote areas. Between 1869 and 1879, the colonial government sold more than 400,000 acres (625 square miles) of Crown land, bringing in more than £1 million to the government accounts.[3] In the upper reaches of the Mahaweli catchment area—particularly in the regions of Maskeliya and Adam's Peak—plantations proliferated. During the planting year 1872/1873 alone, close to 30,000 new acres were put into production, an increase of some 15 percent of the total coffee plantation area.[4] Planters charred out their new fields at higher elevations, at 5,000 and even 5,500 feet, well above the previously accepted agronomic limit of 4,500 feet.

The Onslaught of *Hemileia vastatrix*

But at the same time that the coffee industry expanded, a bright-reddish-orange parasitic fungus, later known as coffee rust or coffee leaf-disease,

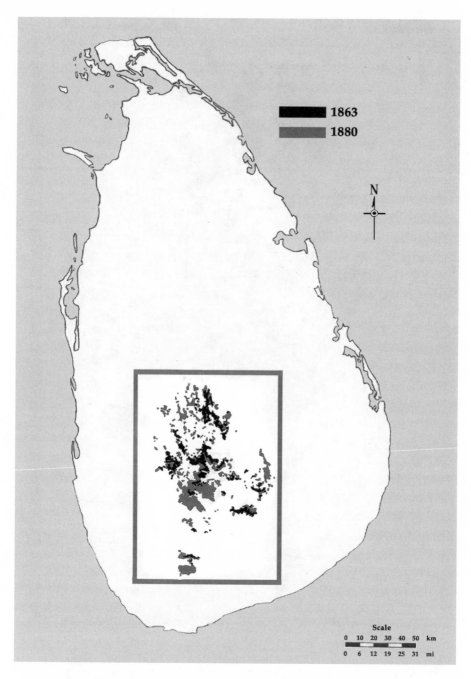

Map 5. *Change in the Extent of Coffee Plantations between 1863 and c. 1880*

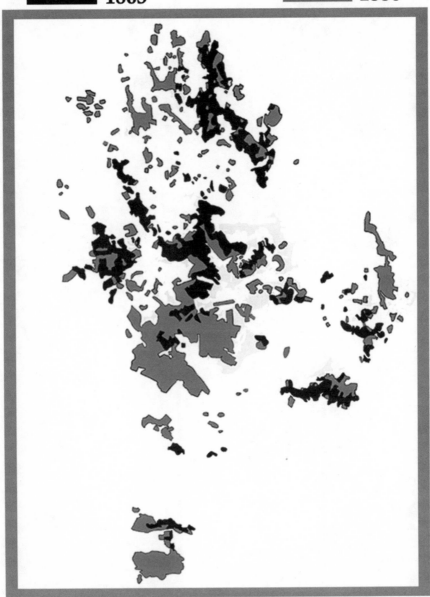

Map 6. *Enlarged Detail of Coffee Plantations. Data on the coffee plantations in 1863 and c. 1880 are from a map entitled "The Principal Coffee Estates in c. 1880," published for A. M. Ferguson, Ceylon Observer Office, London, by J. Hodden & Co., London.*

became noticeable on the estates. The fungus first appeared in 1869 on a new estate in the Madulsima region in the southeast. It reappeared the following season, causing extensive leaf-fall and a moderate-to-severe decrease in yield from the affected shrubs. Over the next season or two, the coffee rust spread to other estates and to Kandyan forest gardens.

The onset from one season to the next was highly unpredictable. Often the fungus disappeared for a season or so, and the coffee shrubs returned robust yields. The initial attack of the fungus *Hemileia vastatrix* was faltering, and most planters whose fields became infected did not initially express alarm. Coffee rust seemed to be simply another of the natural blights—like "bug" and "grub"—with which coffee planters had had to contend. The planters expected that the coffee-leaf disease would simply disappear or that experimental remedies would prove efficacious against the blight.

As early as 1872, when *Hemileia vastatrix* was extending its range through the highlands, Thwaites undertook an investigation. At Peradeniya, he discovered the fungus growing on the indigenous *Coffea travancorensis*, which grew wild in the rainforest and was closely allied to the *Coffea arabica* of commerce.[5] The uniformity of the coffee plantations seemed to present nearly ideal conditions for the spread of the parasitical fungus. He was led to the conclusion that the fungus might well never disappear from the island and that it was probable that the intensity of the coffee disease would continue to vary by location and by year.[6] He advocated for the diversification of the export economy and presciently suggested experimentation with new crops. He also moved to introduce other varieties of coffee plants to test their vulnerability to *Hemileia vastatrix*. Liberian coffee plants, introduced in 1873, were immediately hit hard by the blight.[7]

Not surprisingly, among the coffee-planting community, Thwaites's scientific opinion about the poor long-term prospects for the eradication of the fungus was extremely unpopular. Lives and fortunes had been invested; the coffee sector was the pillar upon which the colonial economy balanced; and it seemed almost to border on treason to predict a continuation of blight. Moreover, there were powerful economic forces that worked in favor of the status quo. As the blight spread, prices for coffee rose to levels far above those of the 1850s and 1860s. Thus, ironically, the profitability of the estates remained healthy well into the 1870s, even as more and more of the coffee shrubs became diseased. Indeed, coffee planters continued to expand their acreage in coffee production, even after the appearance of *Hemileia vastatrix* on an estate and even as yields fell (with wide annual fluctuations). And the continuing profitability of the estates also disposed planters to experiment in an effort to boost yields. Many planters tried applications of manures, which forced growth in the coffee shrub at the same time that the plant was struggling with the fungoid parasite. Thwaites himself initially thought that this might enable the shrub to sustain the attacks of the fungus better,[8] but by the late 1870s it was clear that this was not the case.

There was a certain built-in dynamism to the spread of the fungus. When *Hemileia vastatrix* rendered a coffee estate flatly unprofitable, an owner generally abandoned the property. In some areas this produced a checkerboard landscape of abandoned and cultivated estates.[9] This pattern allowed for the abandoned shuck estates to act as centers of disease transmission. By the late 1870s, the extent of the unfolding disaster was apparent to all. Daniel Morris, the assistant director of RBG-Peradeniya, in 1879 visited leading planters in every coffee district in an effort to determine if elevation, climate, rainfall, differences in systems of cultivation, differences in soils, or in manuring practices had an influence on either mitigating or exacerbating the severity of the disease. He investigated the full range of products applied to the infected coffee leaves in hopes of finding an effective antifungoid. Caustic coral lime worked well, as did preparations of sulphur crystals and sulphur and lime. But the costs of treatment were prohibitively high, and successful treatment did not protect against reinfection. He decided that the best course of action was aggressively interventionist—to root out all trees on abandoned or neglected plantations, sickly trees in forest gardens, by the roadsides, and indeed in all places they could be found.[10] This of course would have necessitated unprecedented government destruction of personal property, and because of the extensive infestation it may well have been impossible to accomplish by the time it was proposed. Be that as it may, there was little else to be proposed, and again in 1881 Morris expressed his conviction that until the shuck estates were taken in hand by the government, there could be no hope for ending the infestation.[11] The coffee rust continued to spread and the cumulative effect of repeated attacks finally brought about industry-wide declines in productivity. By the early 1880s, yields had decreased by roughly 80 percent across the full extent of the highland plantations.[12]

The hopelessness of the planters' plight was underlined by the research mission of an academic specialist from Cambridge University. H. Marshall Ward was sent in 1880 to the RBG at Peradeniya to study the fungus. He produced three scientific reports concerned with the life cycle of the parasite and did not address the planters' practical concern with how to eliminate it. These

Table 5.1. Volume and Value of Coffee Exports, 1849–1899 (in cwts. and £)

Year	Volume (cwt)	Value (£)
1849	337,526	456,663
1850	322,760	657,118
1851	287,911	592,416
1852	408,007	751,861
1853	322,994	637,595
1854	434,086	902,751
1855	483,599	972,462
1856	438,599	971,580
1857	529,442	1,296,736
1858	556,391	1,377,727
1859	601,595	1,488,019
1860	635,062	1,598,304
1861	613,490	1,565,306
1862	600,546	1,534,870
1863	807,345	2,069,125
1864	656,580	1,715,293
1865	929,065	2,358,111
1866	886,762	2,247,038
1867	868,273	2,240,668
1868	1,007,321	2,566,758
1869	1,004,508	2,593,996
1870	1,013,904	2,647,818
1871	955,051	2,480,399
1872	727,455	1,858,722
1873	988,407	2,578,072
1874	600,233	2,655,599
1875	988,328	4,358,604
1876	688,434	3,369,834
1877	927,093	4,662,192
1878	627,246	3,354,153
1879	824,058	4,273,867
1880	654,217	3,324,137
1881	452,032	2,199,892
1882	563,498	2,191,415
1883	262,303	1,159,744
1884	311,969	1,226,904
1885	310,922	1,210,541
1886	220,106	863,933
1887	177,665	1,141,975
1888	138,010	882,897
1889	87,164	480,712
1890	87,144	560,630
1891	88,780	568,684
1892	42,256	323,440
1893	54,674	421,359
1894	31,197	277,321
1895	65,857	339,194
1896	22,160	99,725
1897	18,123	145,303
1898	11,693	85,471
1899	19,094	134,932

Source: John Ferguson, *Ferguson's Ceylon Handbook and Directory for 1900–1* (Columbo, 1901), 632–33.

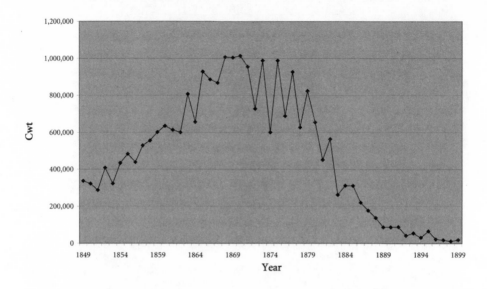

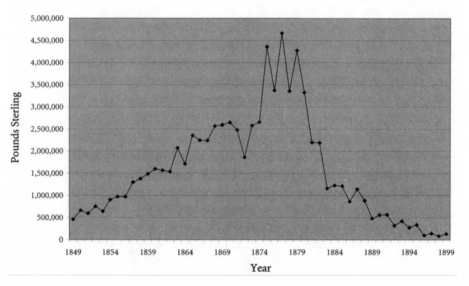

Above: **Table 5.1 Graph a.** *Volume*
Below: **Table 5.1 Graph b.** *Value*

reports constituted a landmark study of the relationship between a parasite and its host, a milestone in the scientific study of fungi, and one that is considered to have begun the field of tropical mycology.[13] Ward directly implicated the wholesale clearing of the coffee plantations in the spread of the fungus. He estimated that, at Peradeniya, a fungal spore of *Hemileia vastatrix* could travel only fifty feet, although he allowed that the distances could be much greater on hills. Thus, the parasitical spore must have traveled from tree to tree across the estates. Outbreaks were coincidental with the monsoons; the rain and wind, respectively, facilitated the germination and transmission of the disease.[14]

Thus the patterned deforestation of the highlands, that reduced or eliminated forest shelterbelts between the estates, was directly implicated in the transmission of the wind-borne fungus. As a government report stated in 1882:

> It is from the ill-considered clearing of trees from the ridges, and from the absence of forest to break the force of the wind, that coffee growers suffer so much. The narrow belts of trees, one to two chains wide, reserved along the summits of the main ridges were, even had they remained standing, quite inadequate to check the force of the south-west gales. In felling and burning the forest on either side, the trees were allowed to fall on and break those belts. No care was afterwards taken to prevent the fire getting in, so that now the ridge-belts of trees exist either only in name or in the shape of a few stag-headed trees. But even broader belts on the main ridges only would not have been sufficient to check the wind. What was required was that on all the higher spurs a broad belt of forest should have been left to keep off the wind, which now sweeps across the ridges, and tears along the treeless slopes during the five months of the south-west monsoon.[15]

There were secondary effects as well from the absence of shelterbelts. Once diseased, the weakened condition of the coffee shrubs made them more vulnerable to natural forces. High wind stripped the trees of their leaves, which in turn clogged the drains and led to increased wash.[16] And in their weakened state, the coffee trees were susceptible to additional parasites. Circa 1885, *Coffea arabica* fell prey to a new species of scale bug, *Lecanium viride*, which is thought to have been introduced inadvertently with Liberian coffee plants. This new parasitical insect was the subject of intensive study by the entomologist at RBG-Peradeniya, but no remedy was discovered to mitigate the effect of the infestation, and the scale bug delivered the final blow to the coffee industry.[17] The coffee disaster ruined many planters, and capital fled the island. John Ferguson—publisher of the *Colombo Observer*, founder of the *Tropical Agriculturalist*, and a planter himself— estimated that of some 1,700 planters engaged in coffee production before the flight, 400 quit the island for northern Australia, Fiji, Borneo, the Straits Settlements, Burma, California, Florida, and elsewhere.[18]

The origin of the *Hemileia Vastatrix* blight remains unknowable. Botanical and mycological experts could not at the time and in fact cannot today pronounce with certainty from whence the fungus came. The view expressed by the director of Kew Gardens a generation later, in 1892, is still generally accepted: that the fungus was probably indigenous, had probably maintained its existence upon some native *Rubiaceous* plant (belonging to the same family as *Coffea arabica*), and had by happenstance encountered its new host about 1869, which enabled it to develop on a grand scale. *Hemileia vastatrix* seems to have simply drifted into an extensive food source and proliferated rapidly. This explanation was not emotionally satisfying to all whose livelihoods were threatened. Ferguson thought that the blight was the revenge of nature.[19]

The fungoid disaster that crippled the coffee industry of Sri Lanka was not long confined to the island. It soon spread across the Straits of Mannar to South India, where it arrived in the early 1870s, perhaps borne on the clothing of coolies returning from the coffee estates. There the blight was particularly severe in South Coorg, a region that included the largest planting district in Coorg Province and where, with the exception of a few temple lands, the expanse of cultivation was a continuous unbroken tract.[20] To compound the planters' woes in South India, another parasitic fungus, known as coffee rot, judged to be equally or more injurious than *Hemileia vastatrix*, simultaneously struck the coffee plantations.[21]

The possibility of a pantropical fungoid disaster emerged as a clear and present danger. At the request of J. D. Hooker, director of the Royal Botanic Garden at Kew, Thwaites at Peradeniya drew up a list of queries about the coffee rust, and Hooker wrote to the Colonial Office and suggested that the inquiries be sent to all British colonies, the Indian government, and all foreign countries where coffee was cultivated.[22] Information received in response to the inquiries was made publicly available.[23] The coffee blight visited southern Africa, eastern Africa, Java, Fiji, and Queensland, Australia.[24] It remained exclusively a blight of the Eastern Hemisphere until the last third of the twentieth century, when it became established on the coffee plantations of the New World.

The Great Cinchona Experiment

During the early 1860s, well before the onset of the coffee rust, the Royal Botanic Garden at Peradeniya undertook experimental trials with varieties of *Cinchona*, a tropical tree species that grew wild in South America on the eastern slopes of the Andes and whose bark contained alkaloids, including quinine, that were known to be effective against malarial fevers. The Sri Lankan trial of cinchona was part of a larger project of European imperial botany whose goal was to establish a supply of cinchona bark within the boundaries of European empire, independent of the South American producers.

Although Europeans had known of cinchona alkaloids for more than two centuries, the adoption of quinine as either a cure or prophylaxis was faltering. The first imperial effort to establish plantations of cinchona in the Eastern Hemisphere took place in the early to mid-1850s, when both the Dutch and the British covertly carried away specimens of cinchona seeds and plants from the Andes. The Dutch succeeded in introducing cinchona to Java; but the British attempts to establish it in India failed. British interest in cinchona planting, however, revived later in the decade, in the aftermath of a massive uprising against colonial rule. In 1857 and 1858, both Hindu and Muslim recruits within the armies of the British East India Company in northern India began a revolt against British East India Company rule that spread beyond the military camps and destabilized the foundations of company rule in South Asia. After two years of bloody fighting and shocking brutality on all sides, troops loyal to the British finally suppressed the rebellion. The debacle resulted in the dissolution of the British East India Company, and the former company territories passed to the control of the British government. The new British Raj acknowledged the abuses of the discredited East India Company and sought policies that would justify the continuation of British rule.

One promising prospect was to intervene in the realm of public health. Malaria was endemic to much of the tropics, but quinine purchased in South America was expensive. Indeed, the attempt to import quinine in the early 1850s had been intended to reduce the cost of this medicine to the East India Company. The high cost of quinine meant that its distribution had been largely confined to British officials and British troops in tropical service. In 1858, the reconstitution of British rule in India seemed a propitious moment to make another attempt at the establishment of cinchona plantations in the British tropics, in order to provide an inexpensive antimalarial drug that could be made available to the subject populations.

In 1859, the Indian government engaged Clements R. Markham, a government clerk with extensive experience in the Andean region, to travel to South America and to return with cinchona seeds. British Indian authorities chose a site at Ootacamund, in the Nilgiri Hills of South India, for experimental trials, and later that year the search for a suitable ecological zone in which to grow cinchona widened to include the highlands of Sri Lanka. Dr. Cleghorn, the conservator of forests in the Madras Presidency, visited Peradeniya to consult with Thwaites at the Royal Botanic Garden. Thwaites proposed the establishment of an experimental station in the upper highlands; Cleghorn endorsed the proposal; and it was duly authorized by the colony's governor.[25] In November 1859, Thwaites scouted out likely sites and recommended one at an elevation above 5,500 feet that would become the Hakgala garden.[26] In short order, a gardener named MacNicoll, recommended by RBG, Kew, arrived to direct the new satellite botanical establishment in the upper highlands.

The Hakgala garden awaited its cinchona allotment. The first plants from the Andes arrived in Bombay (Mumbai) in October 1860. They were, however, in a highly compromised condition and were shipped directly to Ootacamund.[27] The Sri Lankan branch of cinchona experiments began a few months later, in February 1861, when Thwaites received a package of cinchona seeds from Superintendent William McIvor of the government cinchona plantations at Ootacamund. From these seeds, and others sent by professional botanists in government employ who were collecting in the Andes, MacNicoll at Hakgala raised eight hundred plants. Other cinchona seed, from Dutch colonial government plantations on Java, arrived in Sri Lanka via Calcutta. In addition, MacNicoll planted out the two specimens of *Cinchona calisaya* from Kew, via Calcutta, that reached the highlands in a healthy state.[28]

MacNicoll experienced great success in reproducing cinchona from first-generation cuttings. The two varieties that seemed most promising were the *succirubra*, or red bark, and the *condaminea*, which would become known as *officinalis*, or yellow crown bark. And even as early as 1863, the *officinalis* promised to open up some new planting prospects, because it became clear that it could grow at an elevation above that tolerated by coffee, whereas the *succirubra* seemed to be suited to the same elevations as coffee itself. The Hakgala garden made *succirubra* plants available for sale. In 1863, a small number were sold at five shillings each, and later in the year the price was dropped to one shilling. But even this price was prohibitively high, and in 1864, in response to a letter from R. J. Corbet, an influential planter who wished to undertake cinchona planting on a large scale, Thwaites instructed Hakgala garden to give away cinchona plants for free.[29] This proved highly and rapidly successful, and by 1865 the Hakgala garden had given away more than 129,000 plants, of which three-quarters were *succirubra* and one-quarter *officinalis*. The methods of propagation were so simple that Thwaites recommended that planters establish their own nurseries and suggested that planters might send an ordinary coolie laborer to Hakgala for a few days to be taught how to do so.

Fig. 5.1
From John Eliot Howard, The Quinology of the East Indian Plantations *(London, 1869–1876): Plate 11: Cinchona officinalis (colored plate by W. Fitch)*

Fig. 5.2
From John Eliot Howard, Illustrations of the Nueva Quinologia of Pavon *(London, 1862): Plate 8: Cinchona succirubra (colored plate by W. Fitch)*

Markham traveled to the highlands of Sri Lanka and wrote enthusiastically of the very promising outlook for the introduction of cinchona, particularly *succirubra*.[30] The grand experiment had begun, although Thwaites still had not received from Kew the laboratory results of the chemical analyses of the different cinchona varieties.[31]

The following year, the initial chemical results on *succirubra* and *officinalis,* undertaken by the preeminent quinologist Dr. J. E. Howard, became available. They were somewhat encouraging, although the sample size, as Howard noted, was insufficient to assure accuracy. Indeed, for *succirubra,* only the bark from a single tree was available for analysis. Howard expressed a favorable opinion of the prospects for *officinalis*—"this is evidently the sort to cultivate in Ceylon"—and Thwaites was sanguine that *succirubra,* too, would produce good marks upon further analysis.[32]

Experience would show that *succirubra* did indeed have some strongly positive attributes: it was hardy and it had a great capacity for adaptation to new environments. But the percentage of quinine alkaloid in the red bark was low,

Fig. 5.3

From William Graham McIvor,
Notes on the Propagation and Cultivation of the Medicial Cinchonas
or Peruvian Bark Trees *(Madras,*
1863): Plate I: Propagation By Layers

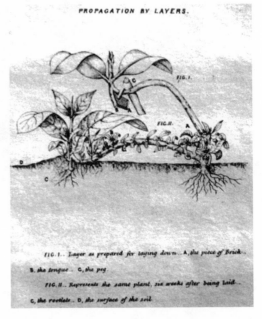

PROPAGATION BY LAYERS.

FIG. I.. Layer as prepared for laying down . A, the piece of Brick.
B. the tongue . C, the peg.
FIG. II.. Represents the same plant, six weeks after being laid .
C, the rootlets . D, the surface of the soil.

although this was not immediately apparent. Only in 1866 did Ootacamund receive the services of a chemist, and his charge was not specifically to investigate the selection of the best type of cinchona.[33] Thwaites, at Peradeniya, for his part was not enthusiastic about securing the services of a chemist, as had been done in Java. He thought that the site of Hakgala, while appropriate for the formation of cinchona nurseries, was unfavorable for the growth of larger trees, and thus he feared that poor results from the analysis of Hakgala bark might prejudice planters against cinchona.[34] It was botanical intuition, and over time it was to be proved wrong. But in the meanwhile, large-scale investments continued to be made in the red-bark cinchona, a tall tree that would grow to heights of fifty to eighty feet, and in the yellow crown bark, a tree of moderate stature that grew more rapidly to thirty feet or more, and at higher altitudes.[35] A very small first shipment of cinchona bark to London took place in 1867.[36]

Prices for cinchona bark proved strongly encouraging, and more coffee planters became willing to plant out experimental fields. This in turn drove up the demand for stock plants. When the cinchona boom gained momentum during the early 1870s, Hakgala went into large-scale production of *succirubra* and *officinalis* stock. From 1 April 1873, cinchona plants were sold at five rupees per thousand, and the demand was such that from 1 September 1873 the price doubled to ten rupees per thousand.[37] The great expansion of cinchona planting in the highlands proceeded apace. Coffee was still king, but the fact that

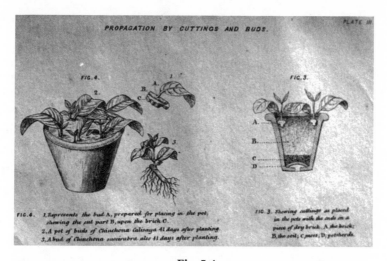

Fig. 5.4
From William Graham McIvor, Notes on the Propagation and Cultivation of the Medicial Cinchonas or Peruvian Bark Trees *(Madras, 1863):*
Plate III: Propagation By Cuttings and Buds

officinalis could grow at higher elevations promised new possibilities for highland expansion.[38]

Agronomy on the Cinchona Plantations

Cinchona, unlike coffee, was difficult to grow from its tiny seed (more than one-quarter million per pound). Much of the cinchona seed simply failed to germinate.[39] McIvor at Ootacamund had developed some effective techniques known as propagation by "slips" and "eyes," and it is likely that these were the techniques adopted by MacNicoll and taught to the estate coolies sent to the Hakgala garden.[40] But once the cinchona seedlings established themselves in the nurseries, the highland workers planted them out using the same techniques that had been successful for coffee. They dug a hole for each plant, and they eliminated the weeds.

Once planted out, however, the agronomic requirements of cinchona proved somewhat different from those of coffee. Of critical importance was the necessity for drainage. Indeed, nothing was so injurious to the cinchona tree as "wet feet." The rainfall of the highlands could be evacuated in most years, but in exceptionally wet years, such as that of 1878, the viability of the entire cinchona project was suddenly called into question. As Daniel Morris, the assistant superintendent at Peradeniya, noted in 1878:

> At Hakgala the cinchona plantation has suffered very severely from the unusually wet season we have had. Nearly all of the large trees, 20 or 30 feet high, and about 12 years old, are dying; the stock plants and about 300,000 cuttings have been killed. We hope to recover ourselves in time and by opening out new ground and starting fresh nurseries there is every probability of being able to meet the demand for plants. The private plantations have suffered very severely and just now there is a feeling among planters that cinchona cultivation is not likely to prove so successful in Ceylon as was once expected.
>
> Great care is required in selecting the aspect, soil, and exposure to which the plants are likely to be subjected. If these are carefully considered and we have moderate seasons, the plantations are in a fair way to succeed. On the other hand, if we have many seasons of continuous wet weather like the last, the plants will suffer very seriously and the planters will abandon their cultivation.[41]

The greater sensitivity of cinchona to waterlogged subsoils led to more aggressive draining practices. With coffee, estate managers designed the drains to minimize soil loss. With cinchona, workers built drains to evacuate rainwater as quickly as possible, at the expense of additional erosion. Specialists recommended drains at a gradient of one in ten or even greater; experience taught that at lesser gradients the drains would silt up. And instead of replacing the eroded surface and subsoils captured above the drains as was the practice with coffee, cinchona planters put the dug-out soils below the drains, so that the effort would not have to be repeated.[42]

Additional agronomic challenges were posed because it was the bark of the tree, rather than its fruit, that was harvested. In Sri Lanka, the planters decided that it would not be economical to prune the cinchona tree back to a shrub, as was the case with coffee. This meant that the cinchona needed to be sheltered from strong winds, which not only tore off the large and tender leaves but sometimes twisted and damaged the entire plant.[43] One approach was to stake the tree, which prevented the wind from working the trunk around in a circle, thus forming a pocket that would fill with water and produce rot. Like coffee, cinchona could play host to various pests. The oleander caterpillar, the cockshafer beetle, a small slug, and seed-bed worms sapped the health of the cinchona plant.[44]

The first large-scale plantings were harvested after five years. One early approach was to coppice, but many planters were reluctant to chop down five years' growth, and the suckers that grew up from the stem were not always promising. Other planters opted to chop down the tree and strip the bark or simply to uproot the entire tree. They abandoned this technique when it became apparent that, in addition to the disincentive of the costly investment of time and labor required to replant, cinchona replanted on the same land would fail.[45]

One successful technique, pioneered by McIvor and that enjoyed success in the Nilgiris, was to cut off tree limbs and to strip the bark.[46] Another, which emerged from Dutch experience in Java, was to shave the bark and then immediately patch the wound with moss.[47] By the early 1870s, cinchona planters in the Nilgiris had adopted the Java techniques and were peeling off three strips of bark, amounting to one-half of the total bark, once every nine months. In the Sri Lankan highlands, this did not prove practicable, and a technique of radical stumping was adopted. As G. H. K. Thwaites noted in his annual report for 1872:

> In Ceylon, however, it having been found that in some localities the cinchona trees show a tendency to become unhealthy, or even to die off, after they have arrived at a certain stage of growth, attributable, it is supposed, to the subsoil not suiting them, it has been found safer to cut down the trees, and allow them to throw out fresh shoots from the stump, the new roots for the nourishment of which fresh shoots will be developed near the surface of the ground, and so not be injuriously affected by the character of the subsoil. In this case all the bark can of course be removed from the felled trees; that of the branches too being also saleable.[48]

Ledgeriana in the Highlands

During the early years of the great cinchona experiment, seed from a new type of cinchona, which would later become known as *ledgeriana,* made its way, in 1865, to the Royal Botanic Garden at Kew, which was just closing down its auxiliary cinchona establishment as a result of the reported successes at Ootacamund in the Nilgiris. The botanists at Kew declined the seed, but through an unusual series of events involving the sale of seed to an Anglo-Indian planter, some *ledgeriana* seed did find its way to McIvor at Ootacamund. There, however, it had adaptation problems and did not thrive.[49] Other seed was sold to the Netherlands government, which transferred it to the government plantations at Java, where it succeeded well, and ultimately became the foundation of the dominant quinine industry in the world.[50]

The divergent outcomes of *ledgeriana* planting in the Nilgiris and on Java were in part the outcome of different approaches to cultivation. Cinchona trees of all varieties had a pronounced tendency to "sport"—to produce a proliferation of subvarieties, even from seeds of an individual tree. Indeed, this was true even of cuttings taken from a single plant.[51] In addition, there was considerable variation in the quantity and composition of the four alkaloids in the barks of individual trees.[52] The British judged that hybridization might produce higher yields, and it was on this path that McIvor embarked. By contrast, the Dutch in Java, after numerous disappointments and failures, decided upon regular chemical analyses of samples of bark. This allowed them to develop a practice of continuous selection, destroying all but the highest-yielding specimens, and eventually produced plantations of cinchona with yields of quinine far in excess of those produced in either a natural or nonselective plantation environment.[53]

The Dutch success in Java was also owing to a more favorable natural-resource endowment: the newer volcanic soils of Java were more suited to cinchona cultivation than the older granitic soils of Sri Lanka and southern India. And indeed, for purposes of cinchona cultivation, the highland soils of Sri Lanka were held to be inferior even to those of the Nilgiris.[54] In many areas, the core problem was that the Sri Lankan highland subsoils were too damp for ongoing cinchona cultivation. Experience showed that the wet subsoils would produce a die-off of some sixty-six percent within three to five years, and this meant that planters had to harvest the cinchona bark sooner, when it was less productive of useful alkaloids. By contrast, in Java, harvesting did not begin until the trees were six or seven years of age.[55]

As early as 1873, the Dutch had demonstrated the superiority of *ledgeriana*, exporting bark with an unprecedented 5.5 to 6.5 percent quinine content. In 1874, one *ledgeriana* bark sample contained an astonishing 11.01 percent quinine. Surprisingly, the Dutch colonial government was not concerned about limiting the diffusion of the rare *ledgeriana*. The following year, private planters obtained *ledgeriana* seeds and planted them out in the highlands. In 1876, in response to a request from the Sri Lankan government, the Dutch sent a case of 185 rooted plants to the RBG at Peradeniya; about 45 were healthy on arrival, but these did not thrive.[56] Only six reached Hakgala, and only one sickly survivor was alive in 1880. In 1878 the Dutch sent three subvarieties of *ledgeriana* seed, labeled after the Dutch system, to the RBG at Peradeniya.

Thwaites had a tiny amount sown at Peradeniya; he gave some seed to a private planter of repute; and the rest he had sent to Hakgala.[57]

But, extraordinarily, at Hakgala, MacNicoll's long-serving successor, another Thwaites—the superintendent E. J. Thwaites (1868–81)—intermingled the subvarieties and did not proceed with any urgency toward their propagation.[58] Indeed, when interrogated by Dr. Henry Trimen, who took over the directorship of the RBG at Peradeniya in 1880, E. J. Thwaites explained that he was devoting his energies to the propagation of *officinalis* and *Cinchona vera*.[59] Because of the large potential significance of *ledgeriana*, this was a lapse that might have had major repercussions for the colony. The Hakgala superintendent had undoubtedly botched the affair, but the responsibility for oversight of the ongoing cinchona project had been that of the recently retired G. H. K. Thwaites at the RBG at Peradeniya, who by dint of personal predilection himself was notoriously averse to labeling plants.[60]

Highland planters did establish some small private plantations of *ledgeriana*, but by 1880 these made up only a tiny percentage of the cinchona industry.[61] W. T. Thistleton-Dyer, the assistant director of the RBG at Kew, asked the Colonial Office for additional assistance, and cuttings from the one assuredly-authentic *ledgeriana*, in the possession of the quinologist J. E. Howard, were to be struck at Kew and sent to Sri Lanka and Jamaica.[62] But this was not only a matter of being too late with too little. The core problem that could not be overcome was the unsuitability of the highland subsoils.

Trimen forced E. J. Thwaites into early retirement from Hakgala in 1881. He ordered cuttings from the difficult-to-grow *ledgeriana* to be grafted onto *succirubra* stock and advised all growers to keep their *ledgeriana* separate from other varieties and to rely upon chemical analysis of the bark of individual trees; in short, to adopt the Java method.[63] But Trimen drew the cinchona experiment at Hakgala itself to a close. He reduced its size from 950 acres to 100 or 150 acres, and laid out for it a broad program of experimental culture with extratropical and hill plants.[64] Hakgala's promise was now to help determine the best exotics to introduce to the highlands to cope with the extensive deforestation.[65] Indeed, the significance of this role for Hakgala would be highlighted by the phenomenal expansion of tea cultivation in the highlands in the 1880s and 1890s.

Meanwhile, because of the long lag between the planting and harvesting of cinchona, the great expansion of the cinchona exports continued apace, even while the high-yielding selections of Java-grown *ledgeriana* threatened to drive all competition from the market. Exports of the low-yielding *succirubra* and *officinalis* rose, and soon prices fell to levels that began to render the cinchona

Table 5.2. Varieties and Quantities of Cinchona Plants Sold at Hakgala Garden in the Years 1876–1880

Year	Succirubra	Officinalis	Calisaya (Darjeeling)	Ledgeriana	Totals
1876	286,000	938,000			1,224,000
1877	81,000	617,000			698,000
1878	41,000	123,000			164,000
1879	20,000	14,000	4,000	95	38,000
1880		50,000	1,000	1,260	52,260

Source: Archives, RBG-Kew, miscellaneous reports, 5.21, Ceylon. Cinchona. 1859–1880. Trimen, "Report on Cinchona *Ledgeriana*," sent to Colonial Office, 20 Aug. 1880. This table, included in the report, was prepared by E. J. Thwaites.

Table 5.3. Volume and Value of chinchona Exports, 1877–1900

Year	Volume (in lbs.)	Value (in Rupees)
1877	72,127	88,738
1878	186,797	171,292
1879	507,368	519,086
1880	1,161,989	1,267,141
1881	1,314,554	1,264,615
1882	4,655,944	3,859,171
1883	7,589,005	4,493,403
1884	11,865,280	4,025,450
1885	12,325,642	4,128,753
1886	14,007,302	4,064,125
1887	15,892,678	4,028,579
1888	12,499,949	1,809,323
1889	9,455,641	1,687,600
1890	8,779,140	1,053,497
1891	5,595,977	669,430
1892	6,846,741	821,609
1893	3,440,715	275,257
1894	2,529,261	202,391
1895	919,820	73,585
1896	1,377,180	68,849
1897	591,136	32,512
1898	977,760	97,776
1899	683,228	47,826
1900	590,692	64,976

Source: Customs accounts, via John Ferguson, *Ferguson's Ceylon Handbook and Directory for 1900–1* (Colombo, 1901), 70–1.

enterprise uneconomical. The shipping and processing costs per ton of the inferior grades were several times the costs for the *ledgeriana* bark from Java. Nonetheless, Sri Lanka came briefly to dominate the world market, albeit with an inferior product. In 1883, Trimen at Peradeniya estimated that 128 million cinchona trees were growing in the highlands.[66] By 1884, at the height of the cinchona experiment, Sri Lanka's acreage in production was almost double that of India and Java combined, and the colony had approximately three-quarters of

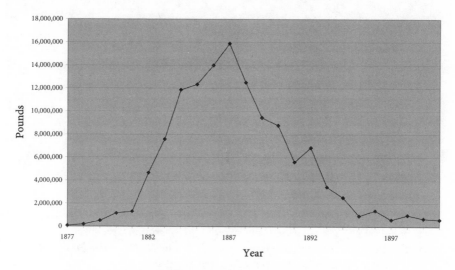

Table 5.3, Graph a. *Volume*

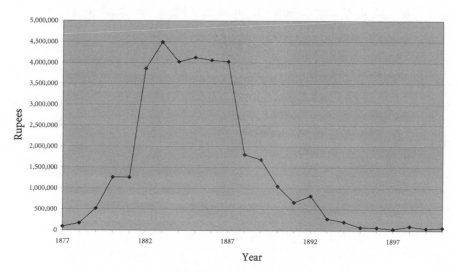

Table 5.3, Graph b. *Value*

Fig. 5.5
From John Ferguson, The Abbotsford Album (photographs by W. H. L. Skeen):
"Forest Being Felled By Singhalese (Who excel in this operation), preparatory to a good
burn in February, and holing and planting in April–August. The 'fellers' hut' hidden in
dense shade on the left. Taken November, 1875."

the world's production.[67] Thereafter it spiraled into decline, and by the early 1890s was an insignificant producer for the world market.

Although the great cinchona experiment ended in failure, it played a significant role in preparing the way for the cultivation of tea. Cinchona grew at elevations of 3,000 feet and higher, and it could be interplanted with coffee, up to the limit of *Coffea arabica* at 5,000 feet. It could be planted alone or interplanted with tea at even higher elevations. The high prices for quinine in the 1870s (reaching their peak in 1877) and into the early 1880s encouraged planters to burn off the forests above 5,000 feet. Cinchona led the way up, and tea followed.

Tea Cultivation in the Highlands

Although experimentation with tea—and its presence in the Royal Botanic Garden at Peradeniya—date from the early era of coffee cultivation, only a

Fig. 5.6

From John Ferguson, The Abbotsford Album *(photographs by W. H. L. Skeen):*
"Tea, Coffee, and Cinchona Nurseries. In sheltered valley below Assistant's Bungalow.
Reticulated objects in foreground are shade platforms for young plants. A waterfall, 'Falls
of the Aber,' tumbles down the steep hill behind, which is planted up to the limits of the
forest belt with Coffee, Tea, and Cinchona. Taken during a drizzle in November, 1875."

Fig. 5.7

From John Ferguson, The Abbotsford Album (photographs by W. H. L. Skeen):
"General View of the Estate, Looking northwards towards the Nuwara Eliya range of
mountains. Tea and cinchona nurseries in the near foreground; then two sets of cooly lines,
the school-house and bungalow, glimpses of the store, two more sets of cooly lines, and As-
sistan't bungalow. This view is interesting, as shewing a plantation in all stages; rows of cof-
fee bushes three and-a-quarter years old to right of cooly lines in foreground, shading away
to one and three-quarter year old coffee above Assistant's bungalow, with felled and stand-
ing forest beyond, up the sides of the range which divides the Estate from Nuwara Eliya."

Fig. 5.8
From John Ferguson, *The Abbotsford Album* (photographs by W. H. L. Skeen):
*"Near View of Cinchona. (The large-leaved C. Succirubra in the foreground) growing
luxuriantly to the top of 'Knock Ferrol,' 5,200 feet above sea-level. Taken November, 1875."*

Fig. 5.9
From John Ferguson, *The Abbotsford Album* (photographs by W. H. L. Skeen):
*"The Bungalow. Near view of the front, taken November, 1875 (in an interval between
showers), when the Australian, Himmalayan, and other trees and shrubs in the garden
were, generally, three and-a-quarter years old."*

Fig. 5.10
From L. E. Douffet, The Ceylon Coffee Album. A Collection of Sixteen Photographs, illustrating the various details of coffee planting in Ceylon (Nuwara Eliya, 1881): Plate VI. Harvest Pickers at Work in the Field

Fig. 5.11
From L. E. Douffet, The Ceylon Coffee Album. A Collection of Sixteen Photographs, illustrating the various details of coffee planting in Ceylon (Nuwara Eliya, 1881): Plate VII. Pulping the Cherries

Fig. 5.12

*From L. E. Douffet, The Ceylon Coffee Album. A Collection of Sixteen Photographs, illustrating the various details of coffee planting in Ceylon (Nuwara Eliya, 1881):
Plate VIII. Drying and Cleaning "Parchment Coffee"*

Fig. 5.13

*From L. E. Douffet, The Ceylon Coffee Album. A Collection of Sixteen Photographs, illustrating the various details of coffee planting in Ceylon (Nuwara Eliya, 1881):
Plate IX. Bullock Carts Conveying Coffee to the Railway Station*

very small number of highland planters shared an interest in experimentation with *Camellia sinensis*. This was owing in part to general unfamiliarity with the growth requirements of the plant and how to process its leaves. The major source of supply for tea was China, and from the late eighteenth century the British had plied the waters between northeastern India and southern China and the United Kingdom. The British East India Company had used tax revenues from Bengal to purchase opium in India and then to exchange this opium for tea at Canton. Roughly coincident with the First Opium War (1839–42), which resulted in the continuation of opium imports to China against the wishes of the government of China, some British planters began to experiment with tea cultivation in both India and Sri Lanka. The experiments in India were initially the more successful. By the 1850s, tea estates flourished in Assam in the foothills of the Himalayas.[68]

The modern era of tea planting in Sri Lanka was given a significant impetus by Arthur Morice, a highland planter who was the largest owner of land in the area known as the Wilderness, near Adam's Peak. In 1865 Morice wrote to Governor Hercules Robinson and expressed his interest in opening the upper highlands—lands that were too high for coffee—for new plantations of cinchona and tea. Morice expressed his willingness to undertake an exploratory mission to the tea district of India to explore all aspects of the tea business—that was to say, not just the horticultural and botanical—if government was willing to pay his way.[69] G. H. K. Thwaites was generally optimistic about the future of tea, in particular because it could grow at higher altitudes than coffee, and he backed Morice's idea.[70] Governor Robinson duly supported the mission on the condition that Morice furnish a report on the tea industry that would be satisfactory to the director of the RBG at Peradeniya.[71] This gave critical momentum to a new, and decisive, round of experimentation with tea. In 1866, Thwaites distributed two hundred pounds of seed free to planters and encouraged them to set up their own tea nurseries.[72] In 1867, the government press published Morice's favorable report on the prospects for tea on the island and Thwaites began to import hybrid Assam tea seed from the Royal Botanical Garden at Calcutta for distribution to planters.[73]

The tea juggernaut, however, was slow to get up speed: well into the 1870s, coffee was still king. Only during the final years of the decade, as coffee succumbed to blight and as cinchona rotted waterlogged in the fields, did more than a few planters begin to lay out extensive fields in the new crop. The historical records do not permit an exact rendering of the numbers of planters and the acreage under tea production in the early years, but it is clear that the

Table 5.4. Highland Acreage in Coffee, Cinchona, and Tea, 1867–1900

Year	Coffee	Cinchona	Tea
1867	168,000	50	10
1868	176,000	75	200
1869	176,467	100	250
1870	185,000	200	250
1871	195,627	350	250
1872	206,000	500	260
1873	219,974	1,500	280
1874	237,345	2,000	350
1875	249,604	3,000	1,080
1876	260,000	4,200	1,750
1877	272,243	5,578	2,720
1878	275,009	10,000	4,700
1879	265,000	20,000	6,500
1880	252,431	33,568	9,274
1881	252,431	45,000	13,500
1882	220,000	55,000	22,000
1883	174,000	64,000	32,000
1884	150,000	56,000	70,000
1885	127,000	48,000	102,000
1886	98,000	39,000	150,000
1887	78,000	32,000	170,000
1888	70,000	26,000	183,000
1889	56,000	19,000	205,000
1890	50,000	15,000	220,000
1891	39,000	9,500	250,000
1892	35,000	7,000	262,000
1893	31,000	5,000	273,000
1894	26,000	4,000	289,000
1895	22,000	3,500	305,000
1896	18,000	2,500	330,000
1897	16,000	1,500	350,000
1898	14,000	1,189	364,000
1899	10,000	1,400	378,000
1900	8,265	1,650	384,000

Source: John Ferguson, *Ferguson's Ceylon Handbook and Directory for 1900–1*, 31, 44, 70. 1862–69 for coffee listed as "doubtful estimates." The datum for coffee in 1870 is likewise an estimate. For 1868, 1871, and 1884, for cinchona I have used intermediate values rather than "missing datum." For 1870 and 1871, for tea, I have used the value for 1870.

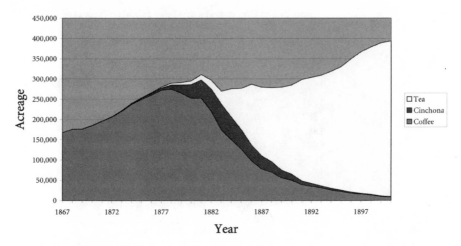

Table 5.4 Graph. *Highland Acreage in Coffee, Cichona, and Tea, 1867–1900*

totals were not large. The value of tea exports, while rising annually, remained at less than 1 percent of the total value of the major highland cash crop exports (coffee, cinchona, and tea) until 1881, and less than 10 percent until 1885. Then tea began its meteoric rise to a position of complete dominance of the highland export economy. By 1890, *Camellia sinensis* exports contributed more than three-quarters of highland exports, and by the end of the century, close to 99 percent. Tea had utterly replaced coffee; cinchona had failed; and planters had edged their plantations up to the very summits of the highlands, where coffee had never been able to grow.

By the end of the century, tea cultivation extended throughout the highlands. The early expansion was a process of substitution, as fields that had suffered through the coffee blight and the collapse of the cinchona industry were replanted with tea from Assam. Toward the end of the century, high prices encouraged planters to open up new lands. In the period 1895–1900, some 87,000 new acres were brought into production. This eventually produced a brief period of overproduction, and planters reduced their total acreage under tea cultivation by abandoning the poorer, lower-yielding fields. This retrenchment was particularly marked in 1897, 1898, and 1899, when a tea leaf blight attacked the shrubs and planters concentrated their efforts on the better-yielding tea fields.[74]

The importance of tea cultivation was not confined to the large estates. Tea, like coffee, became a moderately important cash crop for the highland villager. This process unfolded without any assistance from the government. Trimen, at RBG-Peradeniya, in fact thought it ill-advised to encourage villagers to grow

Table 5.5. Coffee, Cinchona, and Tea as Percentages of Major Highland Exports, 1878–1901

Year	Coffee	Cinchona	Tea
1878	99.4	0.5	0.1
1879	98.4	1.3	0.3
1880	95.7	3.6	0.7
1881	93.1	5.5	1.4
1882	80.2	17.2	2.6
1883	71.4	23.7	4.9
1884	67.9	23.8	8.3
1885	64.4	20.8	14.8
1886	45.7	25.1	29.2
1887	51.6	11.0	37.4
1888	34.9	8.1	57.0
1889	23.4	6.6	70.0
1890	19.3	3.5	77.2
1891	15.5	1.8	82.7
1892	9.0	2.2	88.8
1893	9.4	0.6	90.0
1894	5.7	0.4	93.9
1895	5.5	0.1	94.4
1896	3.9	0.2	95.9
1897	3.0	0.1	96.9
1898	1.8	0.2	98.0
1899	1.5	0.1	98.4
1900	1.1	0.1	98.8
1901	1.1	0.1	98.8

Source: A. C. L. Ameer Ali, "Cinchona Cultivation in Nineteenth Century Ceylon," *Modern Ceylon Studies* 5, no. 1 (1974), 105. Based on reported *Blue Book* values.

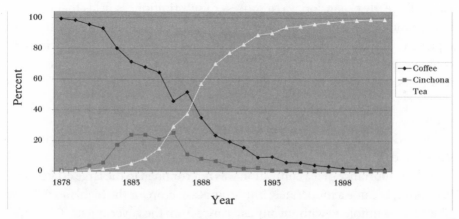

Table 5.5 Graph. *Coffee, Cinchona, and Tea as Percentages of Major Highland Exports, 1878–1901*

Table 5.6. Volume and Value of Tea Exports, 1873–1900

Year	Volume in pounds	Value in Rupees	Year	Volume in pounds	Value in Rupees
1873	23	58	1887	13,834,057	8,300,434
1874	492	1,900	1888	23,820,723	12,624,990
1875	1,438	2,402	1889	34,345,852	17,859,840
1876	757	1,907	1890	45,799,519	22,899,759
1877	2,105	3,457	1891	67,718,372	30,474,245
1878	19,607.5	20,900	1892	72,279,985	32,527,136
1879	95,969	85,229	1893	82,269,535	40,723,329
1880	162,575	150,641	1894	85,376,322	46,103,214
1881	348,157	322,993	1895	98,581,061	49,290,530
1882	697,268	591,805	1896	110,095,194	51,337,388
1883	1,665,768	916,172	1897	114,466,318	46,931,190
1884	2,392,973	1,435,784	1898	122,395,518	47,734,252
1885	4,372,722	2,842,269	1899	129,661,908	51,864,763
1886	7,849,888	5,102,427	1900	149,264,602	53,735,257

Source: John Ferguson, *Ferguson's Ceylon Handbook and Directory for 1900–1* (Colombo, 1901), 45.

tea. Trimen argued that the preparation of the commercial product required care and nicety beyond the powers of the villager, and that the small-scale cultivation of the villager would not be able to compete against the tea plantation. In addition, he noted that, because of the ease of theft from the plantation, European planters objected to villagers growing the same raw product. Trimen held that the proper course for the Royal Botanical Garden was to encourage the production of forest-garden crops such as cloves, nutmegs, pepper, and cacao.[75]

The movement to tea also marked a shift in the nature of the Indian coolie-labor supply. Tea was a perennial and had to be cultivated around the calendar year. The oscillating supply of labor that had characterized the coffee era was to be no more. Planters needed a permanent labor supply, and coolies who signed on to work on the tea plantations generally stayed, for life. Over time, these laborers made cultural accommodations to their new environment and began to develop a distinctive dialect of Tamil, distinguishable from that of southern India. In this manner, the new agronomic demands of the tea estate gave birth to the new ethnicity of the "estate Tamils."

Tea was an extraordinarily versatile crop. It could be grown at all elevations on the island, from the summits of the upper highlands to the coastal lands. Most tea, however, was planted on the former coffee and cinchona estates. This

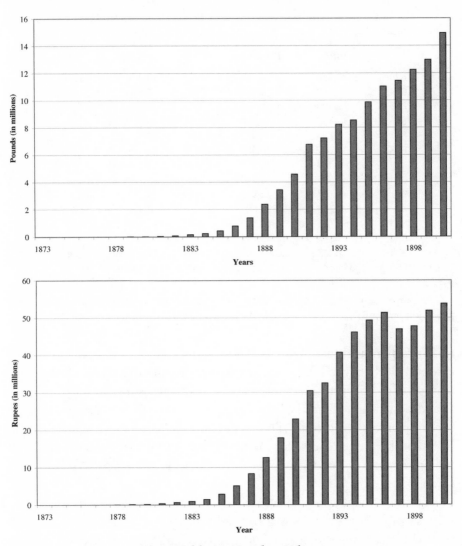

Above: **Table 5.6, Graph a.** *Volume*
Below: **Table 5.6, Graph b.** *Value*

process involved more soil disturbance than had the earlier cash crops, because both in the abandoned coffee and cinchona fields and in the newly felled and burned forests it was necessary, in order to plant tea in close lines, to uproot all vegetation. The possibility to create a bearing tea bush out of what would have grown into a tree, however, eventually produced some marked advantages. The tea bush, cropped to a height of two to three feet, sent out lateral roots to a distance of ten or twelve feet from the stem, which helped to stabilize the soil. This was in contrast to the coffee bush, which, although it, too, was pruned down from its normal growth pattern as a tree, depended principally upon a taproot. In addition, the tea bush's growth pattern was far more compact. An individual tea plant could be allocated a scant twelve square feet, compared with the twenty-five to forty square feet for a coffee bush. This close planting produced high yields per acre and gave the tea landscape its characteristically green-carpet quality, but it came at an initial cost of more extensive soil disturbance and more severe erosion than had the earlier cash-crop regimes. The initial soil loss was great, but this soil loss would have largely abated after the green carpet closed over the landscape had it not been for the practice of aggressive clean weeding, in which workers scraped away the weed growth and with it the topsoil. Ultimately, the lateritic subsoils were exposed. Fortunately they proved to be exceptionally stable and to contain nutrients adequate for the growth of the tea plant. This saved the tea industry from death by self-inflicted wounds.

Tea could be plucked almost continuously, year-round, and this in itself provided some protection against pest infestations. If the tea leaves fell for any reason, the planter could expect a fresh leafing within a few weeks. And because the tea industry processed the leaves ("two leaves and a [leaf] bud") rather than seed, former coffee planters were liberated from their concerns that rainfalls might damage the crop's flowers and reduce yields, as had been the case with coffee. The leaf crop thus had a decisive advantage over the fruit crop. New flushes of tea leaves grew after each plucking, and moreover, tea would produce a good first crop a mere three years after planting, whereas coffee had taken five.

Stream Reservations and Forest Reserves

The expansion of estates into the upper highlands, with its increasing scale of deforestation, breathed new life into earlier conservation concerns, but with little effect. Planters continued to resist the stream reservations, but—because of an economic twist explained below—the government could do little about it. The hands of government were tied by the rule that those who encroached on the stream reservations, which were Crown land, could be forced to compensate the government for damages; the Crown Timber Ordinance No. 6 of 1878 "reserved" sixty-six species of trees from illegal cutting along the banks of the mountain streams. But the value of the timber cut on site was in good measure a function of its distance from market, and in the upper highlands

Fig. 5.14
Tea fields in the highlands (photograph by the author)

the transport costs could be higher than the value of the timber at market. Since trees in the upper highlands were generally felled and burned, rather than hauled to market, the timber was judged to have no economic value, and thus the government could not prosecute encroachments.[76]

Efforts to stem the environmental consequences of highland deforestation were also crimped by confusion over the extent of the deforestation itself and what land-use practices should be considered as detrimental. At first, chena cultivation was all but excluded from the discussion. In 1873, when Hooker, the director of Kew Gardens, visited Thwaites at Peradeniya and interviewed influential coffee planters, he came to the conclusion that restrictions on the continued expansion of highland estates were necessary. Later in the same year, Governor William Gregory, on the basis of a report from the the colony's surveyor-general, developed a sharply different view on the subject, figuring that only some 395,645 acres had been sold to coffee planters and arguing that only a very small percentage of chena and wastelands were not under vegetation and thus that only a small proportion of the soil was exposed to desiccation. By his calculations, 1,657,620 acres were untouched in the highlands.[77] This estimate was only possible to maintain by ignoring the succession of chena clearances that had become the dominant force in the deforestation of the lower highlands.[78] This line of argument, however, was sufficiently persuasive to cause Hooker to revise his earlier point of view, and he endorsed the "enlightened views and energetic policies" of Governor Gregory.[79]

The environmental consequences of the great deforestation, however, washed into officialdom later in the same decade. Floodings of the Kelani and Kaluganga Rivers in Western Province were attributed to the opening of new coffee districts. These inundations pushed Governor J. Longden in 1879 to promulgate a rule that no Crown forest land above 5,000 feet could be sold or exposed to sale except under unusual circumstances.[80] This was the first major attempt to create forest reserves in the highlands. This prohibition did not, however, affect the use of land previously sold, and thus considerable highland forest clearing continued, even at the higher altitudes. Indeed, in 1881, Governor Longden noted that the large clearings recently opened around Nuwara Eliya at elevations above 5,000 feet were on lands that had been sold about 1850.[81] There was the additional complication that a considerable part of the Crown land above 5,000 feet in elevation was patana, rather than forest. It was determined that the restriction on the exploitation of Crown lands above 5,000 feet did not apply to the high mountain grasslands, which could be leased for dairy farms.[82] Moreover, only one of the highland rivers—the Mahaweli—had its headwaters in the mountains at elevations above 5,000 feet; thus, the other major rivers on the island were not protected to any great extent by this regulation because their main sources were in the mountains generally below 3,000 feet.[83] The prohibition on sales of Crown forest above 5,000 feet did, however, enjoy a limited success in that it created forest reserves—mountain caps—on some of the higher peaks in the upper highlands. These mountain reserves have preserved at least some elements of the biodiversity that once characterized the high elevations.

No general effort to reserve forest lands was considered for the lower and middle highlands, because by the last quarter of the nineteenth century, there was virtually no primary forest left at those altitudes. Demand for railway fuelwood also played a role. For the first years of the Colombo-Kandy railway (1867–77), the authorities purchased supplies from villagers who stacked fuelwood along the railway line. This demand obviously encouraged the cutting of timber in government forests.[84] But this was a minor force for deforestation compared with that of chena. The expansion of the Kandyan farming systems had continued apace during the coffee era and beyond. Below 3,000 feet, chena cultivators had cleared off virtually all of the forests except in the plantation areas themselves.[85]

The larger picture of highland deforestation came into focus with the visit of F. D'A. Vincent, of the Indian Forest Service, in 1882. Vincent produced a detailed report on the status and prospects of the island's forests, identifying chena as the major force for deforestation in the highlands. He noted that, in the lower and middle highlands, the defensive forest belt, which had once protected the Kandyan state from invasion, had utterly disappeared; indeed, not even traces of the perimeter were discernable in the landscape.[86] For Vincent, the near completeness of the loss of primary forest had no parallel in British Asia: "The least observant traveller by rail to Kandy and Náwalapitiya cannot fail to notice the general absence of high forest, the enormous areas of scrub, whole hillsides—one unbroken sheet of dense bushy growth—the annual succession of clearings being marked by the different shades of green, from the grey of the recent clearing, to the bright green of the two or three-year old bushes, and the dark green of those ten years old. . . . The extent of chena, in one unbroken stretch, is such as Burmah or India never saw."[87]

Vincent identified the core problem as a failure of government to prevent the destruction of the forest by chena cultivators.[88] As a result of this failure, the possibility of a larger expansion of the estate sector had been foreclosed. As Vincent wrote: "The almost complete denudation of the hills in the Central Province cannot fail to strike anyone going into the coffee districts, and the fact that out of a total area of 3,850,000 acres, or about 6,000 square miles, there should be few large forests, whilst only one-sixth of the area is cultivated, describes better than any words how far destruction has gone."[89]

With a negligible amount of highland forest left to be saved, discussion within government focused on the creation of forest reserves on steep slopes, mountain crests, and patanas. A contemporary scientific belief held that the massive loss of forest cover would result in a reduction in rainfall, as well as in desiccation of the soil, and thus one of the primary goals of the proposed state forest reserves was to stabilize climate. The colonial government wanted to avoid the problems of drought and aggravated soil erosion that plagued Mauritius and the British West Indies. Other goals were to secure a constant supply of timber and firewood to meet the needs of both Kandyan villagers, the estates, and the railway.[90] Moreover, it was generally accepted that the denudation of the forest landscape had created conditions that facilitated the spread of *Hemileia vastatrix*, the scourge that had brought low the coffee industry. Thus prudence seemed to dictate the establishment of tree plantations on hilltops in order to prevent a similar occurrence, should a fungus emerge that could thrive on the tea plantations. The Forest Ordinance of 1885 on paper created a forest reserve with exactly these goals in view.[91] But political disagreements over the organization of a new forest department, which would see to the implementation of the ordinance, and insufficient funds allocated to the department when it was finally created in the early 1890s, meant that a forest reserve was never implemented.[92]

Reforestation by Exotics

The coffee plantations consumed timber for firewood and for construction. The transition from an export economy based on coffee and cinchona to one based on tea created a far higher demand for wood. The tea factories consumed large quantities of fuelwood in the furnaces that dried the tea leaves. In addition, the final tea product was packed in lead-lined wooden boxes to prevent spoilage by excess moisture. As the tea plantations proliferated, planters found that they quickly exhausted the locally available timber. Highland planters, in collaboration with Trimen, the RBG-Peradeniya director, took matters into their own hands.[93] Trimen turned the capabilities of Hakgala from cinchona propagation to experimentation with exotics: as early as 1880, some Himalayan and other conifers had been successfully raised from seed.[94] Forty-three types of eucalyptus were planted out in 1882, and in 1883 the Hakgala garden began to receive scores of exotic trees from botanical gardens from around the world.[95] By dint of experience, planters found that some exotic trees—among them *Cryptomeria japonica, Cedrela toon,* and *Pinus sinensis*— answered well both for fuelwood and tea boxes. They also found that exotics could be planted in their tea fields to provide accommodation for birds, thus reducing the damage to tea caused by insects.[96]

Another important force driving the reforestation movement was the demand for railroad crossties, or sleepers. The remaining natural forests were remote, and because the natural forests were composed of multiple species with unpredictable patterns of distribution, the costs for harvesting only given target species were high. Moreover, the indigenous species proved largely unsuitable for crossties. The principal problem was dry rot. The island woods had to be replaced every four years, compared with every eight years for creosoted pine, which was imported from Baltic ports. The iron wood eucalypti could perform up to eighteen years, at least in Australia and in Britain.[97] Consequently, the railway imported most of its construction wood. In 1899, for example, the Railway Department imported 20,000 railroad crossties, mostly from Norway and Australia, and used only 2,000 crossties made from local wood.[98] It was hoped that fast-growing exotic tree species would eventually allow this demand to be met within the island.[99]

The general pattern was for the Peradeniya and Hakgala gardens to make specimens of exotic tree species available for planters to experiment with on their private holdings. The man-made forests of exotic trees were designed very much along the lines of the earlier coffee and cinchona plantations. On the patanas, the entire grass cover was removed through clean weeding, and the grasses were sometimes burned. Workers planted the seedlings at six-foot intervals, in holes dug to depths of two feet or eighteen inches. The forest plantations continued to be clean weeded for periods up to eight years.[100] Mass plantings of eucalyptus, conifers, pines, acacias, and camphor trees that took root in the last decade of the nineteenth century led to a vigorous process of experimentation with exotic trees that changed the face of the highlands.[101] These were the harbingers of the systematic planting regimes that date from the second decade of the twentieth century.[102] The new highland forests were stands of exotic trees, simple economic adjuncts to the plantation sector.

Scientific Solutions

The expansion of cinchona and then tea cultivation in the late 1870s, on the heels of the collapse of the coffee sector, took place in a new context—one of heightened concerns about the possible ecological vulnerability of the new undertakings. The Planters' Association of Ceylon took the initiative to lobby for an entomologist, a mycologist, and an agricultural chemist to be appointed to the staff of the RBG-Peradeniya. These applied scientists would investigate the threats to agriculture posed by the natural world.[103] Talented staff were appointed, and scientific research on the major agricultural pests advanced rapidly.

Tea, like coffee and cinchona, was found to be susceptible to a wide variety of parasites. During the boom years of the 1880s and 1890s, tea planters had to contend with a leaf blight, a root disease, and an infestation of "shot-hole borer." Some pests adapted themselves to more than one crop, and thus in 1893 the *Helopeltis antonii*, "native flying bug," which had plagued the lowland cocoa plantations in 1884, began to wreak havoc on tea. Trimen, at RBG-Peradeniya, wrote to the newspapers urging a general attack on the insect by catching and destroying it. The challenge was taken up, and the agricultural damage was limited.[104] The same hands-on approach would not work against fungi or all insect pests, but because the tea bushes were pruned aggressively every one or two years to maintain their productivity, there was opportunity to burn or bury all diseased leaves and branches, and this practice helped to control the severity of pest infestations.[105] The downside to the practice of burying cuttings was that it increased soil disturbance and was implicated in increased soil erosion.

Research at the Peradeniya garden was shaped by Trimen's beliefs that there was rarely a specific cure for a specific disease and that therefore the emphasis should be on prevention.[106] The government scientists at RBG-Peradeniya were not always able to come up with a cost-effective response, but the scientific identification of the pest and the knowledge that research was ongoing helped to foster support for and confidence in the institution among the planting community. In addition, because the colonial government was directly involved in pest control, the government began to look toward administrative measures that would have been unenforceable a generation earlier, during the era of coffee rust disease. Government could compel the compulsory registration of all estates on which a pest was found, and could absolutely prohibit the distribution of tea plants from affected estates, until the estate was certified as free from the disease.[107]

The threat from exotic introductions was also recognized. E. E. Green, the entomologist at RBG-Peradeniya who had written a government report on the coffee scale bug, turned his attention to the importance of establishing a quarantine for all imported plants.[108] Early in the twentieth century, the Insect Pest and Quarantine Ordinance No. 5 of 1901 was adopted.[109] The scientists at the RBG started their own series of scientific publications to disseminate their findings to the broader community.[110]

In 1902, the first sizeable experimental station for tropical agriculture in the British Empire was established at Gannaruwa, on the very site of the early coffee plantation initiated by Governor Barnes in the 1820s. Its goals were numerous: to develop the best methods of cultivation; to prevent and to cure diseases associated with cultivated crops; to introduce new and untried plants of possible economic value; to improve economic plants by selection and other scientific methods; to determine the value of various manures for different crops; to determine the value of shade for each product; and to identify the best trees and the numbers of them to be used.[111] Government was now willing to undertake the responsibility of aiding and guiding the agricultural sector. Beginning in 1907, these scientific findings would be published and widely disseminated through the *Tropical Agriculturalist,* the world's first scientific journal devoted to the problems of agriculture in the tropics.[112]

～

Beginning in 1869, a fungal blight began to afflict the highland coffee plants, causing leaf-fall and reducing yields. Even as the blight spread, however, coffee prices continued to rise, and planters responded by burning-off more forest for coffee. By the late 1870s, as the coffee rust promised to destroy the once-great coffee sector, estate managers began to plant cinchona in the coffee fields and to open up additional plantations for the *C. officinalis* variety at higher elevations. In short order, the great cinchona experiment itself collapsed, owing to poor subsoil drainage; the damp soil caused root rot. Planters fortuitously turned to *Camellia sinensis,* the tea plant, which thrived on poor soils and whose shallow root system was not at risk.

The successive coffee and cinchona crises and the planters' concerns about the ecological vulnerability of the tea estates culminated in new scientific initiatives at the Royal Botanic Garden at Peradeniya. In the late nineteenth century, the government established a research team of scientists at the garden to address the practical problems of the plantation sector (in 1912, the research group at the RBG was reconstituted as the Department of Agriculture).[113] Both government and private planters in the last decade of the nineteenth century began to plant out exotic tree species to reforest the highlands. The original highland forests had disappeared. In their wake were the many-hued chena fields in various stages of ecological succession, the vibrant-green living carpets of tea, and new stands of fast-growing exotic trees.

Conclusion

*E*arly communities in Sri Lanka, using fire and simple agricultural techniques, carried out the transformation of their local natural worlds. As
these communities grew larger, they undertook more complex ecological interventions. Beginning in the first millennium BCE, the rajarata states began the wholesale transformation of the lowland ecologies in the northern
and central Dry Zone through the use of fire to clear forest and manage wild
animal populations and the construction and management of large-scale irrigation works. This work was largely accomplished in the course of the first
millennium CE.

As the political center of these communities shifted to the southwest, following the collapse of the rajarata states in the early centuries of the second
millennium CE, more pioneering work was carried out in the Intermediate
Zone. This work of transformation was then extended up into the highlands,
at least from the fifteenth century onward. The heart of this process was the
conversion of the natural rainforest environment to a complex of partially
managed ecosystems. Sri Lankan farming communities in both the lowlands
and highlands carried out their work as tropical pioneers.

At the beginning of the nineteenth century, rainforests of highly diverse
biological composition still covered most of the highlands of Sri Lanka. The
rainforests themselves were interspersed with mountain grasslands, and
within these mosaics lived populations of tropical animals that were highly
biologically diverse. These floral and faunal communities varied by altitude

above sea level, rainfall pattern, soil composition, and water and nutrient distribution. These mosaics themselves were unstable, perturbed by natural fire, flood, cyclone, and the chaos of competition between species. But the highlands also bore the scars of expanding human settlement. In the centuries immediately prior to British conquest, highland communities had enlarged their agronomic domains—carving new fields out of the sides of mountains, re-engineering the natural floodplains for wet rice cultivation, and burning rainforest patches for nonirrigated agriculture. In the process, they had both simplified the local biotic environments and created niche environments that were highly biologically productive at the edges of human settlements. Owing to agronomic constraints to wet rice and chena agriculture at higher elevations, they had limited this work of transformation to the lower and middle highlands.

Generations of accumulated experience had endowed the villagers with highly nuanced understandings of highland ecological dynamics. The villagers' relationship to the natural world was intimate and profound, and their knowledge of island flora was extensive, expressed in part in the indigenous system of ayurvedic medicine that drew broadly from the natural wealth of the rainforest commissary. Yet these understandings had not allowed the highland farmers, even in good years, to produce more than a modest caloric surplus. Their ecological understandings could not protect them from devastating crop failures, insect infestations, or fungal blights. They lived with the specter of dearth and, in very bad years, famine. The farmers' ecological understandings likewise did not protect them or their livestock from devastating disease. These burdens were mitigated to some extent by the astonishing diversity of microclimates and micro-ecologies and the rudimentary isolation of most highland communities from each other, which meant that the visitations of natural calamities were often local and intermittent.

The rule of a repressive political order had long constrained the rate of expansion of the Kandyan farming communities. But following the suppression of the Great Rebellion (1817–18), the political and social controls of the Kandyan elite progressively unraveled. Kandyan farmers extended their fields of both food and cash crops, specializing in small, uniform plantings of wet rice and the more extensive burning of rainforest lands for dry grains, cotton, vegetables, small patches of coffee, and, late in the century, of tea. Low-country Sri Lankans as well as Kandyans cut rainforest timber for profit. The net effect of these practices was the loss of habitat for large animals—elephant, leopard, wild buffalo, wild pig, and deer, among others—the loss of biodiversity, particularly in the destruction of rainforest canopy habitat, and an increase in habitat for birdlife and small fauna.

The breaching of the protective rainforest barrier around the kingdom of Kandy made possible large-scale ecological transformation. The construction of a road system through the highlands inadvertently broke open what had been more discrete ecological zones. When cart routes were hacked through the dense forest, the increased circulation of humans and animals throughout the highlands became possible. Human and animal diseases began to move up from the coast and within the highlands themselves. Contract laborers from South India, who moved annually in and out of the highlands during the long coffee era, brought successive waves of cholera and smallpox with them. Draft cattle imported from India brought rinderpest, which proved deadly to high-land cattle and buffalo and other highland fauna. In the 1870s, the highland coffee industry was stricken by a tropical fungus. As the coffee plants withered and coffee yields fell dramatically, the highland estate managers turned their efforts toward cinchona. But in short order, the cinchona industry peaked and collapsed. From the 1880s onward, the tea plant proved itself both an economically and ecologically viable crop at all elevations on the island.

The successive booms in coffee, cinchona, and tea resulted in ever greater rainforest clearance at ever higher elevations. This progressive deforestation in the middle and upper highlands was matched by the continuing expansion of chena agriculture in the lower and middle highlands. Slash-and-burn agriculture, the more extensive of the two processes, was, however, the less revolutionary. In large measure this was because it was episodic; and the small, fire-cleared plots, typically only one to several acres in extent, were not contiguous. Initially they were separated by dense forest, and later by lands reverting to scrub jungle. Villagers burned-off patches of forest in order to grow dry cereals, cotton, or vegetables, but the forest soils were so poor that new patches had to be opened up after one, two, or three seasons. Agriculture in the slash-and-burn fields was thus neither perennial nor uniform, and this meant that the opportunities for large-scale insect and fungal infestations were limited. Moreover, because highland villagers lacked the means to restore the fertility of the soil, they simply abandoned their fired fields, which in turn evolved into scrub forest, a process that took many years. By the end of the century, the lower and middle highlands were largely covered by verdant growth of varying height and hue, reflecting the years elapsed since the last conflagration.

The contrasts between the chena fields and the British estate sector were striking. The highland plantations were larger, typically of two to three hundred acres. During the early period of estate expansion, these parcels were generally separated by belts of dense rainforest. But over time, because of the increasing demand for highland terrain, estate managers burned off the shelterbelts, and plantations carpeted much of the middle and upper highlands. Uniform and perennial plantings of exotic trees and shrubs became the norm in this sector. Another dramatic contrast was in the British planters' cultural appreciation of the highland natural world. They were utilitarians; they measured growth and harvest and loss; they introduced exotic flora; they experimented; they noticed ecological damage when it threatened to impinge on present or future revenues.

For these reasons, and because the British were able to mobilize the financial capital to pursue what was very often a chimera of high profits, they wrought more far-reaching ecological change. Tropical deforestation in large blocks to make way for coffee, and then cinchona, and then tea plantations changed the face of the middle and upper highlands, and some change was irreversible. In addition to the ecological consequences that can be ascribed to chena agriculture, such as the loss of habitat for large wild animals and the loss of biodiversity, the British tropical pioneers were responsible for the massive loss of topsoil in the middle and upper highlands. Full-scale forest burning, followed by soil scraping to reduce weeds, had a dramatically more deleterious impact on soil resources than did chena.

The loss of topsoil limited the range of options for later land use. The remaining (sub)soils were high in aluminum, a factor responsible for poor crop growth in many acid soils. Fortuitously, the British planters, who had embarked upon the large-scale cultivation of tea on the newly exposed rainforest soils, later discovered that the tea plant could tolerate high levels of aluminum (indeed, tea needs fairly high amounts of it), a fact that sets the tea plant apart.[1] The extension of tea estates into the upper highlands and the uniform replanting of tea on abandoned coffee and cinchona estates did create new seasons of entomological and mycological vulnerability. But by the last decade of the nineteenth century, in the aftermath of the great coffee rust and cinchona root-rot disasters, advances in scientific understandings allowed for the stabilization of a new tea planting regime, supported by a group of new, practically minded scientists at the Royal Botanic Garden at Peradeniya and, later, by the creation of a specialized institute that focused its research program on the specific problems of the tea estate.[2]

Estate managers finally abandoned the practice of clean weeding during the first half of the twentieth century and mitigated the worst pressures for soil erosion. They thereby achieved in the highlands what might be considered a quasi-stable state of degraded equilibrium. Throughout the twentieth century, the tea industry continued its dominance of the middle and upper highlands, remaining broadly productive and profitable (except during an experiment with nationalization in the 1970s). But during the early years of the twenty-first century, global fluctuations in the supply and demand for beverage stimulants, the prospect of steeply rising production costs as a result of the broadening career opportunities for the children of Tamil tea-estate workers, and new competition from tea producers in Africa with low labor costs suggested a highly uncertain future.

Appendix 1

Sir Joseph Banks, Director of Kew Gardens, on the Principles on Which a Colonial Botanic Garden in Ceylon Should Be Founded [c. 1810]

The true principles on which the plan of a Colonial Botanic Garden should be founded, appears, to be, the collecting together and carefully cultivating all the plants of the Colony and its vicinity known to be useful in Medicine, or in the Arts or in any way advantageous to the interests of Mankind, samples of these in the form in which they are used should be transmitted to the Mother Country in the best state possible, in the hopes of their use being adopted in Europe and of their thus becoming articles of Export Trade, for the advantage of the Colony; if such articles sent by the Gardener under the sanction of the Governor and addressed to proper persons at home who have undertaken to examine and report upon them, are admitted free of Duty levied on all unrated goods, it will hold out great encouragement to the discovery of the unknown resources of the Colony. This may be done by the Treasury under the inspection of the Commissioners of the Customs, who as soon as any article appears to have obtained a market and entered into consumption will be ordered to levy the proper Duty upon it.

The Garden will also be useful in receiving from all parts of the World, Plants likely to be advantageous to the Colony, and it will be the Duty of the Gardener to cultivate and increase such Plants when committed to his care, as extensively as possible, and these may be when sufficiently increased in the Garden, distributed under the orders of the Governor to the Colonists most likely in his opinion to cultivate them to advantage.

In all hilly countries near the Line, there are a variety of climates in which the Plants of different countries will if properly attended to, succeed to perfection. The European Strawberry is abundant in Jamaica; towards the summit of the lowest ridge of Hills, at a somewhat higher elevation Apples, Pears and the Fruits of cold climates attain a considerable degree of perfection; in their arrangement of the Intertropical Plants we find that Coffee and Pimento thrive best in elevated stations, while sugar requires low land and the Cocoa Nut which bears abundantly near the sea, becomes sterile when removed to the first slope of the hills; at Batavia and Malacca the Mangosteen and other delicious Fruits of the East require the richest alluvial soil and the hottest climate that can be found; these observations point out the necessity of small subsidiary Gardens in various parts of the Island under the direction of Native Foremen, but under the immediate superintendence of the Royal Gardener. The Establishment of a Garden for the advance of Botanical knowledge is an undertaking of a nature entirely different from this, it is well suited to a mother country where Scientific Education is carried on, but of no use in a Colony, where those pursuits only should be encouraged that tend to enrich the Individual and enable him to return to his native country and thus add his gains to the amount of Public wealth at home.

The proper person to undertake the management of such a Garden, is a well educated Botanic Gardener, skilled not only in Horticulture, of which he must be a perfect master, but also in the names of Plants; a person of this description will know at sight, a great number of the Native Plants of the Country; those that are new to him, he must send home, where their names will be ascertained and returned to him without hazard of mistake, by Botanists who will derive an advantage by the acquisition of new and rare plants to their collections, sufficient to ensure a regular and zealous cooperation on their Parts.

In order more effectually to secure the cooperation of Botanical Science at home for regulating the nomenclature of the New Garden, a Person in England may be appointed as the correspondent of the Garden at Ceylon; if this person is allowed to represent to the Secretary of State from time to time the state of the Garden, the Information he has received from the Gardener, and his wants and wishes if he has any, in short to be the organ of communication at home between the Garden and the Minister, it will be an appointment much wished for by those who are the head of the Science of Natural History, as it certainly will be an honorable employment and will open a channel for the acquisition of Botanical Treasures important to a Collector both for a Garden and an Herbarium.

Source: The Ceylon Overland Observer, and Fortnightly Precis of Ceylon Intelligence. Supplement to the Colombo Observer, 31 December 1860, 5.

Appendix 2

Sir Joseph Banks's Instructions to William Kerr, First Gardener of the Royal Botanic Garden, Ceylon [1812]

You will be instructed to bring with you from China, a collection of all the choice Fruits of that country not already introduced into Ceylon, and you will be furnished with the best information relative to those already known in Ceylon that can be procured; Peaches, Apricots and Plums, appear particularly desirable, and may, if the hotter parts of Ceylon should not suit them, be cultivated on the sides of the hills where the climate is cooler. The Litchi and the two species of Diospyros, the Ginho and many others will probably be improved by an increase of heat as will the good varieties of the Orange; you will also provide yourself with the Trapa natans, the little Rush with a tuberous root, and all other kinds of useful produce that you can obtain; the funds will be supplied to you from Ceylon to enable you to purchase, if these are considerable enough to buy a number of each kind of Fruit Tree, the Governor and the principal inhabitants of Ceylon will soon reap the benefits of your labors. All woody plants may be carried in Chests, they may be planted almost close together in mould, the lids must be fitted to shut down when necessary to preserve the Trees from the spray of the Sea, and they must be shut whenever the waves turn over and form what sailors call white Caps. The herbaceous plants which will be few, as seeds in most cases answer as well, you will easily find the means of providing for.

Your first care when you arrive in Ceylon, will be, to increase your Chinese cargo, and by degrees to find suitable stations on the more elevated parts of the Island for such as do not thrive in the lower and hotter parts of it. The increase of the Fruit Trees you introduce will as soon as possible be distributed by the Governor's Orders to such persons in the Island, as in his judgement are most likely to preserve and further increase them, for which useful purpose you must give all the advice, instruction and assistance in your power.

Your next business, which however you will proceed upon as soon as the other has been properly put in train, will be to cultivate such plants as the Governor shall direct your attention to, or as he shall on your representation to him approve of, as likely to prove advantageous either in medicine, as a raw material for manufacture, or to be in any way applicable to useful purposes, in the hopes that the produce may be approved of in Europe and in due time become an article for an homeward bound investment; these should be cultivated in sufficient quantity to enable you to learn the best mode of managing them, and the best season for harvesting their produce, in order that specimens of them may be sent home to England in the best possible condition to be subjected there to such experiments as will be likely to ascertain their value and probable future importance, to the interests of the Island, as well as to those of the mother country.

Source: Ceylon Overland Observer, and Fortnightly Precis of Ceylon Intelligence. Supplement to the Colombo Observer, 31 December 1860, 5.

Appendix 3

Burning the Forest

It was about the middle of March that we set fire to Unanse-Galla-tenna, and a grand and imposing spectacle it was, when the entire clearing was one mass of seething scorching flame, surmounted by a vast canopy of black rolling smoke. The wind fortunately was pretty high, and blew directly up the clearing. I had a force of nearly three hundred men at the time, which I divided into two parties, one half to set fire to the place, whilst the other half watched the buildings, and were ready with water chatties to extinguish any burning leaves which might fall on them. Each man of the first gang had about half a dozen *chouls* or torches made of the branches of the kitool tree, and these men were ranged along the edge of the forest at the top of the clearing. At a given signal, the whole applied their lighted torches, and then descended towards the lower part of the estate putting fire to every heap or pile of brushwood as they went along. They had to be quick about their work, for the fire spread with amazing rapidity, and threatened occasionally to surround some of the more tardy in its devouring progress. In less than half an hour the whole two hundred acres were in one great and mighty blaze. The white smoke rising in a vast cloud, and hiding the whole mountain side, through which the huge tongues of flame might be seen leaping and flashing as they hissed like big fiery snakes up the ravines and along the gullies where the timber lay thickest, devouring all that came in their way, was a magnificent and imposing spectacle. Within the dense canopy of smoke and flame there were sounds and noises calculated to convey a very good idea of a miniature pandemonium. The burning timber crackled and hissed and occasionally exploded with a report like field artillery, as the roaring flames rolled over, and fixed on portions more combustible than others, whilst every now and then great masses on the steeper points of the clearing would roll with a noise like thunder to the bottoms of the ravines, sending up, far above the smoke, columns of flames and burning leaves. These falls were occasioned by the branches which held the fallen trees to the stumps and roots on the hill sides being burned away, and their support being thus gone, the whole would roll to the bottom, where they would form heaps, which burned and glowed like huge furnaces, long after the fire ceased on the other points of the clearing.

~

By the time the sun had gone down, the fire had, in great measure, burned it-self out, but when darkness set in, the whole clearing seemed one mass of de-tached furnaces from the numerous heaps of smouldering trees which covered the ground, now bursting here and there into flames, and then dying down to a dull red glow, whilst a dense cloud of black smoke hung like a canopy over the whole.

The burning was a great success and lifted a very heavy load of anxiety off my mind. Very little piling would be necessart [sic], and what was likely to be required would be very easily accomplished. I have had a great deal of piling and burning in my day, and I cannot say that I have any love for this work.

Source: William Boyd, "Ceylon and Its Pioneers,"
Ceylon Literary Register, vol. 2 (1888): 241–42.

Appendix 4

Cinchona Harvesting

The first trees planted on a large scale in Ceylon were allowed to attain to some five years' growth before any decided plan of action was hit upon with respect to the harvesting of their valuable bark. First of all coppicing was tried, but planters did not like to see five years' growth and more laid low; and in some instance, and at some elevations, the suckers sent up from the stool did not grow as well as could be desired; and if the suckers did not come on, by the time that this fact was demonstrated the roots below ground had lost all the valuable properties of their bark, so that in certain localities it was the best policy to uproot the trees bodily. The writer once cut out some 23,000 trees, averaging four years old, and on taking the bark off stem, roots, branch, and twigs, the yield per tree was slightly over 1 lb., whilst over a few thousand of the larger, or five-year-old trees, the yield was 11/2 lb. per tree. Each tree was cut out with its roots attached (the root bark being very valuable); the roots were then carried off to the nearest road, where the roots were sawn off at the stool. These roots were at once carried to a pool of water and cleaned prior to being barked. The man now takes his tree, and cutting off all the branches— on which the women operate (whittling off the bark, taking care, however, not to include wood with the bark), the man being left with the stem only—and proceeds to slice rings around it, about 18 in. apart, and then, making a perpendicular cut between these two rings, he inserts anything that will lift the bark without breaking it—either a piece of flat wood, or a steel instrument with a top like a ladle of a spoon, only flat. The bark, being full of sap, comes off easily, and a good hand will cut out his own trees and bring in about 50 lb. to 60 lb. of bark a day. The bark is now dried in the sun for three or four days, and will lose in the first days, drying about half its green weight, and when thoroughly dry will be about one-third of its original weight. The yield from these 23,000 trees fetched an average price in the London market of 4s. 4d. per lb., and some parts of the stem quill, taken off as described, fetched 6s. 6d.

The planters being in difficulties as to the best mode of harvesting, an Indian authority—Mr. M'Ivor—came to the rescue, advising the leaving of the trees, securing the bark by the stripping process, and covering over the stripped part with moss. This method proved unsatisfactory, being too severe to be put into general use, and has since given way to a much better process in every respect. The trees are now spoke-shaved with a two handled shave, set to any required depth, and the amount of bark that can be secured per man per day is truly astonishing; 200 lb. and more has been taken from the larger variety of cinchona (Succirubra), but I consider 80 lb. per man from three to four year old trees of the Officinalis variety a very good day's work.

With the spoke-shaving process there came a flood of knowledge. First of all it was proved that the second shaving gave a richer yield in quinine than the first, and that each shaving increased in value. It was also proved that two harvests could be secured in fourteen months, and that the sooner it was secured the better, for after an eight months' renewal it began to retrograde. The yield of bark is also found greater on each succeeding shaving, the writer's experience putting it at one-fifth—thus, 25 trees gave 10 lb. on the first shaving, and eight months afterwards gave 12 lb.; these trees were only shaved up to a height of 3 ft. Many planters have gone in for shaving trees that are not quite two years old, and have apparently done no damage. The shaving sells for an average price of 2s. per lb., and from 2 1/2 to 3 year old trees about 3 oz. of dry bark could be counted on with safety. Some planters cover over their shaved trees (the process causing a quicker renewal of bark and a richer secretion of quinine); but I had 150 acres of shaved trees under my charge, none of which were covered, and the bark after such treatment fetched as fine prices as could have been desired.

Source: "Cinchona Culture," TA, vol. 3 (1883–1884): 336–37.

Appendix 5

Superintendents, Assistant Directors, and Directors of the Royal Botanic Garden, Peradeniya, in the Nineteenth Century

Superintendents

1812–1814	William Kerr
1817–1825	Alexander Moon
1825–1827	Andrew Walker (acting)
1827–1830	James Macrae
1830–1832	J. Bird (acting)
1832–1838	J. G. Watson
1838–1840	J. G. Lear (acting)
1840–1843	H. F. Normansell
1843–1844	W. C. Ondaatje (acting)
1844–1849	George Gardner
1849	G. Fraser (acting)
1849–1857	G. H. K. Thwaites

Assistant Directors

1874–1879	M. M. Hartog
1878–1879	Daniel Morris
1900–1904	J. B. Carruthers
1908–1912	R. H. Lock

Directors

1857–1880	G. H. K. Thwaites
1880–1896	Henry Trimen
1896–1912	J. C. Willis

Source: F. A. Stockdate, T. Petch, and H. F. Macmillan,
The Royal Botanic Gardens, Peradeniya, Ceylon, 1822–1922 (Colombo, 1922), 57.

Notes

Acknowledgments

1. James L. A. Webb Jr., *Desert Frontier: Economic and Ecological Change Along the Western Sahel, 1600–1850* (Madison, 1995).

Note on Climatological and Elevational Zones

1. See, for example, George Gardner, "Some General Remarks on the Flora of Ceylon," in E. F. Kelaart, *Prodomus Faunae Zeylanica* (Colombo, 1852), app. A.
2. C. R. Panabokke, *Soils and Agro-Ecological Environments of Sri Lanka* (Colombo, 1996).

Introduction

1. On the biological history of human expansion, see Jared Diamond, *Guns, Germs, and Steel: The Fate of Human Societies* (New York, 1997).
2. The best introduction to the subject remains William H. McNeill, *Plagues and Peoples* (New York, 1976).
3. The path-breaking work on global biological exchanges is Alfred W. Crosby Jr., *Ecological Imperialism: The Biological Expansion of Europe, 800–1900* (Cambridge, 1986).
4. On the disease environment of nineteenth-century India, see Mark Harrison, *Public Health in British India: Anglo-Indian Preventive Medicine, 1859–1914* (Cambridge, 1994).

5. This was accomplished without a transformation in the system of food production. For the contrasting circumstances on the mainland, see Madhav Gadgil and Ramachandra Guha, *This Fissured Land: An Ecological History of India* (Berkeley, 1993), 118.

6. During the twentieth century, the lowlands also underwent extensive ecological transformations. Plantations of rubber and coconut, repioneering settlements replete with extensive slash-and-burn fields, and large-scale dams and irrigation works remade much of the rest of the island and reduced the total forest cover on the island of Sri Lanka from an estimated 70 percent in 1900 to 24 percent in 1989: Natural Resources, Energy, and Science Authority of Sri Lanka, *Natural Resources of Sri Lanka: Conditions and Trends* (Colombo, 1991), 198. The twentieth-century ecological history of the lowlands remains to be written.

Chapter 1
The Natural Ecology of the Island and Processes of Early Ecological Change

1. Since 1972, the island has borne the name Sri Lanka (Sinhala: 'revered island'). During the era of European colonialism (1505–1948), the island was known as Ceylon. The appellation Lanka is of ancient usage, dating back to the Hindu epic, the Ramayana. In this book I have chosen to refer to the island at all historical periods as Sri Lanka.

2. Geologists have determined that the island is constructed of three distinctive and characteristic erosion levels, or peneplains. There is no scientific consensus, however, on how these erosion levels formed. For an overview of the three principal theories of peneplain formation, see P. G. Cooray, *An Introduction to the Geology of Sri Lanka* (Colombo, 1987), 49–51.

3. This section on the physiography of the highlands is based on G. H. Peiris, *Development and Change in Sri Lanka: Geographical Perspectives* (New Delhi, 1996), 26–33.

4. The best introduction to this topic is C. R. Panabokke, *Soils and Agro-Ecological Environments of Sri Lanka* (Colombo, 1996).

5. Since 1881, only three severe cyclones (defined as winds in excess of 74 miles per hour) have buffeted the island. These storms occured in 1907, 1964, and 1978: M. G. B. de Silva, "Climate," in T. Somasekaram et al., eds., *Arjuna's Atlas of Sri Lanka* (Dehiwala, 1997), 16.

6. The meteorological history of Sri Lanka has yet to be investigated fully.

7. W. Erdelen, "Tropical Rain Forests in Sri Lanka: Characteristics, History of Human Impact, and the Protected Areas System," *Monographiae Biologicae* 74 (1996): 505.

8. This introductory section has been broadly informed by the T. Somasekaram et al., eds., *Arjuna's Atlas of Sri Lanka* (Dehiwala, 1997).

9. See P. S. Ashton and C. V. S. Gunatilleke, "New Light on the Plant Geography of Ceylon, I: Historical Plant Geography," *Journal of Biogeography* 14 (1987): 249–85.

10. S. U. Deraniyagala, *The Prehistory of Sri Lanka*, 2 vols. (n.p. [Colombo], 1992), passim.

11. R. C. Bailey and T. N. Headland, "The Tropical Rain Forest: Is It a Productive Environment for Human Foragers?" *Human Ecology* 19, no. 2 (1991): 261–85.

12. William R. Dickinson, "Changing Times: The Holocene Legacy," *Environmental History* 5, no. 4 (2000): 492–93.

13. A. Terry Rambo, "Primitive Man's Impact on Genetic Resources of the Malaysian Tropical Rain Forest," *Malaysian Applied Biology Journal* 8, no. 1 (1979): 59–65.

14. A. W. R. Joachim and S. Kandiah, "The Effect of Shifting (Chena) Cultivation and Subsequent Regeneration of Vegetation on Soil Composition and Structure," *TA* 106, no. 1 (1948): 3–11. On the significance of fire on the South Asian mainland, see Stephen Pyne, *World Fire: The Culture of Fire on Earth* (New York, 1995), 149–70.

15. Robert A. Sterndale, *Natural History of the Mammalia of India and Ceylon* (Calcutta, 1884), 481–86.

16. Charles H. Wharton, "Man, Fire, and Wild Cattle in Southeast Asia," *Annual Proceedings Tall Timbers Fire Conference,* no. 8 (1968): 107–67.

17. J. E. Spencer, *Shifting Cultivation in Southeast Asia* (Berkeley, 1966), passim.

18. There is no scholarly consensus on when the Sinhalese identity formed. On identities in an earlier period, see Sudarshan Seneviratne, ""Peripheral Regions' and 'Marginal Communities': Towards an Alternative Explanation of Early Iron Age Material and Social Formations in Sri Lanka," in R. Champakalaksmi and S. Gopal, eds., *Tradition, Dissent, and Ideology* (Delhi, 1996), 264–312.

19. W. I. Siriweera, *A Study of the Economic History of Pre-Modern Sri Lanka* (Delhi, 1994), 54.

20. W. I. Siriweera, "Floods, Droughts, and Famines in Precolonial Sri Lanka," *Modern Sri Lanka Studies,* special K. W. Goodawardena felicitation volume (1987), 79–85.

21. See, for example, the classic work of John Still, *Jungle Tide* (Edinburgh, 1930), which was required reading in the British colonial school curriculum in Ceylon. See also Sumit Guha, *Environment and Ethnicity in India, 1200–1991* (Cambridge, 1999), 46. Foresters and other professionals could not agree as to whether the scrub forest was the negative consequence of chena agriculture or large-scale irrigation: see R. A. De Rosayro, "The Nature and Origin of Secondary Vegetational Communities in Ceylon, *CF* 5, nos. 1–2 (1961): 34. By the late twentieth century, the issue was largely subsumed by political considerations. The impact of the early large-scale deforestation continues to be little appreciated because of the role that the memory of the hydraulic civilizations play in the contemporary politics of the island. These civilizations are remembered by the majority Sinhala ethnic group as the apex of Sinhalese civilization, in contrast to what are generally held to be the less impressive achievements of the Tamils.

22. T. W. Tyssul Jones, "Malaria and the Ancient Cities of Ceylon," *Indian Journal of Malariology* 5, no. 1 (1951): 123–32. What seems certain is that the rajarata civilizations would have collapsed on their own, even absent the destruction of warfare. All large-scale irrigation-based societies have been confronted the fundamental problem of the salinization of soils, which is a direct consequence of long-term irrigation. In the absence of flooding to rinse the soils of accumulated salts, irrigated soils become too saline to support agriculture. How the rajarata civilizations did or did not attempt to deal with the issue of salinization remains a major topic for historical research.

23. On the general phenomenon, see Joseph A. Tainter, *The Collapse of Complex*

Societies (Cambridge, 1988), passim; on the collapse of the Mayan civilization, see esp. pages 152–78.

24. On the history of the town of Kandy, the principal capital of the highland state, see Nihal Karunaratna, *Kandy—Past and Present* (n.p. [Colombo], 1999).

25. These sections on the political history of Sri Lanka during the period 1250–1500 are based on K. M. de Silva, *A History of Sri Lanka* (Oxford, 1981), 81–112.

26. Andrew F. Watson, "The Arab Agricultural Revolution and Its Diffusion, 700–1100," *Journal of Economic History* 34, no. 1 (1974): 8–35.

27. De Silva, *History of Sri Lanka*, 90.

28. A. J. R. Russell-Wood draws together a wealth of information on the early dissemination of flora and fauna: *The Portuguese Empire, 1415–1808* (Baltimore, 1998), 148–82. The routes that the New World crops took and the agents who carried them remain obscure.

29. K. L. Mehra, "Portuguese Introductions of Fruit Plants into India," *Indian Horticulture* 10, no. 1 (1965): 8–12; 10, no. 3 (1965): 9–12; and 10, no. 4 (1965): 23–35.

30. Om Prakash, *European Commercial Enterprise in Pre-colonial India* (Cambridge, 1998), 27, 37.

31. S. T. Senewiratne and R. R. Appadurai, *Field Crops of Ceylon* (Colombo, 1966), 223.

32. The word *arrack* is derived from the Arabic for perspiration. Variants of the word are found throughout large areas of the world influenced by Muslim traders, from Manchuria and Mongolia through South and Southeast Asia and North Africa, and are used to refer to a wide range of distilled alcoholic beverages. See Col. Henry Yule and A. C. Burnell, *Hobson-Jobson: A Glossary of Colloquial Anglo-Indian Words and Phrases, and of Kindred Terms, Etymological, Historical, Geographical and Discursive*, 4th ed., ed. William Crooke (New Delhi, 1984), 36–37.

33. S. Arasaratnam, "Dutch Commercial Policy in Ceylon and Its Effects on Indo-Ceylon Trade, 1690–1750," *Indian Economic and Social History Review* 4, no. 2 (1967): 128; and S. Arasaratnam, "Ceylon in the Indian Ocean Trade, 1500–1800," in A. Das Gupta and M. N. Pearson, eds., *India and the Indian Ocean, 1500–1800* (Calcutta, 1987), 228–29.

34. Prakash, *European Commercial Enterprise in Pre-colonial India*, 238.

35. Jan S. Hogendorn and Marion Johnson, *The Shell Money of the Slave Trade* (Cambridge, 1986), 39, 50–52.

36. C. G. Uragoda, *A History of Medicine in Sri Lanka* (Colombo, 1987), 55, 71.

37. The earliest speculation on the origins of the patanas is that by R. Abbay, "Note on the Supposed Cause of the Existene of Patanas, or Grasslands, of the Mountain Zone of Ceylon," *JRASCB* 6, no. 20 (1879): 59–60. Abbay proposed that a particular band of patana between Pundala Oya and Ramboda was caused by a substratum of brackish rock.

38. As A. F. Broun, the conservator of forests, wrote in 1900,

> The patanas were probably at one time covered with trees . . . but fires and grazing have destroyed the majority of these, except in sheltered places such as gullies or ravines. The trees which are to be found on the patanas are, at higher elevations,

Rhododendron arboreum, and, from 4000 feet downwards, *Careya arborea,* known in Ceylon as "Patana Oak," *Phyllanthus Emblica, Terminalia Belerica, T. Chebula,* and *Pterocarpus Maruspium.* These are, with few exceptions, the only trees which can stand the heavy grass fires; but in the gullies, where they are more sheltered, other species, which are less robust and which are the same as those found in forests at the same elevations, are able to live and to reproduce themselves.

A. F. Broun, "On the Forests and Waste Lands of Ceylon," in Henry Trimen, *A Handbook of the Flora of Ceylon* (London, 1900), pt. 5, app. 2, 355.

39. De Rosayro, "The Montane Grasslands (Patanas) of Ceylon," *TA,* pt. 2 (1946): 7–8.

40. In a classic series of articles, R. A. De Rosayro imparted his research knowledge about patanas. See his "The Montane Grasslands (Patanas) of Ceylon," *TA* 101, no. 1 (1945): 206–13; pt. 2: 102, no. 2 (1946): 4–16; pt. 3: 102, no. 2 (1946): 81–94; pt. 4: 102, no. 3 (1946): 139–48. De Rosayro did not subscribe to the "grass-fire theory" of patana creation: In "Montane Grasslands," pt. 3:89, we read:

It is difficult to visualize great stretches of country over 150 square miles in extent, entirely devastated by primitive shifting cultivation or other form of agriculture without any historical evidence in the form of record or local tradition, or even signs such as abandoned tanks &c., of widespread occupation of these lands. It is impossible that neolithic or later primitive man with primitive stone implements could have brought about this tremendous change.

41. N. P. Perera, "The Ecological Status of the Montane Grasslands (Patanas) of Ceylon," *CF* 9, nos. 1 and 2 (1969): 27–52; F. Lewis, "A Descriptive Catalogue of the More Useful Trees and Flowering Plants of the Western and Sabaragamuva Provinces of Ceylon," *JRASCB* 17, no. 53 (1902): 93–94.

42. G. M. McKay, "Ecology and Biogeography of Mammals," in C. H. Fernando, ed., *Ecology and Biogeography of Sri Lanka* (The Hague, 1984), 413–29.

43. During the last of a series of nineteenth-century waves of massive forest-habitat destruction, one knowledgeable hunter estimated an islandwide population of 1,660 leopards, based on 50 percent forest cover and a density of about one leopard per twenty square kilometers. Whatever the size of the populations in the early nineteenth century, it is certain that one major effect of the clearing of forests and scrub jungles during this century was the isolation of subpopulations of leopards, which in turn has resulted in the splitting up of their gene pool. See Charles Santiapillai, M. R. Chambers, and N. Ishwaran, "The Leopard *Panthera Pardus Fusca* (Meyer 1794) in the Ruhunu National Park, Sri Lanka, and Observations Relevant to Its Conservation," *Biological Conservation* 23 (1982): 11–12.

44. Samuel White Baker, *The Rifle and the Hound in Ceylon* (London, 1854; reprint, New York, 1967), 21.

45. John Banks and Judy Banks. *A Selection of the Animals of Sri Lanka* (Colombo, 1995), plates 15 and 16.

46. E. F. Kelaart, *Prodomus Faunae Zeylanicae* (Colombo, 1852), 87–88; Sir J. Emerson Tennent, *Sketches of the Natural History of Ceylon* (London, 1861), 49–50. The *Bos gaurus* was common in the Western Ghats of India in the second half of the nineteenth century. See Robert H. Elliot, *The Experiences of a Planter in the Jungles of Mysore*, 2 vols. (London, 1871), 1:23.

47. J. W. Bews, *The World's Grasses* (London, 1929), 294, 327, 329. Bews held the view that illuk grass *(Imperata cylindrica)* was the most common patana grass, but this is directly contradicted by the observations of George Gardner in "Some General Remarks on the Flora of Ceylon," 8. See also H. C. Sirr, *Ceylon and the Cingalese* (London, 1891), 1:116–88, and 1:152–53.

48. De Rosayro, "Montane Grasslands," pt. 2:9.

49. J. E. Seneratna, "Patana Burning with Particular Reference to Pasturage and Wet Patanas: A Preliminary Note," *TA* 98, no. 4 (1942): 3–4.

50. "Grassland Agriculture in Ceylon," *TA* 111, no. 4 (1955): 253.

51. A. W. R. Joachim, "The Mineral Constituents of Ceylon's Fodder Grasses," *TA* 68, no. 5 (1927): 269–71. See also H. F. Macmillan, "Notes on Pasture Land and Forage Plants," *TA* 36, no. 4 (1911): 331.

52. Jayantha Jayawardene, *The Elephant in Sri Lanka* (Colombo, 1994), 30, 95.

53. J. Forbes, *Eleven Years in Ceylon*, (London, 1840) 2:99, 2:152; Jayawardene, *Elephant in Sri Lanka*, 25.

54. F. D'A. Vincent, "Report on the Forest Administration of Ceylon, *SP* 43 (1882): 5–6.

55. The principal fragment of undisturbed rainforest left in the wet zone today is in the lower highlands and is known as Sinharaja. There, in the 1930s, the general height of the forest was about 35 meters (115 feet), with a few larger trees towering higher. The stems of the trees were remarkably straight and unbranching, and the undergrowth was scanty, simply a nursery for the trees. Strikingly, there was little birdlife in the forest, except in the canopy. See John R. Baker, "The Sinharaja Rain-Forest, Ceylon," *Geographical Journal* 89, no. 6 (1937): 544–47.

56. De Rosayro, "Montane Grasslands," pt. 2:5.

57. R. A. de Rosayro, "Ecological Considerations in the Management of Wet Evergreen Forests in Ceylon, *CF*, n.s., 1, no. 2 (1953): 83.

58. R. A. De Rosayro, "Forests and Erosion, with Special Reference to Ceylon, *TA* 103, no. 4 (1947): 246.

59. Two major floods were recorded at Peradeniya in the 1830s. In 1834, the RBG-Peradeniya superintendent wrote to the colonial secretary, "With regret I have to inform you of the damage the Botanical Garden has sustained by the late heavy Rains and flood, one third of the Botanic Garden was under water and the Road round the Garden is partly washed away and its quite unsafe to drive round the Garden; upwards of two thousand Clove and Nutmeg Seedlings are destroyed, they were very promising Seedlings, all lost nothing but the dead stems are now visible above the ground. In addition to the above losses the best part of the Botanic Garden Store is come down, and the remaining part is unsafe to keep Government Tools and Coffee now in it": SLNA/6/1322: J. G. Watson to CS, 22 Dec. 1834.

In 1837, an apparently even worse flood occurred. The annual report of the RBG stated, "It has only once occured during the memory of its oldest inhabitants that the river has risen as high as to inundate any portion of the premises, and the kings of Kandy, had previously occupied, this same situation for their Royal Gardens": SLNA/6/1405: report on RBG, Ceylon [1838]; another copy of this report can be found in SLNA/10/22. The flood also caused destruction farther downstream. According to the *Ceylon Almanac,* "Extensive innudation; several Bridges carried away on the Kandy road, and upwards of 1200 houses in the neighborhood of Colombo": June 6: *Ceylon Almanac for 1843* (Colombo, 1843), lxiv. In the Dry Zone, it is likely that not only the Mahaweli River but others as well changed course due to flooding in the historical period. The shifting of riverbeds, drying up of riverbeds, and alteration of the course of rivers was far from an unknown phenomenon in South Asia: Siriweera, "Floods, Droughts and Famines in Precolonial Sri Lanka," 80. The nonequilibrium dynamics of the very wet tropics bear comparison with those of the very arid tropics. For a path-breaking critique of the assumptions of equilibrium modeling, see Michael Mortimore, *Roots in the African Dust* (Cambridge, 1998).

Chapter 2
The Highland Ecologies in the Early Nineteenth Century

1. K. M. de Silva, *A History of Sri Lanka* (Oxford, 1981), 203–4.

2. The regalia of the king was seized as booty and later sold at auction in London in 1820. According to a catalog copy of the royal goods, annotated with sale prices and held in the British Library, the Kandyan king's regalia sold for more than £3,000. See Thomas King, *A Catalogue of a Splendid and Valuable Collection of Jewellery, Forming the Regalia of the King of Kandy* (n.p. [London], n.d. [1820]).

3. For the political history of the early British period, see de Silva, *History of Sri Lanka,* 210–19.

4. John Davy, a British medical officer who was in the highlands during the suppression of the rebellion, estimated that one thousand British troops and perhaps ten thousand Kandyans lost their lives during this struggle. He noted, "The sufferings of the natives were of a more severe kind and complicated nature. In addition to the horrors of war in its most appalling shape, they had to encounter those of disease, want, and famine, without any chance of relief": John Davy, *An Account of the Interior of Ceylon* (London, 1821), 331.

5. Henry Marshall, *Ceylon: A General Description of the Island and Its Inhabitants* (London, 1846; reprint, Dehiwala, 1982), 129.

6. The British had earlier built a large fort at the confluence of the Kelani Ganga and the Gooragooya Oya and had used the fort as a staging ground for supplies to be sent into the interior. The fort was forty miles inland from Colombo, and it was possible to travel downriver to Colombo in seven or eight hours: *Ceylon Calendar for 1816* (Colombo, 1817), 156. The problem lay in the arduous overland climb into the highlands along the embassy road.

7. Even the early completion of the rough road from Colombo to Kandy via Kurenagala drastically reduced transport costs to the highlands by more than 80 percent. SLNA/19/111: "Mr. Turnour's Report upon the Settlement of the Grain Tax Effected in Certain Parts of the Kandyan Provinces, and upon the Services Required from the Inhabitants in the Construction and Repair of Roads."

8. P. M. Bingham, *History of the Public Works Department, Ceylon, 1796–1913*, 3 vols. (Colombo, 1921–23), 3:14.

9. James Cordiner, *A Description of Ceylon*, 2 vols. (London, 1807), 1:425; cited by H. J. Suckling, *Ceylon: A General Description of the Island, Historical, Physical, Statistical*, 2:133. Cordiner, a resident on the island of Ceylon from 1799 to 1804, does not provide a date for an "epidemic of distemper." Interestingly, the epizootic of 1800 was not discovered by the Cattle Disease Commission, which issued its report in 1868.

10. Colvin R. de Silva, *Ceylon under the British Occupation, 1795–1833* (London, 1941; reprint, Colombo, 1995), 2:363.

11. Henry Marshall, *Notes on the Medical Topography of the Interior of Ceylon* (London, 1821), 15–16. See also Regulation of Government no. 4 of 1816, which, in an effort to rebuild the animal stocks after the "extensive Mortality," forbade for a period of twelve months the slaughter of any cow, cow calf, or female buffalo in the maritime districts: *CGG*, no. 754, 28 Feb. 1816.

12. C. G. Uragoda, *A History of Medicine in Sri Lanka* (Colombo, 1987), 258–59.

13. Henry Marshall, "Some Account of the Introduction of Vaccination Among the Inhabitants of the Interior of Ceylon, and of an Epidemic Small-Pox which Prevailed in the Kandyan Provinces in 1819," *Edinburgh Medical and Surgical Journal* 19 (1823): 71–72. Vaccination had been carried out in the maritime provinces by the British since 1802, and it was nearly universal among the European and Burgher (people of mixed race who claim Dutch descent) population on the island. Not a single European or Burgher died during the 1819 epidemic. The practice of vaccination was extended into the Kandyan provinces, but it was not made compulsory until 1886. See Uragoda, *History of Medicine*, 201–3, 210. For ayurvedic practice with regard to smallpox, see Donald Obeysekere, "Medical Science among the Sinhalese: Small Pox and Its Treatment," *Ceylon National Review* 3, no. 8 (1909): 29–34.

14. Marshall, "Introduction of Vaccination," 73–77.

15. J. Kinnis, *A Report on Small-pox as it Appeared in Ceylon in 1833–34; with an Appendix* (Colombo, 1835), 21–22.

16. Marshall noted: "Under the native Government, a very strong measure used to be adopted to arrest the dissemination of the disease when it occurred. Every family was placed in a kind of quarantine, and all intercourse among the people interdicted, until the source of contagion had apparently become extinct": Marshall, "Introduction of Vaccination," 74.

17. Thomas Skinner, *Fifty Years in Ceylon* (London, 1891), 18; cited by Uragoda, *History of Medicine*, 204. Skinner was unaware of earlier outbreaks of smallpox in the Kandyan provinces. On the practice of abandonment of those afflicted with smallpox, see also Marshall, "Introduction of Vaccination," 74–75.

18. Proclamation by Robert Brownrigg, *CGG*, no. 908, 13 Feb. 1819.

19. Proclamation by Governor E. Barnes, *CGG*, no. 1051, 5 Jan. 1822. Government also acted to call in all firearms or parts of firearms; these were to be melted down and returned to the owners as iron: *CGG*, supp. 2, 19 Mar. 1821. In Central Province, the British administration attempted to prohibit the seizure of crops, animals, and other moveable property by individuals seeking to assuage a grievance against them: proclamation by Robert Brownrigg, *CGG*, no. 933, 7 Aug. 1819.

20. SLNA/19/107: "Evidence of Major Fletcher upon the past & present condition of the Kandyan Provinces," 21 Sept. 1829, folios 3b-4a.

21. Marshall, *Medical Topography*, 31–32.

22. Simon Casie Chitty, *The Ceylon Gazetteer* (Cotta Church Mission Press: n.p. [Ceylon], 1834), 113.

23. Marshall, *Medical Topography*, 21.

24. Ibid., 33.

25. J. Burnand, "Ancient and Modern State of the Island of Ceylon and Its Agriculture, 1809," *Monthly Literary Register* 3 (1895): 269.

26. Robert Knox cited by George Wall, in his "Introduction to a History of the Industries of Ceylon," *JRASCB* 10, no. 37 (1888): 329.

27. SLNA/19/106: "Evidence of George Turnour Esquire, Revenue Commissioner for the Kandyan Provinces," 2 Sept. 1829, 29.

28. See, for example, the judgments of W. I. Siriweera on the earlier rajarata period, in Siriweera, *Pre-Modern Sri Lanka*, 120:

Monetized exchange played only a small role in the ancient Sri Lankan economy. The remuneration for services rendered to the king, temples, as well as for work related to most of the caste obligations were made in the form of land revenue and not by money exchange. The circulation of goods depended to some extent on the mechanics of taxation, rent and other payments made in kind. The system of barter was an important mode of exchange. Yet, what is important to note is that currency was also widely used at least in the capital city, port cities and other commercial centres and to some extent even in the interior villages.

29. Michael W. Roberts, "Grain Taxes in British Ceylon, 1832–1872: Problems in the Field," *Journal of Asian Studies* 28, no. 3 (1968): 810.

30. Wickrema S. Weerasooriya, *The Nattukottai Chettiar Merchant Bankers in Ceylon* (Colombo, 1973).

31. Credit practices, however, could vary significantly by region. Sir John D'Oyly reported that in some regions (Seven Korles and Nuwerakalawiya) no interest was charged on paddy; and in Dumbera, no interest was paid on money or grain, and this was attributed to a former Kandyan king's order. For details, see Sir John D'Oyly, *A Sketch of the Constitution of the Kandyan Kingdom* (Dehiwala, 1975), 93–95.

32. "Produce, Stock, &c. of Ceylon," in Lieut. Colonel James Campbell, *Excursions, Adventures, and Field-Sports in Ceylon*, 2 vols. (London, 1843), 2:app. C, 482.

33. Consider, for example, the folk tale below, collected in the nineteenth century, concerning the origins of rice:

The story relates how in the beginning of this kalpa the earth was inhabited by two beings who descended to our sphere from the Brahma-lóka, and how they and their children had at first no difficulty in obtaining their food, as the soil itself was rich and fruitful, and they ate of it gladly and thankfully. But as time went on those qualities which made the soil bear palatable food ceased to exist, and a growth, an edible fungus, sprung up, that these early inhabitants were put to the trouble of collecting as their food; hence, it is said, the necessity for work arose, for the reason that wickedness began to appear among the members of this first earthly family, who had originally nothing but good in their hearts. And as the world grew older its inhabitants grew more wicked, and in proportion the greater was the difficulty in obtaining food. For the first growth, which had merely to be collected and eaten, gave place to another,—a species of plant bearing naked grain, in other words, rice, which the people were put to the additional trouble of collecting and cooking before it was fit for eating.

Later on, as the inhabitants grew more numerous and more wicked, "rice" developed a covering or husk and evolved itself into paddy, thereby causing man greater trouble in having to separate the grain from the husk. But this was not the last of the troubles to the future agriculturalist, for now the paddy plant ceased to grow perenially with no help or attention on the part of man, and then came the necessity for the preparation of fields and the sowing of the grain in order to obtain the crop.

W. A. de Silva, "A Contribution to Sinhalese Plant Lore," *JRASCB* 12, no. 42 (1891): 123–24.

34. Chitty, *Ceylon Gazetteer*, 41; SLNA/19/106: "Evidence of George Turnour Esquire, Revenue Commissioner for the Kandyan Provinces," 2 Sept. 1829, 49.

35. Leopold Ludovici, *Rice Cultivation: Its Past History and Present Condition: With Suggestions for Improvements* (Colombo, 1867), 148.

36. See, for example, SLNA/19/03: "Replies of the Principal Modeliars and Native Landholders in Colombo and the Adjoining Districts to the Questions addressed to Them by the Commission of Inquiry Relative to the Agricultural Resouces of the Country."

Folio 12: [Question] "What is the value of the produce of one acre of land cultivated in paddy and the annual income derived from it deducting the expences of Cultivation?

[Reply] "The produce of a paddy field could not be fixed. It is very uncertain. Sometimes it is one-fold. In times of drought or Rain even the expences of sowing are lost. However the produce of one amonam sown may be rated from three Amonams to Twenty, that is from 24 Parrahs to 160. Fields which produce more are very few. The parrah may be sold from six fanams to one Rix dollar. Expences attending the labour of sowing and reaping a field of this extent will amount from 10 to 25 Rds. In order to shew the expences attending the Cultivation of a ground of one amonam extent and its produce, beginning from its lowest production the following account is made.

Three estimates are put forward, each showing the cultivator with a small profit.

37. Rice yields varied greatly, as did estimates of "average" yields. E. Elliott was a rice booster who expressed high optimism for the future of rice cultivation under irrigation on the island and advanced exaggerated estimates of average yields. See his "Rice Cultivation under Irrigation in Ceylon," *JRASCB* 9, no. 31 (1885): 160–70. Majority opinion and objections to Elliott's data and interpretations, can be found in "The 1885 Proceedings of the R.A.S. (C.B.)," in the same journal issue, xcv–cii. The RAS estimates ranged from fourfold to eightfold returns. John Capper estimated a tenfold return (10 percent of paddy kept for seed, with some paddy fed to stock): John Capper, "The Food Statistics of Ceylon," *JRASCB* 5, no. 17 (1871/1872): 23. George Turnour estimated a tenfold to fifteenfold return: SLNA/19/106: "Evidence of George Turnour Esquire, Revenue Commissioner for the Kandyan Provinces," 2 Sept. 1829, 54–55.

The diversity of returns is the bane of agricultural economists and others who would like to find a lower degree of stochasticity in the historical record. R. L. Lewis in 1848, in reference to Sabagamaruwa Province in the wet southwest foothills of the highlands, recorded returns of forty-eightfold in "many parts of the Meda Korale, while in the Kaduwiti Korale, from two to six fold only is taken from the land": R. L. Lewis, "The Rural Economy of the Sinhalese, More Particularly with Reference to the District of Sabaragamuwa, with Some Account of Their Superstitions," *JRASCB* 2, no. 1, 4, (1848): 31–52. The evidence will not permit exact quantification. As one late-nineteenth-century colonial administrator, for example, estimated: "The average yield of paddy over the whole year, in fair years, is about 15-fold in Kotmalé, about 10-fold in Uda Héwáheta, and about 9-fold in Walapané": Cecil J. R. Le Mesurier, *Manual of the Nuwara Eliya District of the Central Province, Ceylon* (Colombo, 1893), 80.

38. Studies conducted in the 1956/57–1962/63 period indicated that both lack of water and flooding were the major causes of rice crop failure. S. T. Senewiratne and R. R. Appadurai, *Field Crops of Ceylon* (Colombo, 1966), 10. For nineteenth-century observations of the effect of weather on grain production, see the planting reports in the island newspapers (e.g., *KHPWC* and *COOFPCI*).

39. Rice is affected by about fifteen different diseases: blast, brown spot, narrow leaf brown spot, stem rot, and others, as well as by physiological disorders: D. V. M. Abeygunawardena, *Diseases of Cultivated Plants* (Colombo, 1969), 84–106.

40. Henry W. Cave, "The Terraced Hillsides of Ceylon," from *The Times of Ceylon, 1910 — Christmas Number,* reproduced in Pandula Endagama and K. A. S. Dayananda (comps.), *Traditional Agriculture of Sri Lanka* (n.p. [Hector Kobbekaduwa Agrarian Research and Training Institute], n.d. [1998]), 96.

41. Interestingly, even this generalization must be qualified by the observation that in some areas, at least, buffalo would not eat rice straw. See Cattle Disease Commission [1869] report, app.: "Evidence on First Journey," 7.

42. Cave, "Terraced Hillsides," 94–95.

43. I would like to thank C. M. Madduma Bandara, Nimal Gunatilleke, Nimal Wickramaratna, and Siril Wijesundera for their helpful suggestions on this topic at a colloquium organized in the Department of Geography at the University of Peradeniya in November 1998.

44. Jacques Pouchepadass, "British Attitudes Towards Shifting Cultivation in

Colonial South India: A Case Study of South Canara District, 1800–1920," in David Arnold and Ramachandra Guha, eds., *Nature, Culture, Imperialism: Essays on the Environmental History of South Asia* (Delhi, 1995), 123–51.

45. Chena is principally a lowland phenomenon in Sri Lanka. In other Asian countries, it is usually found on the hills of wet evergreen forests where the slope of the land does not permit the use of animal-drawn implements: R. A. De Rosayro, "Some Aspects of Shifting Cultivation in Ceylon," *TA* 105, no. 2 (1949): 51.

46. Samuel White Baker, *The Rifle and the Hound in Ceylon* (London, 1854; reprint, New York, 1967), 75–76.

47. For a statement of the argument that chena was marginal but indispensable to highland communities, see Eric Meyer, "Les Forêts, les Cultures Sur Brûlis, les Plantations et l'État Colonial à Sri Lanka (1840–1930)," *Revue française d'histoire d'outre-mer* 80, no. 299 (1993): 195–218. This argument dates to the mid-nineteenth century, when it was first advanced by British civil servants in the highlands.

48. Ludovici, *Rice Cultivation*, 144.

49. Mesurier, *Manual of Nuwara Eliya District*, 80–81. Some authors have argued that chena cultivation was "respectful of the environment." See, for example, Eric Meyer, "Forests, Chena Cultivation, Plantations, and the Colonial State in Ceylon, 1840–1940," in Richard H. Grove, Vinita Damodaran, and Satpal Sangwan, eds., *Nature and the Orient* (Delhi, 1998), 797–98.

50. De Rosayro, "Shifting Cultivation," 57.

51. Senewirtane and Appadurai, *Field Crops of Ceylon*, 125–27. Kurrakan is the most important crop of the Dry Zone chenas and it plays a major role in Malaysia and India. In the former State of Mysore, in the 1960s it was the most important grain crop.

52. As Simon Casie Chetty explained in the early 1830s: "Among the dry grains sown in the high lands, corakan forms a material portion of the diet of the lower orders; and when the crops of paddy fail, it tends greatly to alleviate their wants. It is ground into flour with hand-mills, and made into flat cakes and into puddings; but it is not reckoned a very wholesome food": Chitty, *Ceylon Gazetteer*, 41. This attitude is also expressed in the late-seventeenth-century treatise by Robert Knox:

> Besides this, tho far inferior to it, there are divers other sorts of Corn, which serve the People for food in the absence of Rice, which will scarcely hold out with many of them above half the Year. There is Coracan, which is a small seed like Mustard-seed, This they grind to meal or beat in a Mortar, and so make Cakes of it, baking it upon the Coals in a potsheard, or dress it otherwise. If they which are not used to it, eat it, it will gripe their Bellies; When they are minded to grind it, they have for their Mill two round stones, which they turn with their hands by the help of a stick: There are several sorts of this Corn. Some will ripen in three months, and some require four. If the Ground be good, it yields a great encrease; and grows both on the Hills and in the Plains.

Historical Relation of the Island of Ceylon in the East Indies (London, 1681; reprint, New Delhi, 1984), 11–12.

53. H. F. Macmillan, *Tropical Planting and Gardening With Special Reference to Ceylon,* 4th ed. (London, 1934), 299; the Indian forester F. D'A. Vincent suggested even higher returns to seed—up to 120-fold to 500-fold: F. D'A. Vincent, "Report on the Conservation and Administration of the Crown Forests in Ceylon," *SP* 43 (1883): 11.

54. Abeygunawardena, *Diseases of Cultivated Plants,* 106–8.

55. W. C. Ondaatje, "Notes on the District of Badulla," *JRASCB* 3, no. 12 (1860/61): 396.

56. Interestingly, Robert Knox, in *Historical Relation* (14 and 18), provides a fascinating description of the fruits and vegetables that were exploited by Kandyan villagers, but he makes no mention of the "forest garden" per se:

These [jack fruit] are a great help to the People, and a great part of their Food. . . . Another Fruit there is which I never saw in any other Part of India, they call it Jombo. In tast it is like to an Apple, full of Juice, and pleasant to the Palate, and not unwholsom to the Body, and to the Eye no Fruit more amiable, being white, and delicately coloured with red, as if it were painted.

Also in the wild Woods are several sorts of pretty Fruits, as Murros, round in shape, and as big as a Cherry, and sweet to the tast; Dongs, nearest like to a black Cherry. Ambelo's like to Barberries. Carolla cabella, Cabela pooke, and Polla's, these are like to little Plums, and very well tasted. Paragidde, like to our Pears, and many more such like Fruits.

Here are also, of Indian Fruits, Coker-nuts; Plantins also and Banana's of divers and sundry sorts, which are distinguished by the tast as well as by the names; rare sweet Oranges and sower ones, Limes but no Lemons, such as ours are; Pautaurings, in tast all one with a Lemon, but much bigger than a mans two fists, right Citrons, and a small sort of sweet Oranges. Here are several other sorts of Lemons, and Oranges, Mangoes of several sorts, and some very good and sweet to eat. In this sort of Fruit the King much delights, and hath them brought to him from all Parts of the Island. Pine-apples also grow there, Sugar Canes, Water-Melons, Pomegranates, Grapes both black and white, Mirablins, Cadjeu's, and several other. . . .

They have all of our English Herbs and Plants, Colworts, Carrots, Radishes, Fennel, Balsam, Spearmint, Mustard. These, excepting the two last, are not the natural product of the Land, but they are transplanted hither; By which I perceive all other European Plants would grow there: They have also Fern, Indian Corn Several Sorts of Beans as good as these in England: right Cucumbers, Calabasses, and several sorts of Pumkins, &c. The Dutch on that Island in their Gardens have Lettice, Rosemary, Sage, and all other Herbs and Sallettings that we have in these Countreys.

57. See Jayaindro Fernando and Thivanshi Fernando, *A Selection of the Fruits of Sri Lanka* (Colombo, 1997), for descriptions of eighty-five common fruits, the majority of which are not indigenous to the island.

58. D. J. McConnell, *The Forest-garden Farms of Kandy, Sri Lanka* (FAO: Rome, 1992), 2–3, 12.

59. Kelaart, *Prodomus Faunae Zeylanicae*, 87.

60. A. S. Chandra Segra, *Notes on the Management of Cattle in India and Ceylon and Their Diseases* (Jaffna, 1909), 52–53.

61. Robert Percival, *An Account of the Island of Ceylon* (London, 1803), 285–88.

62. M. Crawford, "The Influence of the Various Mineral Constituents on Animal Nutrition, and the Effects of Deficiencies and Evidence of Such in Ceylon," *TA* 68, no. 5 (1927): 277. Edward Ives reported that he and his companions killed six oxen at Trincomalee and that their total weight was 714 pounds: *A Voyage from England to India* (London, 1773), excerpted in Major R. Raven-Hart, trans. and ed., *Travels in Ceylon, 1700–1800* (Colombo, 1963), 39.

63. Sir H. Marcus Fernando, "The Need for the Improvement of Cattle in Ceylon," *TA* 66, no. 6 (1926): 298–99. The importation of breeds of cattle from the temperate zones was first begun on a large scale in 1943, when the government imported three hundred cows and thirty-six bulls from Australia: P. Mahadevan, "An Analysis of the European Herds of Dairy Cattle at Ambewela and Bopatalawa," *TA* 113, no. 1 (1957): 45.

64. Marshall, *Medical Topography*, 15.

65. Frederic J. Mouat, *Rough Notes of a Trip to Reunion, the Mauritius, and Ceylon; With Remarks on the Eligibility as Sanataria for Indian Invalids* (Calcutta, 1852), 125.

66. John D'Oyly, *A Sketch of the Constitution of the Kandyan Kingdom* (Dehiwala, 1975), 53.

67. R. Sukumar, "Ecology of the Asian Elephant in Southern India, II: Feeding Habits and Crop Raiding Patterns," *Journal of Tropical Ecology* 6 (1990): 33–53.

68. Jayawardena, *Elephant in Sri Lanka*, 71.

69. For a broad investigation of the principles of ethnobotanical classification, see Brent Berlin, *Ethnobiological Classification: Principles of Categorization of Plants and Animals in Traditional Societies* (Princeton, 1992).

70. De Silva, "Sinhalese Plant Lore," 113–18.

71. Comment by Dr. Henry Trimen in de Silva, "Sinhalese Plant Lore," 143–44.

72. De Silva, "Sinhalese Plant Lore," 131. For other folk stories concerning flora, see Perera and Jain, *Fountains of Life*, 27–40.

73. This discussion of Sinhala terminology about forests is based on conversations with Professor P. B. Meegaskumbura, chair of the Department of Sinhala at the University of Peradeniya, in August 1998.

74. Ralph Pieris, *Sinhalese Social Organization: The Kandyan Period* (Colombo, 1956), 46–49.

75. SLNA/18/3751: no. 301. GA, Kandy, to CS, 1 Sept. 1837.

76. See, for example, the note on the prohibited forest of Udavattekale in Sir John D'Oyly's *Sketch of the Constitution of the Kandyan Kingdom* ("Addenda—Notes, &c.," n.a., dated 27 Oct. 1827), 99:

> The forest of Udawatte Keley near the Palace was strictly interdicted, so that people were not allowed even to gather firewood in it—Hantanne was like wise an interdicted forest, but yet people were permitted to get firewood, withes, &c.,

from it—The forests belonging to the King in the more distant parts of the Country, were likewise under prohibition, but not so strictly watched, and the Inhabitants of the neighbourhood were at liberty to fell timber in them, but not to clear any part for chena.

For a study of the forest of Udavattekale, see Nihal Karunaratna, *Udavattekäle: The Forbidden Forest of the Kings of Kandy* (Colombo, 1986). This text makes the point that the forest of Udavattekale was considered a protected forest. Curiously, the author does not explain why the forest Udavattekale (Sinhala: "Upper Garden Forest") received this name. The appellation would suggest that the forest was exploited by the king of Kandy, rather than left as a nature preserve.

77. Interestingly, some writers did not draw a distinction between the full rainforest and the secondary forests that had grown up after recent chena cultivation. Some used the terms *forest* and *jungle* interchangeably, but others drew an important distinction between the two. A forest had not been burned and was what mid-twentieth-century American ecologists would have called a "climax forest." A jungle was something else altogether. As Lieutenant De Butts explained in his *Rambles in Ceylon* (1841): "The term 'jungle,' as understood in Ceylon, applies to ground covered with thick and nearly impervious underwood. Large trees seldom occur in a jungle of this description, which is, therefore, per se, an uninteresting object; but when it clothes a wild and mountainous country, its uniformity does not displease, because it seems to harmonize with the stern sombre character that belongs to such a landscape": Lieutenant De Butts, *Rambles in Ceylon* (London, 1841), 190. In this sense, *jungle* was synonymous with *connaught*. See Thomas Skinner, *Fifty Years in Ceylon* (London, 1891), 165.

78. James Johnson and James Ranald Martin, *The Influence of Tropical Climates on European Constitutions* (New York, 1846), 88.

79. Anthony Bertolacci, *A View of the Agricultural, Commerical and Financial Interests of Ceylon* (London, 1817; reprint, Dehiwala, 1983), 4–5.

80. Samuel White Baker, *Eight Years' Wanderings in Ceylon* (London, 1855), 75. For a similar view, see also Charles Pridham, *An Historical, Political, and Statistical Account of Ceylon and Its Dependencies*, 2 vols. (London, 1849), 2:686–87.

81. On the general phenomenon of elevated European mortality in the tropics, see Philip D. Curtin, *Death by Migration: Europe's Encounter with the Tropical World in the Nineteenth Century* (Cambridge, 1989).

Chapter 3
Early-nineteenth-century Processes of Change

1. John C. Super, *Food, Conquest, and Colonization in Sixteenth-Century Spanish America* (Albuquerque, 1988).

2. James R. Gibson, *Imperial Russia in Frontier America: The Changing Geography of Supply of Russian America, 1784–1867* (New York, 1976).

3. Alan Frost, "The Antipodean Exchange: European Horticulture and Imperial

Designs," in David P. Miller and Peter H. Reill, eds., *Visions of Empire: Voyages, Botany, and Representations of Nature* (Cambridge, 1996), 58–79.

4. Janet Brown, "A Science of Empire: British Biogeography Before Darwin," *Revue d'Histoire des Sciences* 45, no. 4 (1992): 453–75.

5. The European origins of Sri Lankan botany are to be found in the researches of the physician Paul Hermann, who was chief medical officer at the Dutch Hospital in Colombo from 1672 to 1679, when he accepted a position as professor of medicine and botany at the University of Leiden. His collection of plants from Sri Lanka and his research notes, which included the transliteration of the Sinhala and Tamil plant names, were the foundation for the posthumous publication in Latin of his Musaeum Zeylanicum in 1717 and later in 1726. See Dr. D. C. Gunawardena, "Medicinal and Economic Plants of the Musaeum Zeylanicum of Paul Hermann," *JRASCB* 19 (1975): 33–48.

6. James Cordiner, *A Description of Ceylon* (London, 1807), 1:425.

7. Robert Percival, *An Account of the Island of Ceylon* (London, 1803), 121.

8. For a trenchant analysis of the evidence concerning early botanic gardens, see T. Petch, "The Early History of Botanic Gardens in Ceylon, with notes on the Topography of Colombo," *The Ceylon Antiquary and Literary Register* 5, pt. 3 (Jan. 1920): 119–24.

9. Thomas Christie, "His Majesty's 51st Regiment," in "Extracts from the General Medical Report of the Troops Serving in Ceylon For the Month of April 1803" in Cordiner, *Description of Ceylon*, 2:265.

10. Shelton C. Fernando, "History of the Department of Agriculture," *TA* 97 (1941): 216.

11. Cordiner, *Description of Ceylon*, 1:386–88. MacDowell received the assistance of Dr. William Roxburgh, superintendent of the East India Company's Calcutta garden. See Kalipada Biswas, *The Original Correspondence of Sir Joseph Banks Relating to the Foundation of the Royal Botanic Garden, Calcutta and The Summary of the 150th Anniversary Volume of the Royal Botanic Garden, Calcutta* (Calcutta, 1950), 12–14.

12. Banks apparently was acting on the advice of Sir Alexander Johnston, a member of the supreme court in Ceylon. Johnston, in 1806, had appointed a Muslim physician as superintendent of the Native Medical Establishment. Johnston was impressed with native medicinal plants and wrote in the mid-1820s, "The cultivation and improvement of these plants, as well as of all other plants and vegetables on the island which might be used either for food or commercial purposes was one of the great objects for which His Majesty's government, at my suggestion, in 1810, established a royal botanical garden in Ceylon": Alexander Johnston, "A Cufic Inscription Found in Ceylon," *Transactions of the Royal Asiatic Society of Great Britain and Ireland* 1 (1827): 547; cited by Uragoda, *History of Medicine*, 82.

13. *COOFPCI*, supplement to *CO*, 31 Dec. 1860, 5. See app. 5 for an extract of this statement by Banks. The Dutch had also expressed admiration for the Sinhalese practitioners of ayurvedic medicine. See C. G. Uragoda, *A History of Medicine in Sri Lanka* (Colombo, 1987), 69–70.

The RBG in Ceylon was one of only four "Royal" colonial gardens in the British Empire: Donal P. McCracken, *Gardens of Empire: Botanical Institutions of the Victorian British Empire* [London, 1997], ix.

14. Ray Desmond, *Kew: The History of the Royal Botanic Gardens* (London, 1995), 100–101; Ray Desmond, *The European Discovery of the Indian Flora* (Cambridge, 1992), 67–68; *Ceylon Almanac for 1843* (Colombo, 1844), lv. Kerr's principal instructions were to improve the horticulture of Sri Lanka by importing fruit trees from China. But there were additional charges for the royal gardener. After fulfilling his responsibilities to the improvement of horticulture and responding to the instructions of the governor, he was to look after the cinnamon gardens and suggest horticultural improvements, find suitable spots for subordinate gardens, collect beautiful or curious plants, and send seeds back to Kew, particularly seeds for plants that might grow in an English climate. All of the royal gardener's work was to be duly recorded and an annual report to be submitted to the governor for transmission to the secretary of state: *COOFPCI*, supplement to *CO*, 31 Dec. 1860, 6.

15. The main site of the RBG was at Slave Island in Colombo, with satellite gardens in the fort at Colombo (attached to the governor's house), at Mount Lavinia, and perhaps (the evidence is not clear) at the North Esplanade; SLNA/19/01; "Evidence of Mr. James Mac Rae Superintendent of the Royal Botanic Gardens in Ceylon, upon the state of the Botanical Gardens at Peradeniya near Kandy and improvements introduced into the country in the culture of Coffee," 3a. References to a garden at North Esplanade can be found in the correspondence of Alexander Moon in SLNA/6/1027. The Slave Island location was soon discovered to be subject to flooding and was deemed unsuitable; on 8 Aug. 1813, land for the principal garden was purchased in Kalutara, on the southwest coast below Colombo. It was not an entirely promising locale. The site suffered from wet subsoils, and for this reason alone it probably should have been ruled out as unsuitable for a garden. This indeed was the opinion of Thomas Hardwicke, who visited Kalutara in 1815 and reported back to Banks: letter from Hardwicke to Banks, 28 Oct. 1815, British Library, Add. MSS 9869, folio 18; quoted in Desmond, *The European Discovery of the Indian Flora*, 161–62. According to William Kerr's description, some of the 560 acres were in coconut trees, others were marked by the remains of a failed sugar plantation, and yet others by currently cultivated rice paddies, while most of the acreage was covered by "an impenetrable thicket of trees & shrubs in a state of nature," which suggests that these lands had been earlier cultivated and abandoned: SLNA/6/281: William Kerr to John Rodney, 14 Aug. 1813.

16. Captain L. De Bussche, *Letters on Ceylon; Particularly Relative to the Kingdom of Kandy* (London, 1817), 79–80. See also Marshall, *Medical Topography*, 15. Outside of Kandy, the nutritional status of the British troops remained highly compromised. As Marshall noted,

The diet of the soldiers is . . . very uniform. The bazars of the interior have hitherto furnished little variety, at a rate within the compass of the soldier's pay. Fowls are to be procured at most of the stations, but they are in general so dear as to be beyond the means of a soldier to purchase them. The chief, indeed, the only culinary vegetables which the Kandyan bazars afford are brinjauls (a species of melangona) and sweet potatoes. The plantain is almost the only fruit a soldier is able to purchase.

Bread is very high-priced in the Kandyan country. Even in the town of Kandy, where the demand is the greatest, a coarse kind of bread sells at sevenpence per pound. But bread is prepared at only four stations in the interior; it therefore cannot be procured at many of the dependent posts. To new arrivals the want of bread is a great privation.

Marshall, *Medical Topography,* 87.

17. John Christopher Willis, "The Royal Botanic Gardens of Ceylon, and Their History," *Annals of the Royal Botanic Gardens, Peradeniya* 1, pt. 1 (June 1901) 3.

18. SLNA/6/282: letters from Alexander Moon to John Rodney, chief secretary to government, 12 May 1817, 16 May 1817, 15 Dec. 1818, 7 Jan. 1819. The introduction of European fruits and vegetables in the late eighteenth century had enjoyed great success in New South Wales, and this experience likely played a role in the continuation of efforts to establish European horticulture in Ceylon. On New South Wales, see Frost, "The Antipodean Exchange: European Horticulture and Imperial Designs," 58–79.

19. SLNA/6/283: Alexander Moon to Rodney, chief secretary, 20 Sept. 1820.

20. SLNA/6/283: Moon to William Granville, deputy secretary to government, 7 Oct. 1820.

21. Most of the records of the early years of the garden have been lost to damage. Many were destroyed in the first decades of the garden's existence. As Gardner noted in 1845, "I consider it my duty to state that most of the records belonging to the Garden are half rotten from there being no Almirah in which to keep them: one which was applied for and promised, previous to my arrival, has never been received." George Gardner, *Report on the Royal Botanic Garden, at Pérádenia, Kandy, Presented to His Excellency the Governor in August 1845.* (Colombo, n.d. [1845]), 9. The acquisition of Peradeniya also had repercussions in the maritime provinces. It meant that it was possible to rearrange the assets of the RBG. The garden at Slave Island was slated for sale. SLNA/6/283: Moon to Rodney, chief secretary, 14 June 1822. The Kalutara garden continued in existence, although it entered into decline. By the late 1830s, the rare trees and shrubs were going to ruin at Kalutara. Supt. J. G. Watson suggested that Kalutara be instated as a branch of RBG-Peradeniya: SLNA/6/1322: Watson to CS, 14 Oct. 1834. The government garden in the Fort was transferred to the Ceylon Horticultural and Agricultural Society for its temporary use in 1838: SLNA/6/1405: Watson to CS, 17 Feb. 1838.

22. SLNA/6/1027: The first archival entry for the payment of laborers employed on the coffee plantation at Peradeniya is dated 6 Jan. 1824.

23. It is not clear why Moon thought that a horticultural garden in the environs of Kandy would succeed. After long years of effort at growing European fruits and vegetables along the coast, the problems of seed degeneration there appeared insurmountable. Indeed, in 1822, almost exactly coincident with the opening up of the Peradeniya garden, the Sub-Committee on Natural History and Agriculture of the Ceylon Literary and Agricultural Society reported with discouragement on a "Treatise on the State of Horticulture in Ceylon" that there seemed to be no means "for the improvement of the System of Practical Horticulture or the removal of the deterring causes to which its imperfections are attributed." T. Petch, "In Ceylon a Century Ago:

The Proceedings of the Ceylon Literary and Agricultural Society: With Notes by T. Petch," *The Ceylon Antiquary and Literary Register* 8, pt. 2 (Oct. 1922): 171–76.

The Ceylon Literary Society was instituted on 11 December 1820: *Ceylon Almanac for 1843* [Colombo, 1844], lx. It soon changed its name to the Ceylon Literary and Agricultural Society. In 1822, the society obtained garden seeds from Bangalore and Hyderabad and offered them for sale: *CGG* 1822, 89. Moon's optimism may have been based on the success of some British East India Company gardens in Bangalore and Hyderabad, where more equable ecological conditions seem to have produced good results. At all events, with a continuing official demand for European fruits and vegetables, the horticulture initiative ground on.

24. SLNA/6/1322: J. G. Watson to CS, 27 July 1835.

25. SLNA/53/37: Normansell to W. T. Hooker, 12 Feb. 1842.

26. SLNA/53/1: CS to supt., RBG-Peradeniya, 18 Jan. 1842. By 1843, there was a sufficient local market for European vegetables and fruits that the acting supt., W. C. Ondaatje, was able to arrange for the daily sale of fruits and vegetables from the office of the GA in Kandy and, monthly, of plants and seeds from the Kandy Kutchchery [District Government Office]: SLNA/6/1743: Ondaatje to CS, 20 Nov. 1843. Ondaatje also proposed an outreach program for Kandyan farmers to instruct them in the English mode of gardening, agriculture, and the use of agricultural implements; he suggested that small quantities of seeds and plants might be distributed to those who were unable to pay for them: SLNA/53/1: Ondaatje to CS, 15 Feb. 1844. Moreover, Ondaatje looked after an experimental sugarcane plantation at the garden, planted five acres in indigenous and exotic medical plants, established a nursery, and proposed an experimental station in Nuwara Eliya, in order to naturalize useful European plants: "Report on the Royal Botanic Garden, Peradenia, near Kandy. From February to May 1843: By Wm. C. Ondaatje: With an Appendix by Capt. Champion," in "Remarks on the State of Botany in Ceylon . . . in April 1843," *Ceylon Calendar for 1844* (Colombo, 1845), 447–49; SLNA/6/1743: Ondaatje to CS, 13 July 1843; Wm. C. Ondaatje, "Report on the Royal Botanic Garden, Peradenia, near Kandy. From June to December 1843: With an Appendix," (Colombo, n.d. [1844]), v.

27. SLNA/6/1891: Gardner to CS, 20 Apr. 1844; George Gardner to CS, 29 Jan. 1847; Gardner to CS, 28 June 1847.

28. Charles Pridham, *An Historical, Political, and Statistical Account of Ceylon and Its Dependencies,* 2 vols. (London, 1849), 1:372–73, 2:678; *Ceylon Almanac for 1843* (Colombo, 1844), lx; J. W. Bennett, *Ceylon and Its Capabilities* (London, 1843), 399; SLNA/19/106: "Evidence of George Turnour Esquire, Revenue Commissioner for the Kandyan Provinces," 2 Sept. 1829, 49–50.

29. Bennett, *Ceylon and Its Capabilities,* 125, 127, 138, 287–88.

30. SLNA/6/1743: W. C. Ondaatje to CS, 15 Apr. 1843; Ondaatje to CS, 29 Aug. 1843; Ondaatje to CS, 16 Aug. 1843. On the different species and varieties of yam cultivated in Sri Lanka, see H. F. Macmillan, *Tropical Planting and Gardening With Special Reference to Ceylon,* 4th ed. (London, 1934), 289–90.

31. It is not known when these coffee trees were planted, but it is possible that during the period of Dutch rule coffee in the highlands was grown for export. For a

summary of Dutch policies toward coffee and other export crops that were subsidiary to cinnamon, see K. M. de Silva, *A History of Sri Lanka* (Oxford, 1981), 167–69.

32. I. H. Vanden Driesen, "Coffee Cultivation in Ceylon," *Ceylon Historical Journal* 3 (1953): pt. 1, 33–34.

33. The paddy fields and the lands at Race Course Hill were plowed three times and harrowed twice by elephant. The cost of land preparation was high, calculated at £2 3s. and £3 8s., respectively: SLNA/6/1028: G. Bird to deputy secretary of government, 17 Nov. 1830.

34. SLNA/19/118: no. 45. Governor Barnes to Earl Bathurst, 11 June 1827, Colombo; SLNA/19/1: "Evidence of Mr. James Mac Rae Superintendent of the Royal Botanic Gardens in Ceylon, upon the State of the Botanical Gardens at Peradeniya near Kandy . . . and Improvements Introduced into the Country in the Culture of Coffee," 4a.

35. SLNA/19/102: "Evidence of George Bird Esquire, upon agriculture in the Kandyan Provinces," 2b.

36. The original Gampola estate was sold in 1846 to a British firm, Hudson Chandler & Co., to farm on the English model—uprooting the coffee trees and planting guinea grass with the intention of raising superior breeds of horses and cattle. This concern collapsed during the financial crisis of 1848, and the estate reverted to the control of the Bird family. A new coffee plantation was established, without shade trees, on the lines of those of the West Indies: "Kaduganava," *COOFPCI*, n.s., 6, no. 146 (1858); republished from *CO*, 6 Dec. 1858.

37. "Coffee Planting" and "Letter by S. Northway," *OOFSI*, no. 2, 12 Oct. 1840, 2. By 1840, the coffee trees in Barnes's various experimental plantings were being destroyed to make room for the West Indian model. As a visitor to the Gangaruwa plantation noted,

> When this Plantation was established the cultivation of Coffee was but little understood in Ceylon, and Sir Edward being rather fond of experiments, all sorts of experiments have accordingly here been tried. Tall thin and lanky plants will first be observed, very like hot house plants at Home. These were reared amid a dense shade, the trees forming which are now girdled (i.e. cut slightly all round near the root) falling and crumbling in all directions.

"A Trip Into the Interior. Coffee Planting, Etc.," *OOMPCI*, no. 4 (12 Dec. 1840).

38. The exact location of all of the Peradeniya coffee fields is not known, but some (the majority?) were directly across the road from the entrance to the garden on the Kandy-Colombo road, next to the racetrack. See map of RBG-Peradeniya in 1828 drawn by draftsman Harmanis de Alwis Seneviratne, in *Cingalese Sketches*, a collection of drawings by de Alwis held by the Lindley Library of the Royal Horticultural Society in London.

39. SLNA/6/1322: J. G. Watson to CS, 30 Oct. 1835.

40. These coffee lands were let on lease from Henry Wright and made up by far the greater portion of the garden under cultivation: SLNA/6/1405: "Report on the Present State of the Royal Botanic Garden Ceylon" [1838].

41. SLNA/6/1487: Henry Normansell to CS, 18 Sept. 1840.

42. Wm. C. Ondaatje, *Report on the Royal Botanic Garden, Peradenia, near Kandy. From June to December 1843: With an Appendix* (Colombo, n.d. [1844]), v.

43. Supt. Gardner, shortly after his appointment, proposed that all lands at the garden that were not necessary for botanical and experimental work be put into coffee production: SLNA/6/1891: Gardner to CS, 27 May 1844. Gardner's principal interest in coffee production was to produce revenue to support his botanical research.

44. "Ceylon Sugar," *COCA*, 362, 19 June 1843; "Sugar Planting," *COCA*, 490, 9 Sept. 1844; Charles Pridham, *An Historical, Political, and Statistical Account of Ceylon and Its Dependencies*, 2 vols. (London, 1849), 1:375; Bennett, *Ceylon and Its Capabilities*, 34. The cost of transport in 1837 was estimated at the rate of 17s. going and 8s. 6d. returning for a cart carrying 1,100 lbs.: *Ceylon Chronicle* 1, no. 16 (26 June 1837): 1.

45. George Gardner, "Report on the Royal Botanic Garden-Pérádenia, from July 1846 to August 1847" (Colombo, 1847), 12–13.

46. Samuel White Baker, *Eight Years' Wanderings in Ceylon* (London, 1855), 55. In the late 1860s, the sugar plantation at Peradeniya, owned by the Baring Brothers and consisting of 346 acres, was the only sugar plantation in Central Province: A. M. Ferguson, *Supplement to Ferguson's Ceylon Directory and Handbook for 1866–68* (Colombo, 1869), 79.

47. Moon labeled the "China Tea" as *Thea Bohea*. Alexander Moon, *A Catalogue of the Indigenous and Exotic Plants Growing in Ceylon* (Colombo, 1824), 42.

48. The Portuguese introduced tea from Macau to Brazil in 1814, along with Chinese tea farmers. Experiments with tea continued for decades, but without much success: Warren Dean, *With Broadax and Firebrand* (Berkeley, 1995), 171–72.

49. SLNA/6/1147: J. G. Watson to P. Anstruther, deputy secretary to government, 29 Aug. 1833.

50. SLNA/10/22: Lear to governor, 6 Nov. 1839 and 23 Nov. 1939.

51. SLNA/6/1487: Henry Thomas Normansell to acting CS, 25 Apr. 1840.

52. SLNA/53/1: CS to supt., RBG-Peradeniya, 11 May 1840.

53. SLNA/6/1487: Normansell to CS, 18 Nov. 1840.

54. SLNA/6/1743: Normansell to CS, 15 Apr. 1842. Normansell provided details in his annual report, SLNA/06/1743, 1 Aug. 1842.

55. [Planters' Association], *Planters' Association of Ceylon, 1854–1954* (Colombo, 1954), 12.

56. "Ceylon Tea," *OOMPCI*, no. 57 (10 June 1845):

We are happy to learn that the Tea plants brought from China by Messrs. Worms, are growing in great perfection on their Estate at Pusellawa. These gentlemen have also healthy nurseries of young plants raised from the seeds of the trees thus originally introduced, and which give promise of the most perfect success.— Care was taken, we understand, in China to select those species which produce Tea of the finest quality, known by the name Sactung-fun, and indigenous to the hills of Wohea and Fokein. Messrs. Worms we believe to be the first persons who have imported the plant direct from China to Ceylon; and will probably be also the first exporters of Tea from this Island to England; and may thus prove the originators of what may ere long become another important branch of our colonial trade.

57. SLNA/6/1891: Gardner to CS, 18 May 1847.

58. Barnes cultivated a variety of exotic vegetables, fruit trees, and flowers, including potatoes, tomatoes, mulberry trees, citron, orange, lime, vines, myrtle, geraniun, lupins, cabbage, turnip, peas, Windsor beans, French beans, carrots, pumpkin, nasturtium, peach trees, cherry, apple, rose, fir, filbert, lavender, marjoram, artichokes, cauliflower, red cabbage, brocoli, Brussels sprouts, knole kole, sweet and common turnips, red beet, white beet, parsley, celery, lettuce, radishes, leeks, onion, stocks, mignionette, pinks, carnations, poppies, and leucat peas: *Colombo Journal*, no. 9 (4 Feb. 1832).

59. Other features of the upper highlands, such as the wet patana lands that supported elephant populations, were decidedly unlike Scotland. European visitors found the presence of elephants most striking. One mid-nineteenth-century traveler to the upper highlands even suggested that depredations by elephants must have brought about a human exodus from the region. Dr. W. Hoffmeister, *Travels in Ceylon and Continental India* (Edinburgh, 1848), 167.

60. Baker, *Eight Years' Wanderings*, 25.

61. Ibid., 26–29.

62. Highland horticultural production for urban markets on the island remains important into the twenty-first century. Gardeners in the upper highlands supply markets in Colombo, Kandy, and other cities.

63. E. F. Kelaart, *Prodomus Faunae Zeylanica* (Colombo, 1852), 58.

64. "Newera Ellia: Convalescent Station in the Island of Ceylon," *COCA*, 294, 24 Oct. 1842:

> Cattle are becoming very abundant on the plain. On their first being brought up from the lower country, they fall off in condition, but after two or three months they become acclimatised, and getting accustomed to the coarse grass, they recover their good looks, and thrive as well as in any part of the Island. Sheep are found to do equally well—but they require more care, for unless housed by night, they will soon die, besides the chance of being carried off by the Cheetah, which inhabits the neighboring jungle; indeed, even by day, they require to be watched to prevent their straying into the jungle—A scarcity of birds was much noticed by early settlers at this place, but they are daily becoming more common. The black bird, with its yellow beak and legs, maybe seen in every garden, the Tom Tit hopping from tree to tree—The Tit Lark is very common, and latterly the eye has actually been cheered by the sight of a genuine Robin-red-breast.
>
> There is little to amuse the sportsmen at Nuwera Ellia—Snipe there certainly are in abundance, in the season; jungle fowl are also plentiful at certain times, particularly when the Nilloe, a shrubby kind of Balsam, sheds its seed, which it does every third year.

In 1839 a few wood cock were shot. . . . Elks are very numerous, but only to be got at with good dogs—Some years ago a subscription pack of hounds was kept and then a great many Elks were killed. The elephant is also frequently seen, but he is generally a traveller, and does not remain.

65. SLNA/18/2751: diary entry, AGA for Badulla K. MacKenzie, at Yattipalata, 29 Mar. 1848.

66. Baker, *Eight Years' Wanderings*, 28.

67. Marshall, *Ceylon*, 20.

68. SLNA/18/2490: P. W. Braybrooke to CS, 3 May 1859.

69. SLNA/18/17:

Advertisement. Notice is hereby given that it is the order of His Excellency the Lieutenant Governor with a view to the preservation of useful Timber and to secure a supply of that necessary Article for the public Service that from the publication of this order no chenas shall be cut in the Government Forests nor any new high ground cleared within the Kandyan Provinces without the previous written License of the Revenue Commissioner and no such Licenses will be granted until after a previous inspection and Report Shall have been made as to the good Timber Trees which are Standing upon the ground proposed to be cut and should the number thereof be such as to render it desirable to preserve the Timber the License is to be refused and such Licenses will be invariably refused for clearing any chena within a mile of any River or road by which Timber can be conveyed to any one of the Principal Posts.

The people of Uderatte will apply for Licenses directly to the Cutcherry of Kandy and the people of other Provinces will apply for their Licenses through the Accredited Agents of their respective Districts and will order the necessary inspection to make their Report.

Published at the Cutcherry of Kandy this 15th day of August 1821

70. Regulation no. 2, 1822: "For the Protection of the Revenue of Government derived from Timber growing in the Royal Forests, and also to restrain the felling of Jack Trees which is the species of Timber usually cut in Lands being private Property," *CGG*, no. 1051, 5 Jan. 1822.

71. See, for example, SLNA/18/1751: diary entries, AGA for Badulla K. MacKenzie, at Yattipalata, 29 Mar. 1848: "[The headman] Is of opinion that the Fields have been generally improved and increased in extent since 1832. . . . Considers that the cultivation generally has been greatly improved since 1832. attributes the improvement to the abolition of compulsory labour. and the increase of the population."; and at Kaltaboa, 23 Feb. 1848:

This is a particularly fine village. the people are Moors or Mohammedans. there is considerable attention paid by the people to cultivating useful Fruit Trees in their Gardens. The fields attached to this and the adjoining villages are very extensive and in full cultivation. Nearly the whole of the large Forest, in this

Neighbourhood has been cut down for Chena cultivation. There has not been much Chenah cultivation this year in consequence they say of the abundance of rain that enabled them to cultivate their fields.

72. In addition, the import duties on agricultural and manufacturing implements were abolished. Vanden Driesen, "Coffee Cultivation," pt. 1, 37–40.

73. Michael W. Roberts, *Caste Conflict and Elite Formation: The Rise of a Karava Elite in Sri Lanka, 1500–1931* (Cambridge, 1982), 102–3; Edmund C. P. Hull, *Coffee: Its Physiology, History, and Cultivation: Adapted as a Work of Reference for Ceylon, Wynaad, Coorg, and the Neilgherries* (Madras, 1865), 15.

74. Letter of R. N. Tytler, dated Pitakanda, 7 Aug. 1845, in *COCA*, 597, 18 Sept. 1845.

75. Dean, *With Broadax and Firebrand*, 181–82.

76. SLNA/18/2490: G. Turnour to CS, 4 Jan. 1837.

77. For an analysis of ordinance no. 12 itself, see K. M. de Silva, "Studies in British Land Policy in Ceylon—1," *CJHSS* 7, no. 1 (1964): 28–42.

78. SLNA/18/2490. For evidence of the expansion of chena into new lands, see the testimony of Kandyan political figures about chena in two documents, dated Kandy, 10 May 1843 and 16 Nov. 1844. The first includes testimony from some Kandyan nobles about the expansion of chena in the period since the British accession. See, for example, the testimony of Madugalle Late Basnayake Nilame, who stated, "I am about 84 years old. In the time of the Kandyan King no one was allowed to cut down the mukalana (forest) but the inhabitants cultivated chenas near the paddy fields and other places. But since the accession the forests have been cleared and cultivated to a great extent." The second records the views of the ratamahatmayas of Yati Nuwara, Udunuwara, Harispattu, Upper Dumbera, Lower Dumbera, Hewaheta, and Uda Bulatgama: "They say that the forests were Crown property but that the people, they admit, have cut them down, but that there were also other lands which have been chenas during the Kandyan Kings' time also."

79. The official response to the expansion of chena was decidedly ambivalent. Because chena agriculture in Sri Lanka was a core activity of sedentary agriculturalists, there was no press of policy to forbid slash-and-burn agriculture, in contrast to the prohibitions that were levied in some areas of British India. See, for example, Jacques Pouchepadass, "British Attitudes Towards Shifting Cultivation in Colonial South India: A Case Study of South Canara District 1800–1920," in David Arnold and Ramachandra Guha, eds., *Nature, Culture, Imperialism: Essays on the Environmental History of South Asia* (Delhi, 1995), 123–51.

80. An overall empirical assessment of the impacts of the implementation of ordinance no. 12 of 1840 over the course of the nineteenth century is well outside the scope of this book. The difficulty of interpreting the surviving evidence has discouraged historians from this undertaking. To date an overall empirical assessment has not even been attempted.

81. On the preference for gold:

I lose no time to acquaint you that the supply of silver in my possession is reduced to £400, and that I am under the painfaul [*sic*] necessity of restricting the issue whereby a great deal of inconvenience is experienced by the public. I have caused a notice to be published that I am ready to receive silver in exchange for gold in the hope that natives in the country would avail themselves of the opportunity to suit their own convenience and thereby bring a large sum of the former coin into circulation. Hitherto however my endeavor has not proved successful. At the present moment the want of silver is very much to be lamented.

SLNA/18/12609: no. 281. Kandy, 28 Nov. 1839: J. Mooyart to CS.

On the introduction of paper currency:
I have the honor to bring herewith to the notice of Government that the demand for silver is daily increasing while payments are beginning to be made in paper currency. Not only are the holders of drafts clamorous to receive the consideration in specie, but daily applications are made for the latter, in exchange for notes.—The natives are reluctant I understand to receive paper currency in payment of Coffee, and specie, according to the information I receive, is everywhere hoarded up, which accounts for the constant drain on the Treasury. Pending the present reference I have determined on issuing only one fourth of the sum applied to be exchanged in silver, and to pay no more than one half of drafts in the said currency. And I hope to be favored with instruction as to the course I shall have to adopt in future.

SLNA/8/122: letter from J. Mooyart, GA, Central Province, to CS, dated Kandy, 25 Oct. 1839.
82. Weerasooriya, *The Nattukottai Chettiar Merchant Bankers in Ceylon,* passim.
83. From a letter written by Skinner on 9 June 1849:

It is during the last eleven years that the influx of European capital, and the extensive cultivation of coffee, has thrown a large amount of specie into circulation in the interior; I think that it is estimated at three millions sterling. As a very large portion of the money has been paid in specie for labour, it followed that temptations to, and examples of intemperance, and vice of every kind were rife; the most profligate of the low country Singhalese flocked from the maritime provinces into the interior, and spread far and wide their contaminating influences over a previously sober, orderly, honest race.

Skinner, *Fifty Years in Ceylon,* 220.
84. Michael W. Roberts, "Grain Taxes in British Ceylon, 1832–1878: Theories, Prejudices, and Controversies," *Modern Ceylon Studies* 1, no. 1 (1970): 115–46.
85. "The villagers barter with the Tavelam people, but they give money too. They are not in want of money": SLNA/18/1751: diary entry of the AGA for Badulla, at Pallawelle, 18 Sept. 1847.
86. Sir J. Emerson Tennent, "Report of Sir J. Emerson Tennent on the Finance and Commerce of the Island of Ceylon," in "Ceylon. Reports on the Finance and

Commerce of the Island of Ceylon, and Correspondence Relative Thereto," British parliamentary paper, session 1847–48, vol. XLII.105, paper 933, 49.

Chapter 4
The Transformation of the Middle Highlands

1. Philip D. Curtin, *Two Jamaicas: The Role of Ideas in a Tropical Colony, 1830–1865* (Cambridge, Mass., 1955; reprint, New York, 1970), app. C. By 1847, 465 coffee plantations in Jamaica, totaling more than 188,000 acres, had been abandoned: Douglass Hall, *Free Jamaica, 1838–1865: An Economic History* (New Haven, 1959; reprint, London, 1969), 184.

2. Prior to 1835, East Indian coffee had been assessed a tariff of 9d. per lb., against a tariff of 6d. per lb. for West Indian and British plantation coffee.

3. In 1832, coffee dealers in Liverpool began to mix coffee with chicory and other roasted vegetable matter in contravention of the law and to sell the mixture as coffee. The lords of the treasury intervened, however, and did not allow the commissioners of excise to institute proceedings against the offending firms. In 1840 a Treasury minute explicitly allowed the mixing of coffee with chicory. The author of an anonymous exposé estimated that in 1851, one-half of the "coffee" sold in Great Britain was chicory: *Statement of the Present Position of the Coffee Trade, with Reference to the System of Adulteration Now in Practice* [London, 1851].

4. Vanden Driesen, "Coffee Cultivation in Ceylon," *Ceylon Historical Journal* 3 (1953): pt. 1, 42.

5. The editors of the *CC* noted, "We have little information on which we can rely respecting the expense of such an undertaking [coffee plantation] in the West Indies, but we have been given to understand that the outlay in Ceylon is wonderfully less" *CC* 1, no. 16 (1837).

6. "Ceylon Miscellany," *COCA*, 332, 6 Mar. 1843.

7. And thus the historical reality of these early years was considerably more complex than the romantic figure of the British pioneer planter (the leading figure in the British construction of Sri Lankan mid-nineteenth-century history), who carves out an estate in the midst of a forest wilderness, would suggest. For a recent celebration of the early planters in India and Ceylon, see John Weatherstone, *The Pioneers 1825–1900: The Early British Tea and Coffee Planters and Their Way of Life* (London, 1986).

8. "Had those gentlemen who, in 1843, looked upon Ambegammoa as a future El Dorado, possessed more experience, or had they been able to secure the advice of competent judges . . . many fortunes would probably have been saved, instead of lost. The too continuous rains of that region, and the stiff, clay-like soil, caused the trees to suffer from what has been termed 'wet feet;' and though, in many instances, the bushes looked luxuriant, they never bore remuneratively, and bad times ensuing, the abandonment of most of these properties followed": William Sabonadière, *The Coffee Planter of Ceylon* (Guernsey, 1866), 5.

9. Ibid., 13.

10. Some low-country Sinhalese were also involved with highland forest clearance; see John Capper, *Old Ceylon: Sketches of Ceylon Life in Olden Times* (Colombo, 1877), 32.

11. Even with the Kandyan labor-saving forest-clearance practices, the expense in labor and in wages of forest clearance was high. In the early period of European coffee planting, clearing a three-hundred-acre plantation was estimated to involve the labor of one hundred men for one year at a total labor cost of £900. Lieutenant De Butts, *Rambles in Ceylon* (London, 1841), 182–84. This ingenious system of rainforest clearance was also practiced on the mountainous slopes surrounding Rio de Janeiro. Dean, *With Broadax and Firebrand*, 182–84.

12. "Memoranda on Clearing Jungle, Coffee Planting &c," *COCA*, 109, 14 Jan. 1841.

13. For a vivid account of an estate "burn," see app. 3: "Burning the Forest."

14. T. C. Owen, *The Cinchona Planter's Manual* (Colombo, 1881), 55–56.

15. Editorial, *CHGA*, no. 363, 11 Mar. 1842.

16. Capper, *Old Ceylon*, 37–38.

17. The profitability of the coffee estates was a direct function of their distance from Colombo and from carriage roads. In the early years, for example, the costs of bringing estates into production in Ambagamuwa was estimated at twice that of other districts: "Coffee Planting," *COCA*, 299, 10 Nov. 1842. Transport costs were a high percentage of total costs of producing coffee for market. In the 1840s, proprietors of coffee estates in outlying districts paid twice as much in transport costs to move their goods out of the highlands to Colombo as they did from Colombo to London. This meant that the cost of inland transport per mile was approximately thirty-two times the cost of oceanic transport via the Cape of Good Hope: Capper, *Old Ceylon*, 44.

18. John Hughes, *Coffee Soils and Manures* (London, 1879), 14.

19. E. C. P. Hull, *Coffee Planting in Southern India and Ceylon* (London, 1877), 51–52.

20. P. D. Millie, *"Thirty Years Ago": Reminiscences of the Early Days of Coffee Planting in Ceylon* (Colombo, 1878), chapter 2 (original text, n.p.).

21. "On opening an estate, the manager must look for his best soil and fell the forest in patches of not more than 30 acres in area. Some plantations have fields of two or three hundred acres and I believe in one instance there are one thousand acres in one clearing, but that is, to say the least, a very hazardous plan, for on such properties it is not a rare occurence to see several acres together blasted by the wind and either permitted to run to jungle again, or dragging on a blighted, sickly existence at an enormous and profitless outlay of capital."

C. R. Riggs, "On Coffee Planting in Ceylon," *Journal of the Indian Archipelago and Eastern Asia* 6 (Mar. 1852): 134.

22. "There is great objection amongst Superintendents to leaving belts or patches of forest; mainly on the ground that they afford cover to destructive animals, chiefly rats, which periodically invade the Estates and do much damage by eating the tender shoots of the young Coffee": editorial note, *COOFPCI* 14, no. 325 (30 May 1866): 146.

23. *Supplement to the Overland Observer*, 15 Nov. 1858.

24. "Memoranda. October 1848" [n.a.], KGA, misc. reports, Ceylon, coffee, 1848–94.

25. Earlier historians have judged that these imported techniques accounted for

the success of the coffee sector. See Vanden Dreisen, "Coffee Cultivation,": pt. 1, 31–61; pt. 2, 156–72.

26. P. J. Laborie, *The Coffee Planter of Saint Domingo* (London, 1798). This text was also reprinted in an abridged form during the coffee era: William Graham McIvor, *An Abridgement of The Coffee Planter of St. Domingo by Laborie and Notes on the Propagation and Cultivation of the Medicial Cinchonas or Peruvian Bark Trees* (Madras, 1863).

27. Many variations on the eighteen-inch cube were experimented with before this became the norm: Hull, *Coffee Planting*, 108, 111–15, 122.

28. [George Wall], "A Paper on Pruning by a Member of the Planters' Association," Central Province, June 1859, in McIvor, *Abridgement of the Coffee Planter*, 49–50.

29. As William Graham McIvor, the gifted director of the government cinchona plantation in the Nilghiris, put it: "It must be borne in mind that, in Ceylon, the great varieties of soil and climate, frequently compel the planter to adjust his practice. . . . The rule observed in Kornegalle and Kadugannawa with the best possible results, has been found unsuitable for Dimbola, Kotmalie and Maturatta. In Pusilawa again, we hear of further modifications, suited to the pecularities of that locality": *An Abridgement of the Coffee Planter of St. Domingo by Laborie and Notes on the Propagation and Cultivation of the Medicial Cinchonas or Peruvian Bark Trees* (Madras, 1863), i.

30. R. Abbay, "Coffee in Ceylon," *Nature* 16 (31 Aug. 1876): 376.

31. App.: memo by R. B. Tytler, "Upon the Application and Beneficial Effects of 'Sombreorum' on Coffee Estates," 23 Nov. 1868, in Abraham Joseph, *A Cummi Poem on Coffee Planting with English Translation* (Jaffna, 1869), 15–16.

32. For an early statement of the issues, see Rudolph Gygax, "Remarks on Some Analyses of the Coffee of Ceylon, with Suggestions for the Application of Manures," *JRASCB* 2, no. 5 (1849): 131–34.

33. Hull, *Coffee Planting*, 252–53; for methods of applying manure, 254–59.

34. A. S. Chandra Segra, *Notes on the Management of Cattle in India and Ceylon and Their Diseases* (Jaffna, 1909), 3.

35. As Riggs ("On Coffee Planting," 140–41) noted:

It is almost impossible for hill planters to work their own cattle [for transport], as the native drivers neglect them and often use them to their own profit, so the transit is generally effected by contracting with a Moorman drover. Absentees urge on their representatives that they should keep plenty of cattle for home use, but they little know the difficulty of purchasing stock and the heretofore almost impossibility of keeping them. The grass land on the hills, produces an herb quite unfit for the food of neat cattle, the native takes no interest in the white man's stock and disease is prevalent amongst them.

36. White, *Coffee Culture*, 13–14.

37. Ibid., 18–19.

38. Ibid., 275.

39. After leaving the island and returning to Scotland, R. B. Tytler developed "sombreorum" (from the Tamil word for manure and the island of Sombrero, from

which phosphates were first imported for experimentation). His formula was based on the analyses of Professor Brazier of Aberdeen University: Tytler, "Application and Beneficial Effects," 16.

40. The collection of human waste on the plantations proved highly problematic because of caste distinctions among the Tamil laborers. After outcaste ("pariah") laborers used the accommodations built to collect excrement, nonoutcaste laborers would refuse to do so. There was also the significant danger of typhoid fever: Arnold H. White, *Coffee Culture in Ceylon, Manuring of Estates* (Colombo, 1875), 9.

41. Hull, *Coffee Planting*, 126.

42. As early as the late 1840s, George Gardner, supt., RBG-Peradeniya, noted:

The following are well-known to have escaped from the Botanical gardens at Colombo or Peradenia during the last five-and-twenty years. The small white flowered *Passiflora foetida*, now so common a weed everywhere, is a native of the West Indies and Brazil, and was only introduced to the Island, by Mr. Moon, so short a time ago as 1824. Two species of *Crotalaria*—*C. Brownei*, a native of Jamaica, and *C. incanna*, a native of the Cape of Good Hope; the Mexican Coreopsis-like *Cosma caudata;* the Peruvian blue-flowered *Nicandra physaloides;* and the South American sensitive plant (*Mimosa pudica*), are now not only common weeds about Peradenia and Kandy, but are fast extending themselves in all directions, the first-mentioned species having now nearly reached as far as Rambodde on the Newera-Ellia road. *Brucea Sumatrana,* a shrubby native of the Eastern Islands, and an escape from the Peradenia gardens, now forms part of the low jungle on the neighbouring Hantane range: and *Baddleia Madagascariensis*, a native of Madagascar, and two small kinds of Passion flower (P. Suberosa and glauca) both natives of the West Indies, are fast following. *Ageratum conyzoides,* everywhere a common weed, and one of the great pest of the Coffee Planter, is of American origin, though now thoroughly naturalized in all tropical countries.

George Gardner, "Some General Remarks on the Flora of Ceylon," in Kelaart, *Prodomus Faunae Zeylanica*, app. A, 13–14.

43. See, for example, the letter from R. J. Corbet to members of the Planters' Association, 13 Feb. 1874, Newera Ellia, in *Proceedings of the Planters' Association of Ceylon for the Year Ending February 17, 1874* (Colombo, 1874), 27:

I am sure that many experienced planters will agree with me that it is better to sacrifice a portion of the crop, on a thoroughly clean estate, than to allow weeds to seed and spread; the loss in one case affects one year's return only, in the other it extends over years, deteriorating and perhaps eventually ruining the property. You cannot grow crop and weeds together successfully, although too many have, involuntarily perhaps, tried the rather costly experiment. You have only to look at a really weedy estate in crop time, the leaves faded and yellow, hanging listlessly to the branches as if they took no further interest in the crop; the berries themselves half yellow and half red or black, as if ashamed of their abortive appearance; the secondaries black and shrivelled at their extremities; the ground under the trees, if you carry your investigation so far, covered with black and half-matured berries, while the weeds ride rampant and exultant over all, as if glorying in their triumph. If your curiosity is still unappeased, stroll towards the works, enter the Pulping House, watch the pulpers grinding away at the half-ripened, or dry discoloured berries, picked in extremis to save their lives; note the "floatings" in the cisterns, showing the large percentage of light coffee, and finally cast an eye over the discoloured heaps of brownish, unsightly parchment on the barbecues or in the Stores, and you have a tolerable insight into what a Coffee estate ought not to be.

44. Aberdonensis, "Planting in Ceylon and Southern India," *TA*, 1 Aug. 1885, 85.

45. W. L. Strange, "Irrigation in Ceylon," in F. A. Stockdale, "Soil Erosion," *TA* 61, no. 3 (1923): 136.

46. [Fanny Emily Farr Penny], *Fickle Fortune in Ceylon* (Madras, 1887), 12; T. Petch, "Plants and Trees of Ceylon, *The Ceylon Antiquary and Literary Register* 3, pt. 3 (Jan. 1922), 169. Although reviled at first, British planters developed an appreciation for the lantana by the end of the century. *CF* noted:

Before the Lantana was introduced, and had overrun the country, the jungle which grew up could not be again cut for 15 to 20 years, as the villagers do not manure, and kurakkan is a very exhausting crop to the soil. Now-a-days the "Lantana" grows up very rapidly and recoups the soil so much, that a second crop of kurrakan &c. can be grown on land in a seven years' rotation. As a result, a smaller quantity of land is required, and the forests are not so recklessly felled as they were years ago. In our opinion "Lantana" in Ceylon has been a blessing rather than a curse, but we shall be glad if any of our readers can give us any opinions to the contrary and their reasons for their views.

"Is the Lantana a Friend or an Enemy?" *CF* 2, no. 2 (1896) 18.

47. "Weeds on Coffee Estates in Olden Times," *TA* 2 (1882–83): 779–80.

48. Millie, *"Thirty Years Ago,"* chapter 4. The breakthrough in drainage design seems to have come only in the twentieth century, when contour drains with locks at gentle gradiants were combined with steep downhill drains; see E. O. Felsinger, "Memorandum on a System of Drainage Calculated to Control the Flow of Water on Up-Country Estates, with a View to Reducing Soil Erosion to a Minimum," *TA* 71, no. 4 (1928): 211–14.

49. Macmillan, *Tropical Planting*, 425; Hull, *Coffee Planting*, 137.

50. D. V. M. Abeygunawardena, *Diseases of Cultivated Plants* (Colombo, 1969), 28.

51. "Extract from a private letter dated Ambegamowe, 24 October [1842]," *CHGA*, no. 429, 1 Nov. 1842.

52. [Penny], *Fickle Fortune in Ceylon*, 63.

53. On the different species of *Strobilanthes* (all of which are called *nelu* in Sinhala), see Mark Ashton et al., *A Field Guide to the Common Trees and Shrubs of Sri Lanka* (Colombo, 1997), 79–81.

54. Kelaart, *Prodomus Faunae Zeylanica*, 67. See also W. Knighton, *Forest Life in Ceylon* (London, 1854), 1:119.

55. A. F. Broun, "On the Forests and Waste Lands of Ceylon," in Henry Trimen, *A Handbook of the Flora of Ceylon* (London, 1900), pt. 5, app. 2, 362.

56. Hull, *Coffee Planting*, 18, 93–94.

57. J. Evans, *Plantation Forestry in the Tropics* (Oxford, 1992), 341–42.

58. Edmund C. P. Hull, *Coffee: Its Physiology, History, and Cultivation: Adapted as a Work of Reference for Ceylon, Wynaad, Coorg, and the Neilgherries* (Madras, 1865), 20. On the various insect "enemies of the coffee tree," including "white bug," see Sabonadière, *Coffee Planter of Ceylon*, 81–82.

59. E. Sullivan, *The Bungalow and the Tent* (London, 1854), 120–21.

60. A. M. Ferguson, *Ceylon in 1847–1860* (Colombo, 1867), 1.

61. SLNA/6/1891: George Gardner, "Report on the Brown Scale Bug," 4 July 1848.

62. J. Lamprey, "On the Coffee Blight, the Cotton Aphis, and Some New Species of Lac," *JRASCB* 2, no. 8 (1855), appendix: Proceedings of the General Meeting, 1 Feb. 1854, lciii–ci.

63. R. C. Haldane, *All about Grub: Including a Paper on the Grub Pest in Ceylon* (Colombo, 1881).

64. This impact of the highland estates on Kandyan villagers has been a topic of extensive research. For a recent essay that includes a useful survey of the literature, see Eric Meyer, "Enclave Plantations, "Hemmed-in" Villages and Dualistic Representations in Colonial Ceylon," *Journal of Peasant Studies* 20, nos. 3–4 (1992): 199–228.

65. On the villagers' sale of land through middlemen to the British planters, see Eric Meyer, "From Landgrabbing to Landhunger: High Land Appropriation in the Plantation Areas of Sri Lanka during the British Period," *Modern Asian Studies* 26, no. 2 (1992): 321–61.

66. Millie, *"Thirty Years Ago,"* chapter 6.

67. SLNA/18/2611: J. Mooyart to CS, 5 Mar. 1841:

> In transmitting the original letter and connected documents from the Asst. Agent at Badoola my object is to submit the expediency of proceeding with some discrimination in the disposal of forest land in order that the extensive clearing of the forests may not eventually prove injurious to the low paddy lands which may be deprived of the means of irrigation by the drying up of the springs. Such a contingency by no means improbable is not likely to influence the speculators in the coffee cultivation; and for that reason should not be overlooked by the constituted authorities having the disposal of Crown lands within the Colony. It will remain for the consideration of Govt whether any provision should be made in the condition of sale for the preservation of springs by the precaution adverted to, or whether in particular cases the sale of the land applied for may be declined.

68. One case of this nature came to court in the mid-1860s; the court found in favor of the rice cultivator who brought suit. See "Hill Streams: Coffee Pulping and Rice Irrigation," *COOFPCI* 13, no. 307 (1865).

69. One solution to the pasture shortage, proposed to government, was to replant some of the extensive chena and patana lands in the more nutritious exotic grasses. But this would have involved considerable expense as well as a different conception of the patanas as a resource managed by government. See Cattle Disease Commission, "Report of the Commissioners," vii.

70. Cattle Disease Commission report, app., "Letter from the Director of the Royal Botanic Garden on the Grasses of Ceylon, with Suggestions for Their Improvement," 70.

71. Even so, by the 1880s all rice farmers in Central Province still had access to buffalo, although some farmers had to import buffalo for the job and pay a fee for defraying the expenses of the drivers. See "Paddy (Rice) Cultivation in the Central Province of Ceylon. By a Ceylonese," *TA*, 2 Nov. 1885, 354. Indeed, even by the 1920s the reduction in forest pasture does not seem to have resulted in the long-term deterioration of the condition of highland livestock; according to investigations carried out in that decade, the cattle of the planting areas were in no way inferior to the cattle of the nonplanting districts, although the cattle throughout the island were judged generally inferior owing to mineral deficiencies:

> The opening up of large areas under cultivated crops, such as tea and rubber, has undoubtedly lessened the area of jungle and waste land available for grazing in parts of the Island. At the same time, it must be pointed out that there is no evidence that the inferiority of Ceylon cattle dates from the opening up of such cultivated areas; nor are the cattle of the planting districts inferior to those of nonplanting districts. Again, cattle kept on coconut estates in the Western Province, where pasture is generally available practically the whole year round, show the same inferiority. On our Farm at Ambepussa, where of recent years pasture has been ample all the year round, the cattle, although they appear full, do not develop as they should.

Crawford, "The Influence of the Various Mineral Constituents," 273.

72. John Ferguson, *Ceylon in 1883: The Leading Crown Colony of the British Empire* (London, 1883), 52.

73. Abbay, "Coffee in Ceylon," 377:

> On one side of a small range the coffee exposed to the south-west monsoon is mostly ripe about November. On the opposite side, four miles away, where it is generally picked three if not four months later, whilst in the most favoured districts in the southern part of the mountain zone where the rainfall is considerably influenced by mountains that lie in the track of the monsoon the crop time lasts through nine months, i.e., from September to May—buds, flowers, green and ripe fruit, being on the tree all at the same time.

74. Not all outbreaks were centered in the highlands. The epidemic of 1866–67 principally devastated Northern Province. Only when the medical establishment im-

posed preventive measures for the isolation of cholera sufferers in hospital or in quarantine were the devastations of cholera reined in. See C. G. Uragoda, *A History of Medicine in Sri Lanka* (Colombo, 1987), 258–61.

75. Ian H. Vanden Driesen, one of the outstanding students of Indian labor migration to Sri Lanka, has written that the three major killers of Indian labor mentioned in the historical documentation were fever, dysentery, and dropsy (accumulation of water in tissue); drawing on the work of Sir Philip Manson-Bahr, he has indentified "fever" as scrub typhus: *The Long Walk: Indian Plantation Labour in Sri Lanka in the Nineteenth Century* (New Delhi, 1997), 29–30. The other major study of nineteenth-century Indian labor is Donovan Moldrich, *Bitter Berry Bondage: The Nineteenth Century Coffee Workers of Sri Lanka* (Kandy, n.d. [c. 1989]).

76. Vanden Driesen, *Long Walk*, 227–30.

77. Cordiner, *Description of Ceylon*, 1:425; cited by H. J. Suckling, *Ceylon: A General Description of the Island, Historical, Physical, Statistical*, 2:133. *Ceylon Almanac for 1843* (Colombo, 1844) reported that in 1800 "murrain carried off four-fifths of the Cattle in the northern province," lii. Interestingly, the epizootic of 1800 was not reported on by the Cattle Disease Commission in its report in 1868.

78. Cattle Disease Commission, "Report of the Commissioners," *SP* 20 (1868): x–xii.

79. "Epidemic amongst the Cattle," *COCA*, 148, 31 May 1841.

80. "Coffee. Carriage &c.," *COCA*, 214, 17 Jan. 1842.

81. "Muscat Donkeys," *COCA*, 204, 13 Dec. 1841.

82. *OOMPCI*, no. 21 (9 May 1842).

83. H. J. Suckling, *Ceylon: A General Description of the Island, Historical, Physical, Statistical, Containing the Most Recent Information* (London, 1876), 2:133.

84. James Steuart, *Notes on Ceylon and Its Affairs during a Period of Thirty-Eight Years, Ending in 1855* (London, 1862), 96. Steuart championed the native cattle, even as he noted their disappearance, but his was apparently a minority view. See also Mr. Woodhouse, "The Causes of the Great Increase of Expenditures on Coffee Estates, and the Means to be Adopted for Reducing It," *COOFPCI* 14, no. 322 (16 Apr. 1866): 96; also A. M. Ferguson, *Souvenirs of Ceylon* (Colombo, 1869), 161–62.

85. Cattle Disease Commission report, "Replies to Questions Relative to Cattle Disease Received Chiefly Through the Planters' Association," 37–46.

86. SLNA/18/2751: diary of the AGA for Badulla, K. MacKenzie, at Yattipalata, 29 Mar. 1848.

87. Cattle Disease Commission report, extracts from annual reports of agents, AAs, and others on cattle disease, 49.

88. Cattle Disease Commission report, extracts, 50.

89. Cattle Disease Commission report, evidence of the ratamahatmaya of Bintenne, 2 Apr. 1868, in app., "Evidence on the First Journey," 9.

90. Cattle Disease Commission report, evidence of the ratamahatmaya of Matale North, 31 May 1868, in app., "Evidence on the Second Journey," 17.

91. Cattle Disease Commission report, evidence, first journey, 3–5.

92. Baker, *Eight Years' Wanderings*, 149–51.

93. The Kandyan state had disposed of what appears to have been a considerable

stock of muskets. These were issued to soldiers during their annual fifteen-day period of military obligation. During the remainder of the year, the farmers were without firepower. This severely constrained the volume of game that fell to their more primitive hunting practices. Even the issuing of muskets to Kandyan soldiers was not a universal practice. Marshall (*Ceylon*, 23) noted that, on the eastern side of the island, the soldiers frequently were armed only with bows and arrows.

94. On earlier Sri Lankan exports to the Delhi sultanate, see Simon Digby, *War-Horse and Elephant in the Dehli Sultanate: A Study of Military Supplies* (Karachi, 1971), 70–73. On the Portuguese and Dutch control of the elephant export trade, S. Arasaratnam, "Ceylon in the Indian Ocean Trade, 1500–1800," in A. Das Gupta and M. N. Pearson, eds., *India and the Indian Ocean 1500–1800* (Calcutta, 1987), 224–39, and S. Arasaratnam, "Dutch Commercial Policy in Ceylon and Its Effects on Indo-Ceylon Trade, 1690–1750," *Indian Economic and Social History Review* 4, no. 2 (1967), 120–23.

95. Forbes, *Eleven Years in Ceylon* (London, 1840), 2:73–74.

96. The history of firearms in Sri Lanka is largely unexplored. Before 1815, Kandyan artisans manufactured firearms for the royal arsenal. Although the British attempted to call in and to destroy all Kandyan firearms after the Great Rebellion of 1817–1818, this initiative is unlikely to have been wholly successful. At least by the 1840s, imported firearms, on which an import duty had been paid, were common in the highlands. In 1848, the government levied a gun tax in the amount of 2s. 6d. for an annual license. Kandyans greatly objected to this measure. Firearms were considered agricultural implements, to be used to protect crops and without which it was too dangerous to open up new lands: M. A. Durand Appuhamy, *The Kandyans' Last Stand Against the British* (Colombo, 1995), 380–82. Sir J. Emerson Tennent noted with regard to the hunting of elephants in the lowlands that "the Singhalese themselves, being more freely provided with arms than in former times, have assisted in swelling the annual slaughter": *Sketches of the Natural History of Ceylon* (London, 1861), 78.

97. Jayantha Jayawardena, *The Elephant in Sri Lanka* (Colombo, 1994), 11.

98. In the five years ending in 1862, sixteen hundred elephants were exported to India: A. M. Ferguson, *The Ceylon Directory; Calendar; and Compendium of Useful Information for 1866–1868* (Colombo, n.d.), 4.

99. Today there are fewer than two thousand elephants on the island: Jayawardena, *Elephant in Ceylon*, 60–61, 96.

100. Committee on the Existing Laws . . . . "Report of the Committee Appointed to Consider and Report on the Existing Laws Relating to the Protection of Game, Elephants, and Buffaloes," *SP* 11 (1889): 1.

101. Charles Santiapillai, M. R. Chambers, and N. Ishwaran, "The Leopard *Panthera Pardus Fusca* (Meyer 1794) in the Ruhunu National Park, Sri Lanka, and Observations Relevant to Its Conservation," *Biological Conservation* 23 (1982): 11.

102. Clements R. Markham, "Report on the Cultivation of Chinchona Plants in Ceylon," *SP* 14 (1866): 4.

103. Archives, RBG Kew. misc. reports. Ceylon. Forests, 1873–1900; W. T. Thisleton-Dyer to R. H. Meade, 23 Aug. 1879, citing the article by the Rev. R. Abbay, fellow of Wadham College, Oxford, in *Nature* 16 (31 Aug. 1876): 375–78.

104. Vincent, "Report on the Forest Administration," 72.

105. George Gardner, *Report on the Royal Botanic Garden, at Peradenia, near Kandy, Presented to His Excellency the Governor in August 1844* (Colombo, 1844), viii.

106. "So much forest is now being cleared for coffee planting, that the extirpation is almost to be feared of some of our indigenous trees; we are therefore using every endeavor to introduce young plants of all our native kinds into these gardens": report of the director, RBG-Pérádeniya (1870), 1.

107. Hull, *Coffee Planting*, 46. The name of the estate was not specified.

108. Consider, for example, the following excerpt from "The Effects of Vegitation [sic] on Climate," which appeared in the *Examiner and Ceylon Journal of Commerce and Agriculture*, no. 126 (13 Mar. 1850):

> Planters can tell you in their experience of the small tributary rivulets which have ceased to present anything of their former character but their rocky channels. Estates newly opened or when the earlier period of the labor obliged the Planter to seek the shade of the forest for his habitation, were unhealthy as they have again become at the period when decomposition of the fallen timber becomes most rife, but the act of clearing has had the effect of drying the atmosphere, and creating an open area in which there were neither objects to retain or to propagate that miasma which has proved so destructive to health at the earlier period of opening the country. Unlike the Prairie Burnings of North America, or the clearances that have rendered Europe an abode for civilization, since the time of the Goths, but very little of this country has been opened compared to its extent, by the Axe of the European Planter, the Chena cultivation and Patna burning progress slower but surer, in producing those changes by which the climate is modified.

109. Henry Dickman, "Remarks on the Climate of the Interior of Ceylon," in Ferguson, *Ceylon Directory*, app. 1, 11.

110. For an authoritative introduction to malaria, see Leonard Jan Bruce-Chwatt, *Essential Malariology* (New York, 1985). On malaria in Sri Lanka, see A. S. Dissanaike, "Ecological Aspects of Some Parasitic Diseases in Sri Lanka," in C. H. Fernando, ed., *Ecology and Biogeography of Sri Lanka* (The Hague, 1984), 353–69. On the 1930s epidemic, see Eric Meyer, "L'épidémie de malaria de 1934–1935 à Sri Lanka: fluctuations économiques et fluctuations climatiques," *Culture et Développement* 14, nos. 2–3 (1982): 183–226, and no. 4: 589–638.

111. De Silva, *History of Sri Lanka*, 277–81; see also Appuhamy's *Kandyans' Last Stand* for a book-length treatment of the 1848 rebellion.

Chapter 5
Into the Upper Highlands

1. Governor Sir Hercules Robinson (1866–72) was enthusiastic about extending the coffee plantations to new lands and he built new roads and bridged rivers, drawing down some of the large financial surpluses realized by increased sales of government

land and the increased customs and railway revenues: I. H. Vanden Driesen, "Some Aspects of the History of the Coffee Industry in Ceylon with Reference to the Period 1823–1886," unpublished Ph.D. thesis, University of London, 1954, 71.

2. The completion of the railway brought about a predictable decrease in carters' rates and a collapse in the price of straw: "Planting News-Letter," *KHPWC*, 2 Apr. 1868. [John Ferguson], *Ceylon and Her Planting Enterprize: In Tea, Cacao, Cardamoms, Cinchona, Coconut, and Areca Palms* (Colombo, 1885).

3. John Ferguson, *Ceylon in 1883: The Leading Crown Colony of the British Empire* (London, 1883), 61. Land prices soared. R. Abbay noted in 1876, "At the present time the upset price is 1£, and the land not unfrequently realises as much as 15£ or 20£ per acre, so prosperous has been the enterprise of late years and so great the influx of English capital": "Coffee in Ceylon," 377.

4. Letter from R. J. Corbet to members of the Planters' Association, 13 Feb. 1874, in *Proceedings of the Planters' Association of Ceylon for the Year Ending 17th February 1874* (Colombo 1874), 25–31.

5. G. H. K. Thwaites, *Report of the Director of the Royal Botanic Garden, Pérádeniya, for 1871* (Colombo, 1872), 5.

6. G. H. K. Thwaites, *Report of the Director of the Royal Botanic Gardens of Pérádeniya and Hakgala* (Colombo, 1872), 6. Thwaites, however, did not initially have an accurate understanding of how the fungus was transmitted, and as the blight spread and economic losses mounted, criticism was leveled against him: see G. H. K. Thwaites et al., "Further Correspondence on the Coffee Leaf Disease," *SP* 1 (1880).

7. Liberian seed was first introduced in 1866, but private experiments were unsuccessful. G. A. Crüwell, *Liberian Coffee in Ceylon* (Colombo, 1878), v–vi.

8. Thwaites, *Report of the Director of the Royal Botanic Gardens of Pérádeniya and Hakgala* (Colombo, 1873), 4.

9. Alfred H. Duncan, *The Private Life of a Ceylon Coffee Planter, by Himself* (Colombo, 1881), pt. 2, 1.

10. Daniel Morris, "Reports upon Experiments Connected with the Coffee Leaf Disease," *SP* 12 (1879). These recommendations were mocked by some coffee planters. See Duncan, *The Private Life of a Ceylon Coffee Planter*, pt. 1, 19 and 59.

11. D. Morris, "Further Correspondence on the Coffee Leaf Disease," *SP* 13 (1880): 2.

12. Ferguson, *Ceylon in 1883*, 58.

13. E. J. Butler, "The Development of Economic Mycology in the Empire Overseas," *Transactions of the British Mycological Society* 14 (1929): 1–18.

14. H. Marshall Ward, "Coffee Leaf Disease: Preliminary Report by the Government Cryptogamist," and "Coffee Leaf Disease: Second Report," in *SP* 17 (1880), and "Coffee Leaf Disease: Third Report," *SP* 17 (1881).

15. Vincent, "Report on the Forest Administration," 70.

16. John Hughes, *Coffee Soils and Manures* (London, 1879), 10.

17. "Retirement of Mr. Green, Ceylon Government Entomologist," *TA* 40, no. 2 (1913): 81.

18. [John Ferguson], *Tea and Other Planting Industries in Ceylon, in 1885* (Colombo, 1885), viii.

19. Ferguson, *Ceylon in 1883*, 62.

20. John Cameron, *The Prevention of Leaf-Disease in Coffee. Report of a Visit to Coorg by John Cameron, F.L.S., Superintendent of Government Gardens in Mysore* (n.p., 1898), 3, 13.

21. M. C. Cooke, *Report on Diseased Leaves of Coffee and Other Plants* (London, 1876).

22. Dr. Hooker to the Colonial Office, 23 Dec. 1874, in J. D. Hooker and G. H. K. Thwaites et al., "Correspondence Relating to the Coffee-Leaf Disease," *SP* 36 (1876); PRO. FO/83/486: Coffee Leaf Disease in Ceylon: Answers to Circular of Feb. 12, 1875.

23. *Report on the Progress and Condition of the Royal Gardens at Kew, during the Year 1876* (London, 1876).

24. "Hemileia Vastatrix in South Africa," *TA*, 1 Dec. 1885, 441.

25. As early as 1850, G. H. K. Thwaites, in the first year of his long tenure as head of the RBG, Peradeniya, had proposed the establishment of a small experimental station at an elevation of 5,000 feet or higher: G. H. K. Thwaites, "Report on the Royal Botanic Garden, Peradeniya, from October 1850 to September 1851, Inclusive"; MS bound with *Miscellaneous RBG Reports, 1843–1860*, at the Rare Book Room of the Department of Agriculture Library, Gannaruwa. As noted in chapter 3, an upper highland garden had been first proposed by W. C. Ondaatje, acting supt. of RBG-Peradeniya, in 1843. Thwaites hoped that tea would also get a full trial at higher elevation; he also foresaw a fuelwood shortage in the highlands and thus was interested in the possibility of introducing firs and other trees that might be suitable for the estates. G. H. K. Thwaites, *Royal Botanic Garden: Report on . . . Pérádeniya, from September 1858 to August 1859* (Colombo, 1859), 5.

26. SLNA/6/2586: G. H. K. Thwaites to CS, 19 Nov. 1859.

27. SLNA/6/2586: Clements R. Markham to G. H. K. Thwaites, 22 Oct. 1860.

28. G. H. K. Thwaites, *Royal Botanic Garden: Report on . . . Peradenia, from September 1860 to August 1861* (Colombo, 1861), 3–4.

29. SLNA/6/2944: G. H. K. Thwaites to CS, 31 July 1863, and G. H. K. Thwaites to CS, 26 Apr. 1864; G. H. K. Thwaites, *Royal Botanic Garden: Report on . . . Peradenia, from September 1862 to August 1863* (Colombo, 1863), 3–4; G. H. K. Thwaites, *Royal Botanic Garden: Report on . . . Peradenia, from September 1863 to August 1864* (Colombo, 1864), 3–4.

30. Clements R. Markham, "Report on the Cultivation of Chinchona Plants in Ceylon," *SP* 11 (1865), and "Report on the Cultivation of Chinchona Plants in Ceylon," *SP* 14 (1866).

31. G. H. K. Thwaites, *Royal Botanic Garden: Report on . . . Peradenia, from September 1864 to August 1865* (Colombo, 1865), 3–4.

32. G. H. K. Thwaites, RBG: report on RBG, "Pérádeniya and Hakgalla" [1866], 4–5. In 1866, MacNicoll suffered health problems and left for the United Kingdom to recuperate; Hakgala was placed temporarily in the care of Thwaites's trusted Sinhalese plant collector.

33. Gabriele Gramiccia, *The Life of Charles Ledger, 1818–1905* (London, 1988), 154.

34. SLNA/6/3510: G. H. K. Thwaites to CS, 31 Oct. 1870. In addition, some bark

from trees issued from the Hakgala gardens had been analyzed and determined to be of "very excellent quality," and Thwaites thought that Hakgala could look for guidance to the reports from the Indian government cinchona plantations. Dr. J. E. de Vrý, at one time chemist for the Dutch cinchona plantation in Java, wrote to Thwaites with his analyses of the highland cinchona barks sent to London. His analysis indicated that *succirubra* had a higher percentage of crystallisable quinine than did *officinalis*. Extracts of the de Vrý letter were sent to the CS: SLNA/53/40: Thwaites to CS, 9 Oct. 1871.

35. It was later discovered that the alkaloid content of the *succirubra* branch and twig bark was considerably inferior to that of the stem bark. In the Nilgiris, for this reason, the branches were not barked: "Latest Sale of Cinchona Bark," *CO*, 10 June 1878.

36. Frederick Lewis, *A Few Pioneer Estates and Early Pioneers in Ceylon* (Colombo, 1927). Ceylon Historical Association: paper no. 10, 10.

37. SLNA/6/4015A: G. H. K. Thwaites to CS, 6 Mar. 1873, and Thwaites to CS, 6 Aug. 1873.

38. G. H. K. Thwaites, Royal Botanic Garden. *Report on . . . Pérádeniya and Hakgalla, from September 1865 to August 1866* (Colombo, 1866), 3–5.

39. The author of a prize-winning essay on cinchona cultivation suggested sterilizing the beds with boiling water to kill insects and their eggs before planting the seed, precautions that were never dreamed of for coffee: Thomas North Christie, *Prize Essay on Cinchona Cultivation Written for the Dikoya Planters' Association* (Colombo, 1883), 3.

40. William Graham McIvor, *Notes on the Propagation and Cultivation of the Medical Cinchonas or Peruvian Bark Trees* (Madras, 1863).

41. RBG Kew, misc. reports 5.21: Ceylon. Cinchona, 1859–90. Letter from Daniel Morris to Professor W. T. Thisleton-Dyer, 14 Feb. 1878.

42. T. C. Owen, *The Cinchona Planter's Manual* (Colombo, 1881), 61–63.

43. McIvor, *Notes on the Propagation and Cultivation of the Medical Cinchonas,* 5.

44. Christie, *Prize Essay,* 10, 22. In Java, the insect *Helopeltis Antonii* was a major scourge, best fought by having plantation workers pick off and destroy the insects by hand: Karel Wessel Van Gorkem, *A Handbook of Cinchona Culture,* trans. Benjamin Daydon Jackson (London, 1889), 182–84.

45. The planter James Taylor developed a system to root out the trees to be barked and to leave seedlings from such trees and those he had intentionally sown in the fields in order to provide a succession of plants of all ages. This system was not widely adopted: "The Great Sale of Ceylon Cinchona, and Cinchona Culture in Ceylon," *CO,* 13 Sept. 1878.

46. This McIvor technique was found superior to stumping every other tree in a plantation and allowing the stumps to regenerate: J. E. De Vrij, *On The Cultivation of Quinine in Java and British India* (London, 1865), 24.

47. Christie, *Prize Essay,* 17; D. McHale, "The Cinchona Tree," in Institute of Biology, *Exploited Plants,* 30 (London, 1990); reprinted from *Biologist* 33, no. 1 (1986).

48. G. H. K. Thwaites, *Report of the Director of the Royal Botanic Gardens of Pérádeniya and Hakgala* (Colombo, 1872), 4.

49. As was the case in Sri Lanka, only the *succirubra* and *officinalis* varieties of cinchona ever thrived in the Nilgiris: SLNA/6/6752: Government of Madras, Revenue De-

partment, 14 Oct. 1882, no. 1116, Revenue: Confidential: Enclosure. From W. T. Thisleton Dyer to Sir Louis Mallet, under-sec. for India, India Office, dated Royal Gardens, Kew, 3 Aug. 1882.

50. The introduction of *ledgeriana* rescued the Dutch cinchona plantations from dismal failure. See M. L. Duran-Reynals, *The Fever Bark Tree* (London, 1947), 174–75; Gramiccia, *Life of Charles Ledger,* 126–30.

51. Owen, *Cinchona Planter's Manual,* 16–17. Specialists were divided over the classification of the cinchona species. On the rancorous debate over classification, see "Wars of the Quinologists," *TA* 3 (1883–84), 27–28, and Henry Trimen, "The Botany of Cinchona *Ledgeriana,*" *TA* 3 (1883–84), 453–54.

52. McHale, "Cinchona Tree," 27–28.

53. See Van Gorkem, *Handbook of Cinchona Culture,* 106–29, for an overview of the history of the chemical analysis. Because *Cinchona ledgeriana* proved particularly difficult to propagate and was slow growing, the Dutch grafted *C. ledgeriana* scions onto *C. succirubra* rootstocks from seed: McHale, "Cinchona Tree," 27–28.

54. "Cinchona Cultivation; Proceedings of the Madras Government Embodying the Report by Colonel Beddome on his Recent Visit to the Island," *SP* 2 (1881).

55. "Ceylon and Her Planting Industry: By a Java Planter," *TA* 3 (1883–84), 146–47.

56. This was part of a pattern of exchanges between the British and Dutch colonies. In 1865, British India had sent two hundred *officinalis* plants to Java, and in 1866 Thwaites had sent *officinalis* from Sri Lanka. The Dutch responded by promising to send a couple of thousand *calisaya* from Bolivia and two hundred of the best calisaya from Java: SLNA/53/10: Secretary-general's Office, Buidenzerg, to CS, Colombo, 14 Feb. 1866.

57. SLNA/53/40: G. H. K. Thwaites to CS, 27 June 1876; R. B. G. Kew, misc. reports 5.21. Ceylon: Cinchona, 1859–80. Dr. Trimen, "Report on Cinchona *Ledgeriana,*" to CS, 20 Aug. 1880.

58. E. J. Thwaites, superintendent of RBG-Hakgala from 1868 to 1881, was, to my knowledge, no relation to G. H. K. Thwaites, director of the RBG-Peradeniya, 1849 to 1880.

59. RBG-Kew, misc. reports 5.21. "Ceylon: Trimen, report on *Ledgeriana,*" 20 Aug. 1880.

60. Ibid.; Sir J. D. Longden to earl of Kimberley, 18 Jan. 1881. Thwaites was never convinced to adopt the suggestions of Dr. Hooker, in particular that "the gardens should be both useful and attractive to the general public, and should contain—(a) A conspicuously ticketted collection of the plants, shrubs and trees of the Colony. (b) A collection, also well ticketted, of all such useful plants as can be cultivated in the Colony": SLNA/53/10: Hooker, "Suggestions for the information of Colonial Governments about to appoint Superintendents of Botanic Gardens, and for the guidance of the Superintendents themselves." [1865]; Lady Gregory, ed., *Sir William Gregory: An Autobiography* (London, 1894), 284. Trimen was quite critical of Thwaites's management of the garden:

The principles of management consistently carried out in these gardens for many years past aimed at the preservation, to as great an extent as possible, of their natural character. The result has been all that could be desired in that respect, and their luxuriant and tropical wild beauty has been a characteristic feature of the gardens. Trees were rarely felled but allowed to decay, new ones were planted without regard to their surroundings, crowded together and never pruned, and the struggle for existence permitted to go on almost unchecked.

The result of this was naturally the predominance of some plants and the more or less complete destruction of others. Few were able to exhibit their full proportions and complete development; even the flower-beds, never weeded, formed dense thickets under the shade of large trees, where it not infrequently happened that rare and interesting species were choked and barely alive from the inordinate luxuriance of some dominant but worthless weed. The same principles forbade any arrangement or systematic classification of the plants in accordance with their affinities, or the attachment to them of any explanatory labels. In short, many portions presented more the appearance of a beautiful wild jungle, where plants from the tropics of all latitudes strove for the mastery, than of a scientific garden for the public utility.

Henry Trimen, *Report of the Director of the Royal Botanic Gardens for the Year 1880* (Colombo, 1881), 1.

61. RBG-Kew, misc. reports 5.21. Ceylon. Cinchona. 1859–80; J. C. Campbell to Sir Joseph Hooker, 16 Dec. 1880.

62. The Campbell brothers estimated that their twenty-five acres of *ledgeriana*, comprising some twenty-five thousand plants, was the largest in the island: RBG-Kew, misc. reports 5.21. Ceylon: Cinchona, 1859–90. Letter from W. T. Thiselton-Dyer to R. A. Meade, Colonial Office, 14 May 1880.

63. Henry Trimen, "Royal Botanic Gardens, Ceylon: Report of the Director for the Year 1880," *CAR for 1880* (Colombo, 1880), 3. In the 1881 New Products Commission report, Trimen did not mention the problems with *ledgeriana* propagation at Hakgala, but instead praised the work of the RBG-Peradeniya, particularly with regard to its work on cinchona. He wrote that the best varieties of cinchona were now in circulation, and he stated his views that Hakgala no longer needed to play a role in the distribution of seedlings and cuttings because it was now known that Hakgala was an inappropriate site for such activities, owing to severe winds and cold, wet subsoils. In this manner, Trimen succeeded in turning attention toward the role that Hakgala might next play in the evolution of the highlands: New Products Commission. "Report of the New Products Commission Appointed to Report on the Question of the Introduction and Cultivation of New Cultures in Ceylon," *SP* 13 (1881): app. A: "Memorandum on the Part Taken by the Royal Botanic Gardens in the Introduction of Useful Plants Into Ceylon," 8.

64. Trimen, "Report of Director for 1881," 2. The phoenix of *ledgeriana* rose again with the outbreak of World War II and the subsequent loss of supplies from Java, which had produced most of the world supply of quinine. Hakgala botanical garden again took up the cause of *ledgeriana* and produced thirty-seven thousand seedlings; these were transplanted into new plantations at Massena, near Balangoda. Another

two thousand plants were grown from seed collected from an old *ledgeriana* tree at Nuwara Eliya: Mudandiram E. Perera, "Hakgala Botanic Gardens," *TA* 102, no. 4 (1946): 224–25.

65. SLNA/6/6046: Trimen to CS, 14 Dec. 1880.

66. Trimen, "Report of Director for the Year 1883," 11: John Ferguson, *Ferguson's Ceylon Handbook and Directory for 1900–1* (Colombo, 1901), 70.

67. A. C. L. Ameer Ali, "Cinchona Cultivation in Nineteenth Century Ceylon," *Modern Ceylon Studies* 5, no. 1 (1974): 99.

68. Weatherstone, *The Pioneers 1825–1900* (London, 1986).

69. SLNA/53/5: Arthur Morice to Sir. H. Robinson, 18 Nov. 1865.

70. SLNA/53/40: G. H. K. Thwaites to CS, 29 Nov. 1865; G. H. K. Thwaites, *Royal Botanic Garden: Report . . . Peradenia, from September 1864 to August 1865*.

71. SLNA/53/10: CS to G. H. K. Thwaites, 29 Jan. 1866.

72. G. H. K. Thwaites, *Royal Botanic Garden: Report . . . Pérádeniya and Hakgalla* (Colombo, 1866).

73. Arthur Morice, "Report of a Visit to Some of the Tea Districts of India, with the View of Ascertaining the Suitability or Otherwise of Ceylon for Tea Cultivation," *SP* 5 (1867); SLNA/6/3302: G. H. K. Thwaites to CS, 11 Jan. 1869.

74. West Ridgeway, *Administration of the Affairs of Ceylon, 1896 to 1903* (Colombo, 1903), 71–73.

75. SLNA/6/6936: Trimen to CS, 6 Nov. 1844; Trimen to CS, 13 Dec. 1844.

76. SLNA/18/3501: no. 1234. CS to GA, Central Provice, 15 Nov. 1882; Deputy Queen Advocate's Office to GA, Central Province, 25 Sept. 1882.

77. Governor Gregory to earl of Kimberley, 31 July 1873, Queen's House, Colombo, reproduced in "Correspondence on the Subject of the Conservation of Crown Forests," *SP* 29, no. 2 (1873):

78. The government, however, did not speak with a single voice on this issue. John Douglas, the acting CS, expressed concern that the "complete denudation of the forests for the purposes of coffee planting" entailed severe consequences for the Sinhalese farmers, who were thereby "debarred from obtaining fence-sticks and wood for building and agricultural purposes": Douglas to CS to the GA, Central Province, 3 July 1873, in "Correspondence . . . Conservation of Crown Forests," *SP* 29,, no. 2 (1873).

79. RBG-Kew, misc. reports, Ceylon: Forests, 1873–1900. Hooker to R. G. W. Herbert, under-sec., 22 Oct. 1873: "This able and exhaustive document has interested me greatly and given me much new information regarding a Colony, in which I have long taken an active interest. I am extremely glad to find from it, that I had exaggerated the amount of forest destruction attributable to Coffee planting, a matter in which it appears that I have been misinformed by some of the most intelligent of the planters with whom I am acquainted, and probably included the chena cultivation in the same category with the coffee."

80. RBG-Kew, misc. reports 5.21, Ceylon: Forests. 1859–1880: Sir J. Longden to Sir M. Hicks Beach, 29 Mar. 1879.

81. RBG-Kew, misc. reports 5.21, Ceylon: Cinchona, 1859–80: Longden to earl of Kimberley, 19 Feb. 1881.

82. SLNA/18/20: diary, GA, Central Province, entry for 10 Apr. 1882; R. A. De Rosayro, "Forests and Erosion with Special Reference to Ceylon," *TA* 103, no. 4 (1947): 250.

83. P. M. Lushington, "Report on the Ceylon Forests in the Year 1921, and Their General Administration," *SP* 12 (1921): 4; F. A. Stockdale, "Soil Erosion," *TA* 61, no. 3 (1923): 134.

84. Vincent, "Report on the Forest Administration," 108.

85. Ibid., 71.

86. "This belt of forest, which protected the Kandyans so effectually, is no longer traceable, and the area occupied by it is now remarkable for the worst devastations of the chena cultivator." Vincent, ibid., 9.

87. Ibid., 12. Vincent also wrote (ibid., 66.): "In the most thickly-populated parts of the Island, and especially in the Kandyan Districts, the people have gone on extending their chena cultivation, year after year getting further from their villages, and gradually swallowing up all the forest on which they have hitherto drawn for their building timber. They have annually encroached on the Crown forest, until not only do they now chena beyond the boundary of the village common-land, but they also cut such timber as they require at great distances from their villages."

88. Vincent was unequivocally clear on this point (ibid., 51): "It is not that all forest has been cleared for coffee, and thus that the enterprise has found its own limits, but large though the extent of coffee estates is, the map shows what immense areas, now only covered with lantana, would be available for fresh development of the enterprise had any foresight or care been shown in preventing forest destruction."

89. Ibid., 70.

90. Ibid., 52. On the problem of railway sleepers and the broad question of the role of the Forestry Department in India, see Madhav Gadgil and Ramachandra Guha, *This Fissured Land: An Ecological History of India* (Berkeley, 1993), 118–45.

91. F. C. H. Clarke, "Report of the Conservator of Forests for 1887," *CAR for 1887* (Colombo, 1887), pt. 4, 17–21.

92. For a summary of legislation re. the Forest Department, see R. S. Troup, *Colonial Forest Administration* (Oxford, 1940), 365–71.

93. As early as the 1860s, G. H. K. Thwaites at Peradeniya had anticipated the need for exotics in highland reforestation. He understood that the scale of deforestation was such that a wood shortage would soon become apparent on the estates themselves. For Thwaites (*Report on RBG-Péradeniya, 1868*, 3), the answer was to convert the patana grasslands to woodlots:

> So much forest having been felled for Coffee planting, and this operation still being extensively carried on, it seems very desirable that the pattanas or savannahs, which occupy so large an area on the hills, and are not suitable for Coffee cultivation, should be planted with trees suitable for firewood and other useful purposes. I have accordingly requested the Conductor of the Hakgala gardens to make experiments with various Australian trees, some of which will probably be found adapted for the required purpose. Should any be found to be so, arrangements will be made for a good supply being available for distribution.

94. Trimen, "Report of Director for 1880," 3.

95. Trimen, "Report of Director for 1882," 4; Trimen, "Report of Director for 1883," 8–9.

96. The growth patterns of some of the exotics were unanticipated. Australian wattle acacias were tried, and the silver wattle, *Acacia dealbata,* was judged to be an ideal tree. It grew from seed at a fast rate, to reach the height of fifty-one feet after only six years, with a stem four feet in circumference at the base. The silver wattle, however, sent up suckers and thus had to be planted away from other cultivations; it was, nevertheless, an extremely valuable source of fuelwood: Trimen, "Report of Director for 1887," 12. The Australian blue gum was found to grow from seed at a rapid rate on some estates above 5,000 feet, reaching the height of 60 feet after only five years: C. F. Gordon Cumming, *Two Happy Years in Ceylon* (London, 1892), 2:285–86.

97. "Sleepers on the Railway," *CF* 3, no. 5 (1897): 350.

98. Committee on Re-organization of the Ceylon Forest Department, "Report of the Committee Appointed to Give Effect to the Recommendation Made by Mr. Fisher on the Re-Organization of the Ceylon Forest Department," *SP* 2 (1899): 4.

99. Frederick Lewis, "Our Forests," *TA* 59, no. 5 (1922): 298–302; P. M. Lushington, "Report on the Ceylon Forests in the Year 1921, and Their General Administration," *SP* 12 (1921): 5.

100. R. A. De Rosayro, "The Montane Grasslands (Patanas) of Ceylon," *TA* 102, no. 3 (1946): 139.

101. S. B. Tennakoon dates the mass plantations to the last two decades (rather than the last decade) of the nineteenth century; this is contradicted by other authorities, however. The experimentation with exotics began in the 1880s at Hakgala, but specimens of exotics do not appear to have been widely disseminated until the 1890s. Tennakoon provides a useful summary of the principal exotics planted out:

> Over 50 species of Eucalyptus were planted out, amongst them were the Tasmanian Blue Gum, *Eucalyptus globulus,* and red gum *Eucalyptus robusta.* In the conifers were a number of genera and species that proved to be valuable as timber, for dyes, for tanning, for obtaining turpentine, for fuel, and even for use as wind belts. Amongst these were the *Cupressa macrocarpa* (The Monetary Cypress of California) planted in 1881, *Cedrela toona* (the Red Cedar of Queensland), *Pinus longifolia* (the Chir Pine of the Himalayas), *Cryptomeria japonica* (the Japanese Pencil Cedar, 1874), *Cupressa knightiana* (the knight's cypress), *Cupressus torulosa* (the towering Cypress of the Himalayas), *Cupressus funebris* (the weeping cypress of China), *Cupressus bermudiana* (the Pencil Cedar of Bermuda), *Cupressus sempervirens* variety *horizontalis* (the spreading Cypress of Crete) and a host of other conifers, besides which there were trees like *Syncarpia glomulifera* (the turpentine tree of New South Wales, 1890), *Grevillia robusta* (the silky oak of Australia), *Tristania conferta* (the Queensland Red box). There was also a collection of Oak, planted in 1883 that produced acorns in 1892. A number of species of Acacias were put on trial and these thrived well. In this way a large number of trees were introduced.

S. B. Tennakoon, "The Centenary of the Botanic Gardens, Hakgala, 1861–1961," *TA* 117 (1961): 200–201.

102. C. H. Holmes, "Weeding in the Up-Country Timber and Fuel Plantations," *TA* 97, May 1941, 274.

103. [Planters' Association of Ceylon], *Jubilee of the Planters' Association of Ceylon, 1854–1904* (Colombo, 1904), introduction by Governor West Ridgeway.

104. Trimen, "Report of Director for 1893," 12.

105. F. A. Stockdale, "Soil Erosion," *TA* 61, no. 3 (1923): 132. Here, Stockdale restates the principal findings of the 1904 Commission for the Kelani Valley, which were published as *SP* 42 (1905).

106. Trimen, "Report of Director for 1896," 4.

107. West Ridgeway, *Administration of the Affairs of Ceylon, 1896 to 1903* (Colombo, 1903), 73.

108. "Retirement of Mr. Green," 81.

109. This was the first of several measures. See J. C. Hutson, "Plant Import Legislation in Ceylon," *TA* 92, May 1939, 288–301.

110. *Annals of the Royal Botanic Gardens, Peradeniya* was launched in 1901. For an overview of the scientific publications in Sri Lanka, see Adrian Senadhira, *History of Scientific Literature of Sri Lanka* (Colombo, 1995).

111. Shelton C. Fernando, "History of the Department of Agriculture," *TA* 97 (1941): 222.

112. The *Tropical Agriculturalist* had been founded a generation earlier by the planter and newspaper publisher John Ferguson. Since its inception in 1881, it had served as a forum for planter opinion and for the discussion of practical agronomy. In 1907, under the direction of John C. Willis, director of RBG-Peradeniya, the publication was relaunched as a scientific journal; it began a new career that continues unbroken today.

113. Fernando, "History of the Department of Agriculture," 135.

Conclusion

1. Johannes Botschek et al., "Agricultural Suitability of Degraded Acrisols and Lixisols of Former Tea Lands in Sri Lanka," *Zeitschrift Fur Pflanzenernährung und Bodenkunde* 161, no. 6 (1998): 629.

2. R. L. de Silva, "A Short History of the Tea Research Institute of Ceylon," *Tea Quarterly* 38, pt. 2 (June 1967): 65–102.

Bibliography

I. Principal Collections of Archival Materials Consulted

1. Sri Lankan National Archives (Colombo)

Series 6. Dossiers 281–83, 1027, 1028, 1147, 1322, 1405, 1487, 1743, 1891, 2280, 2586, 2707, 2944, 3027, 3302, 3510, 3632, 4051A, 5524, 5813, 6046, 6276, 6509, 6752, 6936, 7213.
Series 7. Dossiers 278, 279, 634.
Series 8. Dossiers 19, 52, 63, 95, 122–24, 135.
Series 10. Dossiers 22, 168, 177A, 177B, 199.
Series 19. Dossiers 1–3, 60, 106, 107, 111, 113, 114, 118.
Series 47. Dossier 52.
Series 53. Dossiers 1–40, 60, 89.

2. Sri Lankan National Archives, Kandy Branch

Series 18. Dossiers 4–9, 17, 19, 20, 22–24, 2490, 2555, 2608–614, 2741–745, 2751, 3501, 3540, 3751.

3. Department of Agriculture Library (Gannaruwa)

Rare Book Room. Collection of Reports (some unpublished) of the Royal Botanic Garden, Peradeniya. Annotated by Henry Trimen.

4. Royal Botanic Gardens at Kew

Main Library: Miscellaneous Reports 5.21. Ceylon. Cinchona. 1859–90; Miscellaneous Reports. Ceylon. Coffee. 1848–94; Miscellaneous Reports. Ceylon. Coffee Diseases, 1871–87; Miscellaneous Reports. Ceylon. Forests, 1873–1900.
Economic Botany Library: Rubiaceae. Cinchona.

II. Sessional Papers of the Government of Ceylon

"Correspondence on the Subject of the Conservation of Crown Forests." *SP* 29, 1873.

"Correspondence Relative to the Conservation of Government Forests in Ceylon." *SP* 1, 1874.

"Further Correspondence on the Coffee Leaf Disease." *SP* 1, 1880.

"Papers Relating to the Cultivation of Liberian Coffee." *SP* 14, 1876.

Cattle Disease Commission. "Report of the Cattle Disease Commission, and Appendices." *SP* 20, 1869.

Champion, H. G. "Report on the Management and Exploitation of the Forests of Ceylon." *SP* 7, 1935.

Committee on Soil Erosion. "Report of the Committee on Soil Erosion." *SP* 3, 1931.

Committee on the Existing Laws Relating to the Protection of Game, Elephants, and Buffaloes. "Report of the Committee Appointed to Consider and Report on the Existing Laws Relating to the Protection of Game, Elephants, and Buffaloes." *SP* 11, 1889.

Committee on Re-Organization of the Ceylon Forest Department. "Report of the Committee Appointed to Give Effect to the Recommendations Made by Mr. Fisher on the Re-Organization of the Ceylon Forest Department." *SP* 2, 1899.

Committee on Soil Denudation. "Report of the Committee on Soil Denudation in the Kelani Valley." *SP* 42, 1905.

Commission Appointed by His Excellency the Governor to Inquire into and Report on the Advisability of Establishing a Department of Agriculture. "Report of the Commission Appointed by His Excellency the Governor to Inquire into and Report on the Advisability of Establishing a Department of Agriculture." *SP* 12, 1900.

Dyer, W. T. T. "Despatch from the Right Hon. the Secretary of State Transmitting Observations on the Present Condition of the Coffee Planting Industry in Ceylon and the Demand for Developing New Industries." *SP* 4, 1881.

Fisher, F. C. "Reports on the Present State and Proposed Re-Organization of the Ceylon Forest Department." *SP* 29, 1898.

Forest Committee. "Report of the Forest Committee." *SP* 1, 1928.

Hooker, J. D., and G. H. K. Thwaites et al. "Correspondence Relating to the Coffee-Leaf Disease." *SP* 36, 1876.

Lushington, P. M. "Report on the Ceylon Forests in the Year 1921." *SP* 12, 1921.

Markham, Clements R. "Report on the Cultivation of Chinchona Plants in Ceylon." *SP* 11, 1865.

———. "Report on the Cultivation of Chinchona Plants in Ceylon." *SP* 14, 1866.

Morice, Arthur. "Report of a Visit to Some of the Tea Districts of India, with the View of Ascertaining the Suitability or Otherwise of Ceylon for Tea Cultivation." *SP* 5, 1867.

Morris, D. "Reports Upon Experiments Connected with the Coffee Leaf Disease." *SP* 12, 1879.

———. "Further Correspondence on the Coffee Leaf Disease." *SP* 13, 1880.

New Products Commission. "Report of the New Products Commission Appointed to

Report on the Question of the Introduction and Cultivation of New Cultures in Ceylon." *SP* 13, 1881.

Thwaites, G. H. K. "Remarks on the Coffee Leaf Disease by the Director, Royal Botanic Gardens, Peradeniya, with Extracts from His Annual Reports, 1871–76 inclusive." *SP* 35, 1879.

[Varian, H. W.]. "Report on the Forests of the North-Central Province." *SP* 17, 1879.

Vincent, F. D'A. "Report on the Conservation and Administration of The Crown Forests of Ceylon." *SP* 43, 1882.

Ward, H. M. "Coffee Leaf Disease: Preliminary Report by the Government Cryptogamist." *SP* 17, 1880.

———. "Coffee Leaf Disease. Second Report." *SP* 50, 1880.

———. "Coffee Leaf Disease. Third Report." *SP* 17, 1881.

Wright, Norman. "Report on the Development of Cattle Breeding and Milk Production in Ceylon." *SP* 20, 1946.

III. Unpublished Papers and Theses

Ameer Ali, A. C. L. "Peasant Agriculture in Ceylon, 1833–1893." Unpublished M. Phil. doctoral thesis, University of London, 1970.

Drayton, Richard Harry. "Imperial Science and a Scientific Empire: Kew Gardens and the Uses of Nature, 1772–1903." Unpublished Ph.D. thesis, Yale University, 1993.

Sarkar, N. K. "Demography of Ceylon in the Twentieth Century." Unpublished Ph.D. thesis, University of London, 1954.

Vanden Dreisen, I. H. "Some Aspects of the History of Coffee Industry in Ceylon with Reference to the Period 1823–1886." Unpublished Ph.D. thesis, University of London, 1954.

IV. Books and Articles

Abbay, R. "Coffee in Ceylon." *Nature* 16 (31 August 1876): 375–78.

———. "Observations on *Hemileia vastatrix*, the so-called coffee leaf disease." *Journal of the Linnean Society* 17 (1880): 173–84.

———. "Note on the Supposed Cause of the Existence of Patanas, or Grasslands, of the Mountain Zone of Ceylon." *JRASCB* 6 (1879): 59–60.

Abeygunawardena, D. V. M. *Diseases of Cultivated Plants*. Colombo, 1969.

Abeywickrama, B. A. "The Origin and Affinities of the Flora of Ceylon." *Proceedings, 11th Annual Session, Ceylon Association for the Advancement of Science (D)*, 1956, 99–121.

———. "The Evolution of the Flora of Ceylon." *Proceedings, 14th Annual Session, Ceylon Association for the Advancement of Science (D)*, 1958, 217–24.

———. "The Flora of Sri Lanka." *Spolia Zeylanica* 35 (1980): 1–8.

Abrams, Elliot M., and David J. Rue. "The Causes and Consequences of Deforestation Among the Prehistoric Maya." *Human Ecology* 16, no. 4 (1988): 377–95.

Adams, S. N. "Sheep and Cattle Grazing in Forests. A Review." *Journal of Applied Ecology* 12 (1975): 143–52.

Aiyar, T. V. V. "The Sholas of the Palghat Division, a Study in the Ecology and Silviculture of the Tropical Rain Forests of the Western Ghats." *Indian Forester* (1932): 414–32.

Alles, W. S. "Drought Incidence in Relation to Rain-fed Rice." *TA* 125 (1967): 1–8.

Aliquis. *Coffee-Planting in Ceylon.* London, 1861.

Ameer Ali, A. C. L. "Peasant Coffee in Ceylon during the Nineteenth Century." *Ceylon Journal of Historical and Social Studies* 2, no. 1 (1972): 51–59.

———. "Cinchona Cultivation in Nineteenth Century Ceylon." *Modern Ceylon Studies* 5, no. 1 (1974): 93–106.

Andrews, J. R. T. *A Forest Inventory of Ceylon.* Colombo, 1961.

Anthonisz, Richard Gerald. "How They Travelled in the Olden Days." *Journal of the Dutch Burgher Union of Ceylon* 2, no. 2 (1909): 74–79.

Appuhamy, M. A. Durand. *The Kandyans' Last Stand Against the British.* Colombo, 1995.

Arasaratnam, S. "Dutch Commercial Policy in Ceylon and Its Effects on Indo-Ceylon Trade, 1690–1750." *Indian Economic and Social History Review* 4, no. 2 (1967): 109–30.

———. "Ceylon in the Indian Ocean Trade, 1500–1800." In A. Das Gupta and M. N. Pearson, editors, *India and the Indian Ocean 1500–1800*, 224–39. Calcutta, 1987.

———. *Maritime Trade, Society and European Influence in Southern Asia, 1600–1800.* Aldershot, 1995.

———. *Ceylon and the Dutch, 1600–1800, External Influences and Internal Change in Early Modern Sri Lanka.* Aldershot, 1996.

Ariyapala, M. B. *Annotated Index of the Articles in the Journals of the Royal Asiatic Society of Sri Lanka, 1845–1989.* Colombo, 1989.

Arnold, David. "The Indian Ocean as a Disease Zone." *South Asia* 14, no. 2 (1991): 1–21.

Arnold, Edwin. *On the Indian Hills; or, Coffee-planting in Southern India.* London, 1893.

Arunachalam, P. "Kandyan Provinces." *JRASCB* 22, no. 63 (1910): 103–23.

Asad, M. N. M. Kamil. *The Muslims of Sri Lanka Under the British Rule.* New Delhi, 1993.

Ashton, Mark, Savithri Gunatilleke, Neela de Zoysa, M. D. Dassanayake, Nimal Gunatilleke, and Siril Wijesundera. *A Field Guide to the Common Trees and Shrubs of Sri Lanka.* Colombo, 1997.

Ashton, P. S. "Species Richness in Tropical Forests." In L. B. Holm-Nielsen, I. C. Nielsen, and H. Balslev, editors, *Tropical Forests: Botanical Dynamics, Speciation, and Diversity*, 239–51. London, 1989.

Ashton, P. S., and C. V. S. Gunatilleke. "New Light on the Plant Geography of Ceylon: I. Historical Plant Geography." *Journal of Biogeography* 14 (1987): 249–85.

Austin, W. "General View on the Commencement and Progress of Coffee-Planting in Ceylon." In John Ribeyro, *History of Ceylon*, trans. George Lee, appendix 8, 221–30. N.p., 1847.

Bailey, R. C., and T. N. Headland. "The Tropical Rain Forest: Is It a Productive Environment for Human Foragers?" *Human Ecology* 19, no. 2 (1991): 261–85.

Baker, John R. "The Sinharaja Rain-Forest, Ceylon." *Geographical Journal* 89, no. 6 (1937): 539–51.

Baker, Samuel White. *The Rifle and the Hound in Ceylon.* London, 1854; reprint: New York, 1967.

———. *Eight Years' Wanderings in Ceylon.* London, 1855; 2nd ed. published as *Eight Years in Ceylon,* London, 1891.

Balasingham, S. V. *The Administration of Sir Henry Ward, Governor of Ceylon 1855–1860.* Dehiwala, 1968.

Banks, John, and Judy Banks. *A Selection of the Animals of Sri Lanka.* Colombo, 1995.

Barron, T. J. "George Turnour and British Land Policy in the Kandyan Provinces, 1823–1841." *University of Colombo Review* 1, no. 2 (1982): 1–17.

Barron, T. J. "Science and the Nineteenth Century Ceylon Coffee Planters." *Journal of Imperial and Commonwealth History* 16, no. 1 (1987): 5–21.

Bastiampillai, Bertram. "From Coffee to Tea in Ceylon—the Vicissitudes of a Colony's Plantation Economy." *CJHSS* 7, no. 1 (1964): 43–66.

Bastiampillai, B. *The Administration of Sir William Gregory.* Colombo, 1968.

Bennett, John Whitchurch. *Ceylon and Its Capabilities.* London, 1843.

Berlin, Brent. *Ethnobiological Classification: Principles of Categorization of Plants and Animals in Traditional Societies.* Princeton, 1992.

Bertolacci, Anthony. *A View of the Agricultural, Commercial, and Financial Interests of Ceylon.* London, 1817; reprint, Dehiwala, 1983.

Bertus, A. L. "A Selected Bibliography on Land-Use Problems with Special Reference to Shifting Cultivation." *Ceylon Forester* 4, no. 1 (1959): 80–83.

Bidie, G. *Cinchona Culture in British India.* Madras, 1879.

Bidie, W. "Remarks on the Indian Coffee Leaf Disease." *Journal of the Linnean Society* 18 (1881): 458–61.

Bingham, P. M. *History of the Public Works Department, Ceylon, 1796–1913.* 3 vols. Colombo, 1921–23.

Biswas, Kalipada. *The Original Correspondence of Sir Joseph Banks Relating to the Foundation of the Royal Botanic Garden, Calcutta.* Calcutta, 1950.

Bley, J. "Travel Impressions of a Java Planter in Ceylon." *TA* 20 (1900–1901): 470–73.

Bosanquet, W. D. "Coffee and the General Planting Enterprise of Ceylon." *TA* 3 (1883–84): 128–31.

Bossel, H., and H. Krieger, "Simulation Model of Natural Forest Dynamics." *Ecological Modelling* 59 (1991): 37–71.

Botschek, Johannes, Anni Neu, Armin Skowronek, and Ananda N. Jayakody. "Agricultural Suitability of Degraded Acrisols and Lixisols of Former Tea Lands in Sri Lanka." *Zeitschrift Fur Pflanzenernährung und Bodenkunde* 161, no. 6 (1998): 627–32.

Boulger, G. S. "History of Ceylon Botany." In Henry Trimen, *A Handbook of the Flora of Ceylon,* part 5, appendix 4, 367–81. London, 1900.

Bourget, Marie-Noëlle, and Christophe Bonneuil. "De l'inventaire du monde à la mise en valeur du globe." *Revue Française d'Histoire d'Outre-Mer* 86, nos. 322–23 (1999): 7–38.

Boyd, William. "Ceylon and Its Pioneers." *Ceylon Literary Register* 2 (1888): 217–20, 225–27, 233–35, 241–42, 249–50, 257–58, 274–75, 281–82.

Bremer, J. M. *Memories of a Ceylon Planter's Travels, 1851–1921.* London, 1930.

Brockway, Lucile H. *Science and Colonial Expansion: The Role of the British Royal Botanic Gardens.* New York, 1979.

Brohier, R. L. *Ancient Irrigation Works in Ceylon,* 3 pts. Colombo, 1934–35.

Brohier, R. L. *Land, Maps, & Surveys: A Review of the Evidence of Land Surveys as Practiced in Ceylon from Earliest Known Periods and the Story of the Ceylon Survey Department from 1800 to 1950.* 2 vols. Colombo, 1950–51.

Broun, A. F. *Silviculture in the Tropics.* London, 1912.

———. "On the Forests and Waste Lands of Ceylon." In Henry Trimen, *A Handbook of the Flora of Ceylon,* part 5, appendix 2, 355–63. London, 1900.

———. *Report of the Conservator of Forests.* Ceylon Adminstrative Reports, Colombo, 1890, 1892, 1893, 1894, 1895, 1896, 1898, 1899.

Brown, A. *The Coffee Planters' Manual.* Revised ed. Colombo, 1880.

Brown, Janet. "A Science of Empire: British Biogeography before Darwin." *Revue d'Histoire des Sciences* 45, no. 4 (1992): 453–75.

Brown, Sampson. *Life in the Jungle.* Colombo, 1845.

Brown, Sandra, and Ariel E. Lugo, "Tropical Secondary Forests." *Journal of Tropical Ecology* 6 (1990): 1–32.

Bruce-Chwatt, Leonard Jan. *Essential Malariology.* New York, 1985.

Burnand, J. "Ancient and Modern State of the Island of Ceylon and Its Agriculture: 1809." *Monthly Literary Register* 3 (1895): 206–8, 221–24, 244–47, 269–72; 4 (1896): 1–4.

Burnand, Jacob. "The Memoir of the Late Monsieur Bernand Drawn Up by Him for the Information of Sir Alexander Johnston in the Year 1809." *Ceylon Miscellany* 1–3 (1842): 46–51, 156–69.

———. "Fragments on Ceylon." *The Asiatic Journal and Monthly Register* 11 (1821): 440–48, 553–61; 12 (1821): 3–7, 128–33.

Butler, E. J. "The Development of Economic Mycology in the Empire Overseas." *Transactions of the British Mycological Society* 14 (1929): 1–18.

Campbell, James. *Excursions, Adventures, and Field-Sports in Ceylon.* 2 vols. London, 1843.

Campbell, T. J. Report of the Conservator of Forests for 1904–9 (annual), 1910–11.

Cameron, John. *The Prevention of Leaf-Disease in Coffee. Report of a Visit to Coorg by John Cameron, F.L.S., Superintendent of Government Gardens in Mysore.* N.p., 1898.

Canagaratnam, W. "Chena Cultivation in the East of Ceylon." *TA* 25 (1905–6): 867–69.

Capper, John. "The Food Statistics of Ceylon." *JRASCB* 5, no. 17 (1871/1872): 17–24.

———. "Remarks on the Collection of Statistical Information in Ceylon" *JRASCB* 1 no. 1 (1845): 83–89.

[———]. Sampson Brown [pseud.]. *Life in the Jungle.* Colombo, 1845.

———. "A Descriptive Catalogue of the Woods of Ceylon." *JRASCB* 2, II, no. 5 (1849/50): 135, 155.

―――. "A Brief Notice of the Vegetable Productions of Ceylon." *Journal of the Royal Asiatic Society (Great Britain and Ireland)* 16 (1856): 266–79.

―――. *Old Ceylon: Sketches of Ceylon Life in Olden Times.* Colombo, 1877.

Cave, Henry W. *Golden Tips: A Description of Ceylon and Its Great Tea Industry.* London, 1900; reprint: New Delhi, 1994.

―――. "The Terraced Hillsides of Ceylon." From *The Times of Ceylon, 1910—Christmas Number,* reproduced in Pandula Endagama and K. A. S. Dayananda, compilers, *Traditional Agriculture of Sri Lanka,* Agrarian Research and Training Institute, 94–99. N.p., n.d. [1998].

"Ceylon—Past and Present." *Ceylon Miscellaneous* 2, no. 1 (1855[?]): 1–7.

"Ceylon Past and Present." *Calcutta Review* 26 (1856): 313–44.

Ceylon Planter's "Vade Mecum," The. Colombo, 1881.

Chandra Segra, A. S. *Notes on the Management of Cattle in India and Ceylon and Their Diseases.* Jaffna, 1909.

Chenery, E. M., and R. L. de Silva, editors. "A Century of Ceylon Tea, 1867–1967." *Tea Quarterly* 38, pt. 2 (June 1967): 53–218.

Chitty, Simon Casie. *The Ceylon Gazetteer.* Cotta Church Mission Press: n.p. [Ceylon], 1834; reprint, New Delhi, 1989.

Christie, Thomas North. *Prize Essay on Cinchona Cultivation Written for the Dikoya Planters' Association.* Colombo, 1883.

"Cinchona." *TA* 92 (June 1939): 327–29.

Clark, A. *Report of the Conservator of Forests.* CAR. Colombo, 1900, 1901, 1902.

Clarke, F. C. H. *Report of the Conservator of Forests.* CAR. Colombo, 1887, 1888, 1889.

Codrington, H. W. *Glossary of Native, Foreign, and Anglicized Words Commonly Used in Ceylon in Official Correspondence and Other Documents.* Colombo, 1924.

Codrington, Humphrey William. *Ceylon Coins and Currency.* Colombo, 1924.

Coffee Planting in Ceylon: Past and Present. Colombo, 1855.

"Coffee Planting: Wash and Weeds." *TA* 2 (1882–83): 693.

Conte, C. A. "The Forest Becomes Desert: Forest Use and Environmental Change in Tanzania's West Usambara Mountains." *Land Degradation and Development* 10 (1999): 291–309.

Conte, C. A. "Searching for Common Ground: Reconstructing Landscape History in East Africa's Eastern Arc Mountains." In M. Agnoletti and S. Anderson, editors, *Methods and Approaches in Forest History,* 173–87. New York, 2000.

Cooke, M. C. *Report on Diseased Leaves of Coffee and Other Plants.* London, 1876.

Coomaraswamy, Ananda K. *Medieval Sinhalese Art.* 3rd ed. N.p. [Colombo], 1979.

Cooray, P. G. "Effective Rainfall and Moisture Zones of Ceylon." *Bulletin of the Ceylon Geographical Society* 2, no. 3 (1948): 39–44.

Cooray, P. G. *An Introduction to the Geology of Ceylon.* Colombo, 1967.

Cordiner, James. *A Description of Ceylon.* 2 vols. London, 1807; reprint, Colombo, 1983.

Corner, E. J. H. "Ecology and Natural History in the Tropics." *Proceedings, 24th Annual Session, Ceylon Association for the Advancement of Science,* pt. 2 (D): 261–73.

Craig, Jr., J. Edwin. "The Plantation Crops; The Dry Zone; Foundations of Development." In W. Arthur Lewis, editor, *Tropical Development 1880–1913,* 222–49. London, 1970.

Crawford, M. "The Influence of the Various Mineral Constituents on Animal Nutrition, and the Effects of Deficiencies and Evidence of such in Ceylon." *TA* 68, no. 5 (1927): 272–81.

Crawford, M. "Animal Husbandry in Ceylon, Part II." *TA* 82, no. 1 (1934): 121–35.

Cronk, Quentin C. B., and Janice L. Fuller. *Plant Invaders: The Threat to Natural Ecosystems.* London, 1995.

Crosby, Jr., Alfred W. *Ecological Imperialism: The Biological Expansion of Europe, 800–1900.* Cambridge, Eng., 1986.

Cross, A. L. *First Year's Work on a Coffee Plantation.* Colombo, 1877.

Crusz, Hilary. "Nature Conservation in Sri Lanka (Ceylon)." *Biological Conservation* 5, no. 3 (1973): 199–208.

Crüwell, G. A. *Liberian Coffee in Ceylon.* Colombo, 1878.

Cumming, C. F. Gordon. *Two Happy Years in Ceylon.* 2 vols. London, 1892.

Curtin, Philip D. *Two Jamaicas: The Role of Ideas in a Tropical Colony, 1830–1865.* Cambridge, Mass., 1955; reprint: New York, 1970.

Curtin, Philip D. *Death By Migration: Europe's Encounter with the Tropical World in the Nineteenth Century.* Cambridge, Eng., 1989.

Danson, J. T. *Economic and Statistical Studies, 1840–1890.* London, 1906.

Davy, John. *An Account of the Interior of Ceylon and of Its Inhabitants with Travels in that Island.* London, 1821.

Dawood, Nawaz. *Tea and Poverty.* New Delhi, 1980.

Days of Old, or the Commencement of the Coffee Enterprise in Ceylon: By Two of the Pioneers. Colombo, 1878[?].

Dean, Warren. *With Broadax and Firebrand: The Destruction of the Brazilian Atlantic Forest.* Berkeley, Calif., 1995.

De Bussche, Captain L. *Letters on Ceylon; Particularly Relative to the Kingdom of Kandy.* London, 1817.

De Butts, Lieut. *Rambles in Ceylon.* London, 1841.

De Costam, Noel. "The Evolution of the National Parks." *Loris: A Journal of Ceylon Wild Life* 13, no. 4 (1974): 223–35.

De Lanerolle, J. "An Examination of Mr. Codrington's Work on 'Ancient Land Tenure and Revenue in Ceylon,'" *JRASCB* 34, no. 91 (1938): 199–230.

Denevan, W. M., et al. "Indigenous Agroforestry in the Peruvian Amazon: Bora Indian Management of Swidden Fallows." *Interciencia* 9 (1984): 346–57.

Denslow, J. S. "Tropical Rainforest Gaps and Tree Species Diversity." *Annual Review of Ecology and Systematics* 18 (1987): 421–51.

Deriniyagala, P. E. P. "The Wild Buffalo of Ceylon: A New Subspecies." *Spolia Zeylanica* 27, part 1 (1953): 103–6.

Deraniyagala, S. U. *The Prehistory of Sri Lanka.* 2 vols. N.p. [Colombo], 1992.

De Ransonnet, Baron E. *Sketches of the Inhabitants, Animal life, and Vegetation in the Lowlands and High Mountains of Ceylon, as Well as of the Submarine Scenery near the Coast, Taken in a Diving Bell.* Geneva, 1867.

De Rosayro, R. A. "Some Aspects of Shifting Cultivation in Ceylon." *TA* 105, no. 2 (1949): 51–58.

————. "Notes on the Patanas of Ceylon." *Bulletin of the Ceylon Geographical Society* 9, nos. 3 and 4 (1955): 35–43.

————. "The Soils and Ecology of the Wet Evergreen Forests of Ceylon. Part I." *TA* 198, no. 2 (1942): 4–14, and "Part II. Ecology and Forest Types." *TA* 198, no. 3 (1942): 13–35.

————. "The Montane Grasslands (Patanas) of Ceylon." *TA* 101, no. 1 (1945): 206–13; pt. 2, 102, no. 2 (1946): 4–16; pt. 3, 102, no. 2 (1946): 81–94; pt. 4, 102, no. 3 (1946): 139–48.

————. "Forests and Erosion with Special Reference to Ceylon." *TA* 103, no. 4 (1947): 246–52.

————. "Ecological Conceptions and Vegetational Types with Special Reference to Ceylon." *TA* 106, no. 3 (1950): 108–21.

————. "Ecological Considerations in the Management of the Wet Evergreen Forests in Ceylon." *CF*, n.s., 1, no. 2 (1953): 80–90.

————. "The Silviculture and Management of Tropical Rain Forest with Special Reference to Ceylon." *CF*, n.s., 2, no. 1 (1956): 5–26.

————. "The Climate and Vegetation of the Knuckles Region of Ceylon." *CF*, n.s. 3, nos. 3 and 4 (1958): 201–60.

————. "The Nature and Origin of Secondary Vegetational Communities in Ceylon." *CF* 5, nos. 1–2 (1961): 23–49.

de Silva, C. R. *The Portuguese in Ceylon, 1617–1638.* Colombo, 1972.

de Silva, K. M. "Studies in British Land Policy in Ceylon—1." *CJHSS* 7, no. 1 (1964): 28–42.

————. "The Third Earl Grey and the Maintenance of an Imperial Policy on the Sale of Crown Lands in Ceylon, c. 1838–1852." *Journal of Asian Studies* 27 (1967): 5–20.

————. *A History of Sri Lanka.* Oxford, 1981.

de Silva, M. G. B. "Climate." In T. Somasekaram et al., editors, *Arjuna's Atlas of Sri Lanka,* 16–22. Dehiwala, 1997.

de Silva, R. K. *Early Prints of Ceylon (Sri Lanka), 1800–1900.* London, 1985.

————. *Nineteenth Century Newspaper Engravings of Ceylon-Sri Lanka.* London, 1988.

de Silva, R. K., and W. G. M. Beumer. *Illustrations and Views of Dutch Ceylon 1602–1796.* London, 1988.

de Silva, R. L. "A Short History of the Tea Research Institute of Ceylon." *Tea Quarterly* 38, pt. 2 (June 1967): 65–102.

de Silva, S. B. D. "Plantations and Underdevelopment." In Charles Abeysekera, editor, *Capital and Peasant Production: Studies in the Continuity and Discontinuity of Agrarian Structures in Sri Lanka.* Colombo, 1985, 21–32.

de Silva, W. A. "A Contribution to Sinhalese Plant Lore." *JRASCB,* 12, no. 42 (1891): 113–44.

————. "Rural Agriculture in Ceylon and How It Might be Improved." *TA* 31 (1908): 569–71 and 32 (1909): 69–71.

————. "Some Problems Connected with Village Cultivation in Ceylon." *TA* 40 (1913): 281–83.

————. "Some Primitive Processes of Agricultural Practice and Their Significance." *TA* 44, no. 2 (1915): 133–35.

Desmond, Ray. *The European Discovery of the Indian Flora.* Oxford, 1992.

Devaraja, Lorna Srimathie. "Revenues of the King of Kandy." *JRASCB*, n.s., 16 (1972): 17-24.

Dewaraja, L. S. *The Kandyan Kingdom of Sri Lanka, 1707-1782.* 2nd ed. Colombo, 1988.

De Vrij, Dr. J. E. *On The Cultivation of Quinine in Java and British India.* London, 1865.

Diamond, Jared M. "The Island Dilemma: Lessons of Modern Biogeographic Studies for the Design of Natural Reserves." *Biological Conservation* 7 (1975): 129-46.

———. *Guns, Germs, and Steel: The Fate of Human Societies.* New York, 1997.

Dickinson, William R. "Changing Times: The Holocene Legacy." *Environmental History* 5, no. 4 (2000): 483-502.

Dickman, Henry. "Remarks on the Climate of the Interior of Ceylon." In A. M. Ferguson, compiler, *The Ceylon Directory; Calendar; and Compendium of Useful Information for 1866-1868*, app. 1, 1-20. Colombo, n.d.

Digby, S. *War-Horse and Elephant in the Dehli Sultanate.* Karachi, 1971.

Dissanaike, A. S. "Ecological Aspects of Some Parasitic Diseases in Sri Lanka." In C. H. Fernando, editor, *Ecology and Biogeography of Sri Lanka*, 353-69. The Hague, 1984.

Domrös, M. *The Agroclimate of Ceylon: A Contribution Towards the Ecology of Tropical Crops.* Weisbaden, 1974.

———. "Dry Years and their Relationship to Crop Production in Sri Lanka." *Geojournal* 5, no. 2 (1981): 133-38.

Donovan, William. "Clements Robert Markham and the Introduction of the Cinchona Tree into British India, 1861." *Geographical Journal* 128 (1962): 431-42.

Douffet, L. E. *The Ceylon Coffee Album: A Collection of Sixteen Photographs, Illustrating the Various Details of Coffee Planting in Ceylon.* Nuwara Eliya, 1881.

D'Oyly, John. *Diary of Mr. John D'Oyly.* Introduction and notes by H. W. Codrington. A special publication of *JRASCB*. Colombo, 1917; reprint: New Delhi, 1995.

———. "The Elephant Kraal of 1809." *JRASCB* 34, no. 91 (1938): 240-63.

———. *A Sketch of the Constitution of the Kandyan Kingdom.* Dehiwala, 1975.

Drayton, Richard Henry. *Nature's Government: Science, Imperial Britain, and the "Improvement" of the World.* New Haven, 2000.

Drummond, José. "The Garden in the Machine: An Environmental History of Brazil's Tijuca Forest." *Environmental History* 1, no. 1 (1996): 83-104.

Duncan, Alfred H. *The Private Life of a Coffee Planter, by Himself.* Colombo, 1881.

Duncan, James S. *The City as Text: The Politics of Landscape Interpretation in the Kandyan Kingdom.* Cambridge, Eng., 1990.

Dunlap, Thomas R. *Nature and the English Diaspora: Environment and History in the United States, Canada, Australia, and New Zealand.* Cambridge, Eng., 1999.

Dunn, C. L. *Malaria in Ceylon: An Enquiry Into Its Causes.* London, 1936.

Duran-Reynals, M. L. *The Fever Bark Tree.* London, 1947.

Dyer, W. T. T. "The Coffee Leaf Disease of Ceylon." *Quarterly Journal of Microscopic Science*, n.s., 20 (1880): 119-29.

———. "Coffee Leaf Disease in Central Africa." *Kew Bulletin* (1893): 361-63.

Eisenberg, J. F., and G. M. McKay. "An Annotated Checklist of the Recent Mammals of Ceylon with Keys to the Species." *Ceylon Journal of Science (Biology)* 8, no. 2 (1970): 69–99.

Elliott, C. *Coffee Planting in Ceylon.* Colombo, 1852.

Elliott, E. "Rice Cultivation under Irrigation in Ceylon. *JRASCB* 9, no. 31 (1885): 160–70.

———. "Paddy Cultivation in Ceylon in the Nineteenth Century." *TA* 37 (1911), 225–32, 305–12, 393–97, 501–7; 38 (1912), 21–31, 313–18, 403–8, 506–11; 39 (1912), 21–24, 118–25, 235–38; 40 (1913), 100–102, 115–16, 322–26; 41 (1913), 116–19, 203–5, 286–90, 393–94, 465–67; 42 (1914), 98–100, 286–90, 381–83.

Elliot, Robert H. *Experiences of a Planter in the Jungles of Mysore.* 2 vols. London, 1871.

Erdelen, W. "Forest Ecosystems and Nature Conservation in Sri Lanka." *Biological Conservation* 43 (1988): 115–35.

———. "Tropical Rain Forests in Sri Lanka: Characteristics, History of Human Impact, and the Protected Area System." *Monographiae biologicae* 74 (1996): 503–11.

Evans, J. *Plantation Forestry in the Tropics.* Oxford, 1992.

Extracts of Letters from Ceylon on Courtship; Marriage etc.; with a Peep into Jungle Life. London, 1848.

[Falconer, John, and Ismeth Raheem]. *Regeneration: A Reappraisal of Photography in Ceylon 1850–1900.* London, 2000.

FAO: Forest-Resources Assessment 1990. *Survey of Tropical Forest Cover and Study of Change Processes.* In FAO Forestry Paper 130, 152 pp. Rome, 1966.

Farmer, B. H. *Pioneer Peasant Colonization in Ceylon.* London, 1957.

Ferguson, A. M. *Souvenirs of Ceylon.* Colombo, 1869.

———. *Supplement to Ferguson's Ceylon Directory and Handbook for 1866–68.* Colombo, 1869.

———. *The Abbotsford Album: . . . 20 views on . . . a Mountain Plantation in the District of Dimbulla, Ceylon, Illustrative of the Culture of Coffee, Tea, and Cinchona.* Photographed by W. L. H. Skeen. Colombo, 1876.

———. *Ceylon in 1837–46.* Colombo, 1886.

———. *Ceylon in 1847–60.* Colombo, 1887.

———. "Planting in Ceylon in 1847–1860." *TA* 7 (1887–88): 153–55.

———. *All About Coffee-Leaf Disease.* N.p., n.d.

———. "Ceylon in 1847–1860." *Ceylon Literary Register* 2 (n.d.): 13–16, 22–24, 30–32, 38–40.

———, compiler. *The Ceylon Directory; Calendar; and Compendium of Useful Information for 1866–1868.* Colombo, n.d.

Ferguson, A. M., and J. Ferguson. *Plantation Gazetteer and Summary of Useful Information Concerning Ceylon.* N.p. [Colombo], 1859.

———. *Coffee Planters' Manual.* Colombo, 1872, 1880, 1894.

———. *Planters' Notebook, With Everyday Information for the Tea Planter.* Colombo, 1887.

———. *Pioneers of the Planting Enterprise in Ceylon from 1830 Onwards.* 4th series. Colombo, 1894–1908.

Ferguson, J. *Ceylon in 1883.* London, 1883.

————. *Ceylon in 1884*. London, 1884.

[————]. *Ceylon and Her Planting Enterprize: In Tea, Cacao, Cardamoms, Cinchona, Coconut, and Areca Palms*. Colombo, 1885.

————. *Ceylon in the Jubilee Year*. London, 1887.

————. *The Production and Consumption of Certain Tropical Products with Reference to their Cultivation in Ceylon*. Chamber of Commerce Pamphlet Series, no. 13. London, 1892.

————. "The Production and Consumption of Certain Tropical Products with Reference to their Cultivation in Ceylon." *TA* 12 (1892–93): 337–46.

————. *Ceylon in 1893*. London, 1893.

————. *The Coffee Planter's Manual for Both the Arabian and Liberian Species*. Colombo, 1898.

————. *Ferguson's Ceylon Handbook and Directory for 1900–1*. Colombo, 1901.

Fernando, H. Marcus. "The Need for the Improvement of Cattle in Ceylon." *TA* 66, no. 6 (1926): 297–303.

Fernando, Shelton C. "History of the Department of Agriculture." *TA* 97 (1941): 135–37, 215–28, 275–93.

Fisher, F. C. *Report of the Conservator of Forests*. CAR. Colombo, 1897.

Forbes, Major J. *Eleven Years in Ceylon*. 2 vols. London, 1840.

Forrest, D. M. *A Hundred Years of Ceylon Tea, 1867–1967*. London, 1967.

Frost, Alan. "The Antipodean Exchange: European Horticulture and Imperial Designs." In David P. Miller and Peter H. Reill, editors, *Visions of Empire: Voyages, Botany, and Representations of Nature*, 58–79. Cambridge, Eng., 1996.

Gadjil, Madhav, and Ramachandra Guha. *This Fissured Land: An Ecological History of India*. Berkeley, 1993.

Gardner, George. Untitled essay. *Journal of the Horticultural Society, London* 4 (1849): 31–40.

————. "Report on the 'Brown Scale' or 'Coccus,' so Injurious in the Coffee Plants of Ceylon." *Hooker's London Journal of Botany* 2 (1850): 353–60; and 3 (1851): 1–9.

————. "Some General Remarks on the Flora of Ceylon." In E. F. Kelaart, *Prodomus Faunae Zeylanica*, app. A. Colombo, 1852.

————. *Report Upon "Brown Scale" or "Bug" on Coffee*. Colombo, 1885.

Gibson, I. A. S., and T. Jones, "Monoculture as the Origin of Major Forest Pests and Diseases." In J. M. Cherrett and G. R. Sagar, editors, *Origins of Pest, Parasite, Disease, and Weed Problems*, 139–61. Oxford, 1979.

Gibson, James R. *Imperial Russia in Frontier America. The Changing Geography of Supply of Russian America, 1784–1867*. New York, 1976.

Gómez-Pompa, A. "On Maya Silviculture." *Mexican Studies* 3 (1987): 1–19.

Gómez-Pompa, A., J. S. Flores, and V. Sosa. "The 'Pet Kot': a Man-Made Tropical Forest of the Maya." *Interciencia* 12 (1987): 10–15.

Goonatilleke, H. A. I. *A Bibliography of Ceylon*. 5 vols. Zug, Switzerland, 1970–1983.

Gooneratne, Brendon, and Yasmine Gooneratne. *This Inscrutable Englishman. Sir John D'Oyly (1774–1824)*. London, 1999.

Gordon, Cumming C. F. *Two Happy Years in Ceylon*. London, 1893.

Gramiccia, Gabriele. *The Life of Charles Ledger (1818–1905). Alpacas and Quinine.* London, 1988.

"Grassland Agriculture in Ceylon." *TA* 111, no. 4 (1955): 253.

Great Britain, Colonial Office. *Reports on the Finance and Commerce of the Island of Ceylon and Correspondence Relative Thereto.* Presented to Both Houses of Parliament by Command of Her Majesty, April 1848. 146p. London, 1848. 146p. + report by Sir James Emerson Tennent (pp. 44–146) appendix, nos. 1–12 (pp. 107–46).

Green, Joseph Reynolds. *A History of Botany, 1860–1900; Being a Continuation of Sachs' "History of Botany, 1530–1860."* Oxford, 1909.

Gregory, Lady, editor. *Sir William Gregory: An Autobiography.* London, 1894.

Grigson, E. S. *On the Manuring of Coffee Estates.* Colombo, n.d.

Grove, Richard H. "The Transfer of Botanical Knowledge between Asia and Europe, 1498–1800." In *Journal of the Japan-Netherlands Institute* 3 (1991), 160–76.

Grove, Richard H. *Green Imperialism: Colonial Expansion, Tropical Island Edens and the Origins of Environmentalism, 1600–1800.* Cambridge, Eng., 1995.

Guha, R. "Forestry in British and Post-British India, a Historical Analysis." *Economic and Political Weekly* 18, nos. 44, 45, 46 (1988).

Guha, R. *The Unquiet Woods. Ecological Change and Peasant Resistance in the Himalaya.* Delhi: Oxford University Press, 1990.

Guha, Sumit. *Environment and Ethnicity in India, 1200–1991.* Cambridge, Eng., 1999.

Gunasekera, H. A. de Silva. *From Dependent Currency to Central Banking in Ceylon: An Analysis of Monetary Experience 1825–1957.* London, 1962.

Gunatilleke, I. A. U. N., and C. V. S. Gunatilleke. "Distribution of Floristic Richness and Its Conservation in Sri Lanka." *Conservation Biology* 4, no. 1 (1990): 21–31.

Gunawardena, D. C. "Medical and Economic Plants of the Museum Zeylanicum of Paul Hermann." *JRASCB*, n.s., 19 (1975): 33–48.

Gygax, R. "Remarks on Some Analyses of the Coffee of Ceylon with Suggestions for the Application of Manures." *JRASCB* 2, no. 5 (1849): 131–34.

Haafner, Jacob Godfried. *Travels on Foot Through the Island of Ceylon.* London, 1821.

Haeckel, E. A. *A Visit to Ceylon.* London, 1883.

Haldane, R. C. *All about Grub: Including a Paper on the Grub Pest in Ceylon.* Colombo, 1881.

Hall, B. *Travels in India, Ceylon, and Borneo.* N.p., 1831.

Hall, Douglass. *Free Jamaica, 1838–1865: An Economic History.* New Haven, 1959; reprint: London, 1969.

Hamilton, V. H., and Fasson, S. M. *Scenes in Ceylon.* London, 1881.

Harler, C. R. *The Culture and Marketing of Tea.* Oxford, 1964.

Harrison, Mark. *Public Health in British India: Anglo-Indian Preventive Medicine, 1859–1914.* Cambridge, Eng., 1994.

Hayley, Frederic Austin. *The Laws and Customs of the Sinhalese or Kandyan Law.* Colombo. 1923 [reprint: Delhi, 1993].

Headrick, Daniel R. *The Tentacles of Progress: Technology Transfer in the Age of Imperialism.* New York, 1988.

Hettiarachchy, Tilak. *The Sinhala Peasant in a Changing Society: Ecological Change Among the Sinhala Peasants from 1796 A.D. to 1909 A.D..* Colombo, 1982.

Hewa, Soma. *Colonialism, Tropical Disease, and Imperial Medicine: Rockefeller Philanthropy in Sri Lanka*. Lanham, Md., 1995.

Higman, B. W. *Slave Population and Economy in Jamaica, 1807–1834*. Cambridge, Eng., 1976.

Hoffmeister, W. *Travels in Ceylon and Continental India*. Translated from the German. Edinburgh, 1848.

Hogendorn, Jan, and Marion Johnson. *The Shell Money of the Slave Trade*. Cambridge, Eng., 1986.

Holman, James. *Travels in Madras, Ceylon, Mauritius, Cormoro Islands, Zanzibar, Calcutta, etc., etc.* London, 1840.

Holmes, C. H. "Weeding in the Up-Country Timber and Fuel Plantations." *TA* 97, May 1941, 274–94.

Holmes, C. H. "The Broad Pattern of Climate and Vegetational Distribution in Ceylon, *CF* 2, no. 4 (1956): 209–25.

———. "The Natural Regeneration of the Wet and Dry Evergreen Forest of Ceylon, *CF* 2, no. 4 (1956): 153–64.

House of Commons. "Copy of Correspondence Relating to the Introduction of the Chinchona Plant into India, and the Proceedings connected with its Cultivation from March 1852 to March 1863." E. D. Bourdillon, India Office.

Howard, John Eliot. *Illustrations of the Nueva Quinologia of Pavon*. London, 1862.

———. *Quinology of the East Indian Plantations, Parts I–III*. London, 1869–76.

Hughes, John. *Ceylon Coffee Soils and Manures*. London, 1879.

Hull, Edmund C. P. *Coffee; Its Physiology, History, and Cultivation: Adapted as a Work of Reference for Ceylon, Wynaad, Coorg, and the Neilgherries*. Madras, 1865.

———. *Coffee Planting in Southern India and Ceylon*, 2nd ed. London, 1877.

Hutson, J. C. "Plant Import Legislation in Ceylon." *TA* 92, May 1938, 288–301.

Ievers, R. W. *Manual of the North Central Province*. Colombo, 1899.

Innes, T. E. D. "Is the Lantana a Friend or an Enemy?" *Ceylon Forester* 2, no. 2 (1896): 17–26.

———. "List of Jungle Products Used by the Poor During the Famine, 1896–1897." *TA* 30, no. 6 (1908): 546–48; 31, no. 1 (1908): 33–35; 32, no. 2 (1908): 130–32.

Jackson, J. R. *Commercial Botany of the Nineteenth Century*. London, 1890.

Jacob, V. J., and W. S. Alles. "Kandyan Gardens of Sri Lanka." *Agroforestry Systems* 5 (1987): 123–37.

Jayamaha, G. S. "The Monsoons and Their Influence on the Ceylon Weather." *TA* 110, no. 4 (1954): 275–79.

Jayaweera, D. M. A. "History of Cinchona Culture in Ceylon." *TA* 99 (1943): 91–95.

Jayewardene, Jayantha. *The Elephant in Sri Lanka*. Colombo, 1994.

Jenkins, R. W. *Ceylon in the Fifties and Eighties*. Colombo, 1886.

Joachim, A. W. R. "The Mineral Constituents of Ceylon's Fodder Grasses." *TA* 68, no. 5 (1927): 269–71.

Joachim, A. W. R., and S. Kandiah. "Studies on Ceylon Soils, II: General Characteristics of Ceylon Soils, Some Typical Soil Groups of the Island, and a Tentative Scheme of Classification." *TA* 84, no. 5 (1935): 254–75.

————. "Studies on Ceylon Soils, III: The Red and Yellow Earths, and the Wet and Dry Patana Soils." *TA* 84, no. 6 (1935): 323–34.

————. "The Chemical and Physical Characteristics of the Soils of Adjacent Contrasting Vegetation Formations." *TA* 98, no. 2 (1942): 15–30.

————. "The Effect of Shifting (Chena) Cultivation and Subsequent Regeneration of Vegetation on Soil Composition and Structure." *TA* 106, no. 1 (1948): 3–11.

Johnson, James, and James Ranald Martin. *The Influence of Tropical Climates on European Constitutions.* New York, 1846.

Johnson, Nels. "An Introduction to the Technical Aspects of Biodiversity and Its Conservation." in Simon Tietbergen, editor, *The Earthscan Reader in Tropical Forestry.* London, 1993, 297–316.

Johnston, A. "On the Measures Required for the Improvement of Agriculture in Ceylon (1809)." *Ceylon Literary Register* 1 (n.d.): 263, 264; 271, 272.

Joseph, Abraham. *A Cummi Poem on Coffee Planting with English Translation.* Jaffna, 1869.

Kannangara, P. D. *The History of the Ceylon Civil Service, 1802–1833.* Dehiwala, 1966.

Kandy: Planters Association of Ceylon. *Jubilee of the Planters Association of Ceylon, 1854–1904.* Colombo, 1904.

Karunaratna, Nihal. *Udavattekäle. The Forbidden Forest of the Kings of Kandy.* Colombo, 1986.

————. *Forest Conservation in Sri Lanka From British Colonial Times 1818–1882.* Colombo, 1987.

————. *Kandy—Past and Present.* N.p. [Colombo], 1999.

Karunatilake, H. N. S. "Social and Economic Statistics of Sri Lanka in the Nineteenth Century." *JRASCB*, n.s., 31 (1986/87): 40–61.

Kelaart, E. F. *Prodomus Faunae Zeylanicae.* Colombo, 1852.

King, Thomas. *A Catalogue of a Splendid and Valuable Collection of Jewellery, Forming the Regalia of the King of Kandy.* N.p. [London], n.d. [1820].

Kinnis, J. *A Report on Small-Pox as It Appeared in Ceylon in 1833–34; with an Appendix.* Colombo, 1835.

Knighton, W. *The History of Ceylon from the Earliest Period to the Present Time.* London, 1845.

————. *Forest Life in Ceylon.* 2 vols. London, 1854.

Koelmetyer, K. O. "Climatic Classification and the Distribution of Vegetation in Ceylon, *CF* 3, no. 2 (1957): 144–63, and 3, nos. 3 and 4 (1958): 201–60.

Kumar, Deepak. *Science and the Raj, 1857–1905.* Oxford, 1995.

Lamprey, J. "On the Coffee Blight, the Cotton Aphis, and Some New Species of Lac." *JRASCB* 2, no. 8 (1855). Appendix: Proceedings of the General Meeting, 1 February 1854, lxxxix–cii.

Laborie, P. J. *The Coffee Planter of Saint Domingo.* London, 1798.

Lawrie, A. C. *A Gazeteer of the Central Province of Ceylon.* 2 vols. Colombo, 1896–98.

Le Mesurier, C. J. R. *Manual of the Nuwara Eliya District, Ceylon.* Colombo, 1893.

Lear, J. Correspondence Relating to the Royal Botanic Gardens, Peradeniya in 1838 and Succeeding Years. *TA* 9 (1889–90), 750–54; 782–84; 804–9; 833–35; also *Ceylon*

Literary Register 4 (n.d.): 267, 268; 274–77; 282–84; 289–91; 299–303; 307–10; 316, 317; 323–26; 331–33.

Leiter, N. "Denudation Chronology and Drainage Pattern of the Central Massif of Ceylon." *Bulletin of the Ceylon Geographical Society* 2 (1947): 64–69.

Lewis, Frederick. "A Descriptive Catalogue of the More Useful Trees and Flowering Plants of the Western and Sabaragamuva Provinces of Ceylon." *JRASCB* 17, no. 53 (1902): 89–256.

———. "Our Forests." *TA* 59, no. 5 (1922): 298–302.

———. *Sixty-Four Years in Ceylon.* Colombo, 1926.

———. "The Altitudinal Distribution of the Ceylon Endemic Flora." *Ceylon Journal of Science: Section A. Botany* 10 (1926): 1–130.

———. *A Few Pioneer Estates and Early Pioneers in Ceylon.* Ceylon Historical Association, paper no. 10. Colombo, 1927.

———. *The Vegetable Products of Ceylon.* Colombo, 1934.

Lewis. J. P. *Manual of the Vanni Districts, Ceylon.* Colombo, 1895; reprint: Delhi, 1993.

Lewis, John Penry. *Ceylon in Early British Times.* Colombo, 1914.

Lewis, R. E. *Coffee Planting in Ceylon, Past and Present.* Colombo, 1855.

Lewis, R. L. "The Rural Economy of the Sinhalese, More Particularly with Reference to the District of Sabaragamuwa, with Some Account of Their Superstitions." *JRASCB* 2, I, 4 (1848): 31–52.

Liesching, L. F. *A Brief Account of Ceylon.* Jaffna, 1861.

Loos, James. *On the Nature and Causes of Fevers in Ceylon.* Colombo, 1888.

Ludden, David. "Ecological Zones and the Cultural Economy of Irrigation in Southern Tamilnadu." *South Asia* 1, no. 1 (1978): 1–13.

Ludovici, L. *Rice Cultivation, Its Past History and Present Condition.* Colombo, 1867.

MacKay, David. "Agents of Empire: The Banksian Collectors and Evaluation of New Lands." In David P. Miller and Peter H. Reill, editors, *Visions of Empire: Voyages, Botany, and Representations of Nature,* 38–57. Cambridge, Eng., 1996.

Mackenzie, John, editor. *Imperialism and the Natural World.* Manchester, 1990.

Macmillan, H. F. "Fruit Cultivation in Ceylon." *TA* 25 (1905–6): 486–97.

———. *Illustrated Guide to the Royal Botanic Gardens, Peradeniya.* Colombo, 1906; reprint, New Delhi, 1999.

———. "Acclimatisation of Plants: What Has Been Done in Ceylon." *TA* 29, no. 5 (1907): 374–78.

———. "Notes on Pasture Lands, Fodder Grasses, and Forage Plants." *TA* 36 (1911): 331–37.

———. *Tropical Planting and Gardening With Special Reference to Ceylon.* 4th ed. London, 1934.

Mahadevan, P. "Performance of the Sinhala Cattle." *TA* 108, no. 4 (1952): 37–42.

———. "An Analysis of the European Herds of Dairy Cattle at Ambawela and Bopatalawa." *TA* 113, no. 1 (1957): 45–54.

Mahamooth, T. M. Z. "Eradication and Control of Rinderpest in Ceylon, *TA* 105, no. 1 (1949): 14–21.

Manson-Bahr, Philip H., editor, *Manson's Tropical Diseases: A Manual of the Diseases of Warm Climates.* London, 1921.

Marcus, Millett W. *Jungle Sport in Ceylon.* London, 1914.

Markham, Clements R. *Peruvian Bark: A Popular Account of the Introduction of Cinchona Cultivation into British India.* London: 1880.

Marshall, Henry. *Notes on the Medical Topography of the Interior of Ceylon.* London, 1821.

———. "Some Account of the Introduction of Vaccination Among the Inhabitants of the Interior of Ceylon, and of an Epidemic Small-Pox which Prevailed in the Kandyan Provinces in 1819." *Edinburgh Medical and Surgical Journal* 19 (1823): 71–77.

———. *Ceylon: A General Description of the Island and Its Inhabitants.* London, 1846.

McCann, James C. *People of the Plow: An Agricultural History of Ethiopia, 1800–1990.* Madison, 1995.

McConnell, Douglas. *The Forest Farms of Kandy.* Rome: FAO, 1992.

McCracken, Donal P. *Gardens of Empire: Botanical Institutions of the Victorian British Empire.* London, 1997.

McHale, D. "The Cinchona Tree." In Institute of Biology, *Exploited Plants*, 25–33. London, 1990; reprinted from *Biologist* 33, no. 1 (1986).

McIvor, William Graham. *An Abridgement of The Coffee Planter of St. Domingo by Laborie and Notes on the Propagation and Cultivation of the Medicial Cinchonas or Peruvian Bark Trees.* Madras, 1863.

———. *Notes on the Propagation and Cultivation of the Medicial Cinchonas or Peruvian Bark Trees.* Madras, 1863.

McKay, G. M. "Ecology and Biogeography of Mammals." In C. H. Fernando, editor, *Ecology and Biogeography of Sri Lanka*, 413–29. The Hague, 1984.

McNeill, John R. *The Mountains of the Mediterranean: An Environmental History.* Cambridge, Eng., 1992.

———. *Something New Under the Sun: An Environmental History of the Twentieth Century.* New York, 2000.

McNeill, William H. *Plagues and Peoples.* New York, 1976.

Mehra, K. L. "Portuguese Introduction of Fruit Plants in India." *Indian Horticulture* 10, no. 1 (1965): 8–12; 10, no. 3 (1965): 36–38; 10, no. 4 (1965): 23–35.

Mendis, V. L. B. *British Governors and Colonial Policy in Sri Lanka.* Dehiwala, 1984.

Meyer, Eric. "Between Village and Plantation: Sinhalese Estate Labour in British Ceylon." In Marc Gaboreau and Alice Thorner, editors, *Asie du Sud: Traditions et Changments: Sixth European Conference on Modern South Asian Studies Sevres, 8–13 July 1978.* Paris, 1978.

———. "L'épidémie de malaria de 1934–1935 à Sri Lanka: fluctuations économiques et fluctuations climatiques." *Culture et Développement* 14, nos. 2–3 (1982): 183–226 and 14, no. 4 (1982): 589–638.

———. "The Plantation System and Village Structure in British Ceylon: Involution or Evolution?." In Peter Robb, editor, *Rural South Asia: Linkages, Change, and Development*, 56–23. London, 1983.

―――. "Enclave Plantations, 'Hemmed-in' Villages, and Dualistic Representations in Colonial Ceylon." *Journal of Peasant Studies* 20, nos. 3–4 (1992): 199–228.

―――. "From Landgrabbing to Landhunger: High Land Appropriation in the Plantation Areas of Sri Lanka during the British Period." *Modern Asian Studies* 26, no. 2 (1992): 321–61.

―――. "Les forêts, les cultures sur brûlis, les plantations et 1'état colonial à Sri Lanka, 1840–1930." *Revue française d'histoire d'outre-mer* 80, no. 299 (1993): 195–218.

―――. "Paddy, Garden, Chena, Plantation: Was There a Peasant Strategy in the Kandyan Regions of Sri Lanka before 1940?" In Peter Robb, editor, *Meanings of Agriculture: Essays in South Asian History and Economics*, 182–227. Delhi, 1996.

―――. "Forests, Chena Cultivation, Plantations and the Colonial State in Ceylon, 1840–1940." In Richard H. Grove, Vinita Damodaran, and Satpal Sangwan, editors, *Nature and the Orient*, 793–827. Delhi, 1998.

Millie, P. D. *"Thirty Years Ago," or Reminiscences of the Early Days of Coffee Planting in Ceylon.* Colombo, 1878.

Modder, Frank. *Gazetteer of the Puttalam District of the North-Western Province of Ceylon.* Colombo, 1908; reprint, Delhi, 1993.

Moens, J. C. B. *De Kinacultuur in Azie 1854 t/m 1882.* Batavia, 1882; trans. J. C. Fagginger Auer as *Cultivation of Cinchona in Asia, 1854–1882.* N.p., n.d. [c. 1943].

Moldrich, Donovan. *Bitter Berry Bondage: The Nineteenth Century Coffee Workers of Sri Lanka.* Colombo, 1989.

Moon, Alexander. *A Catalogue of Indigenous and Exotic Plants Growing in Ceylon.* Colombo, 1824.

Moore, M. "The Ideological History of the Sri Lankan Peasantry." *Modern Asian Studies* 23, no. 1 (1989): 179–207.

Morris, D. "Coffee Leaf Disease in Ceylon and Southern India." *Nature* 20 (1879): 557–59.

[―――]. *The Campaign of 1879 against Coffee Leaf Disease (Hemileia vastatrix) by the Coffee Planters of Ceylon.* Assisted and guided by D. Morris. Colombo, 1879.

―――. "Note on the Structure and Habit of Hemileia Vastatrix, the Coffee Leaf Disease of Ceylon and Southern India." *Journal of the Linnean Society* 17 (1880): 512–27.

Mortimer, Michael. *Roots in the African Dust.* Cambridge, Eng., 1998.

Moss, Boyd. "Health and Disease in Ceylon." JRASCB 3, no. 12 (1860/61): 1–12.

Mottau, S. A. W. "Glossary of Terms Used in Official Correspondence of the Government of Sri Lanka, Compiled from Records at the National Archives." *The Sri Lanka Archives: The Journal of the Sri Lanka National Archives Colombo* 3 (1985–86).

Mouat, Frederic J. *Rough Notes of a Trip to Reunion, the Mauritius, and Ceylon; With Remarks on their Eligibility as Sanitaria for Indian Invalids.* Calcutta, 1852.

Munasinghe, Indrani. "The Road Ordinance of 1848 and the Kandyan Peasantry." *JRASCB* n.s., 28 (1983/84): 25–44.

Munasinghe, Indrani. "Modes of Travel in Sri Lanka at the Beginning of British Rule." *The Sri Lanka Archives: The Journal of the Sri Lanka National Archives Colombo* 2 (1984): 61–66.

Muraleedharan, V. R. "Quinine (Cinchona) and the Incurable Malaria: India, c. 1900–1930s." *Parassitologia* 42, nos. 1–2, 2000, 91–100.

Natural Resources, Energy, and Science Authority of Sri Lanka. *Natural Resources of Sri Lanka: Conditions and Trends.* Colombo, 1991.

Nietner, J. *The Coffee Tree and Its Enemies.* Colombo, 1872.

Obeysekere, Donald. "Medical Science among the Sinhalese: Small Pox and Its Treatment." *Ceylon National Review* 3, no. 8 (1909): 29–34.

Oldeman, R. A. A. "Dynamics in Tropical Rain Forests." In L. B. Holm-Nielsen, I. C. Nielsen, and H. Balslev, editors, *Tropical Forests: Botanical Dynamics, Speciation and Diversity,* 3–21. London, 1989.

O'Loughlin, C. L. "The Effect of Timber Removal on the Stability of Forest Soils." *Hydrology* 13 (1974): 121–34.

Ondaatje, W. C. *Observations on the Vegetable Products of Ceylon.* Colombo, 1854.

———. "Notes on the District of Badulla and Its Natural Products." *JRASCB* 3, no. 12 (1860/61): 381–428.

Owen, T. C. *First Year's Work on a Coffee Plantation.* Colombo, 1877.

———. *Cinchona Planter's Manual.* Colombo, 1881.

Pagot, Jean. *Animal Production in the Tropics and Subtropics.* London, 1992.

Panabokke, C. R. *Soils and Agro-Ecological Environments of Sri Lanka.* Colombo, 1996.

Pandian, M. S. S. "Hunting and Colonialism in the Nineteenth-Century Nilgiri Hills of South India." In Richard H. Grove, Vinita Damodaran, and Satpal Sangwan, editors, *Nature and the Orient,* 273–98. New Delhi, 1998.

Park, Malcolm, and M. Fernando. *Diseases of Village Crops in Ceylon.* Colombo, 1941. Peradeniya Manuals, no. 4.

Parkin, J., and H. H. W. Pearson. "The Botany of the Ceylon Patanas, II." *Journal of the Linnean Society* 35 (1903): 430–63.

Parsons, T. H. "Food Crops of the Tropics." *TA.* 80, no. 2 (1933): 285–89.

———. "Items of Interest in the Activities of the Royal Botanic Gardens, Peradeniya, in the Last Quarter Century." 1: 1914 to 1922, *TA* 98, no. 1 (1942): 28–42; 2: 1923 to 1927, *TA* 98, no. 2 (1942): 42–56; 3: 1928–1934, *TA* 98, no. 3 (1942): 37–53; 4: 1935 to 1940, *TA* 98, no. 4 (1942): 26–41.

———. "Records of Interesting Exotic Trees in the Royal Botanic Gardens, Peradeniya." *TA* 100, no. 2 (1944): 92–101.

Payne, Charles Wynn. *The Eastern Empire. Crown Colonies. Ceylon.* London, 1847.

———. *Ceylon, Its Products, Capabilities, and Climate.* London, 1854.

Payne, W. J. A. *An Introduction to Animal Husbandry in the Tropics.* London, 1990.

Pearson, H. H. W. "The Botany of the Ceylon Patanas." *Journal of the Linnean Society of London* 34 (1899), 300–65.

Peebles, Patrick. "Land Use and Population Growth in Colonial Ceylon." In James Brow, editor, *Population, Land, and Structural Change in Sri Lanka and Thailand,* 64–79. Leiden, 1976.

———. *Social Change in Nineteenth Century Ceylon.* Delhi, 1995.

Pegler, D. N. "Advances in Tropical Mycology Initiated by British Mycologists." in Brian G. Sutton, editor, *A Century of Mycology,* 53–80. Cambridge, Eng., 1996.

Peiris, Gerald. "The Physical Environment." In K. M. de Silva, editor, *Sri Lanka: A Survey,* 3–30. Honolulu, 1977.

————. *Development and Change in Sri Lanka: Geographical Perspectives.* New Delhi, 1996.

[Penny, Fanny Emily Farr]. *Fickle Fortune in Ceylon.* Madras, 1887.

Percival, Robert. *An Account of the Island of Ceylon.* London, 1803.

Perera, A. H. "Growth and Performance of Pines in Sri Lanka." In H. P. M. Gunasena, S. Gunatilleke, and A. H. Perera, editors, *Reforestation with Pinus in Sri Lanka.* Proceedings of a Symposium at the University of Peradeniya, July 1988.

————. "A Baseline Study of Kandyan Forest Gardens of Sri Lanka: Structure, Composition, and Utilization." *Forest Ecology Management* 45 (1991): 269–80.

Perera, G. F. *The Ceylon Railway: The Story of Its Inception and Progress.* Colombo, 1925.

Perera, Mario, and Marie Jain. *Fountains of Life.* Oberrieden, Switzerland, 1992.

Perera, Muhandiram E. "Hakgala Botanic Gardens." *TA* 102, no. 4 (1946): 224–25.

Perera, N. P. "The Ecological Status of the Montane Grasslands (Patanas) of Ceylon." *CF* 9, nos. 1 & 2 (1969): 27–52.

————. "Early Agricultural Settlements in Sri Lanka in Relation to Natural Resources." *Ceylon Historical Journal* 25 (1978): 58–73.

————. "Natural Resources, Settlements, and Land Use." In D. H. Fernando, editor, *Ecology and Biogeography in Sri Lanka*, 453–93. The Hague, 1984.

Perera, W. R. H. "The Development of Forest Plantations in Ceylon Since the Seventeenth Century." *CF* 5 (1962): 142–57.

"Periods of Sowing and Reaping the Different Grains Throughout the Island." *Ceylon Almanac and Compendium of Useful Information 1815*, 139–45; *1816*, 164–70; and succeeding issues.

Petch, T. "The Early History of Botanic Gardens in Ceylon, with notes on the Topography of Colombo." *The Ceylon Antiquary and Literary Register* 5, part 3 (January 1920): 119–24.

————. "Plants and Trees of Ceylon." *The Ceylon Antiquary and Literary Register* 3, part 3 (January 1922): 169–79.

————. "In Ceylon A Century Ago. The Proceedings of the Ceylon Literary and Agricultural Society: With Notes by T. Petch." *The Ceylon Antiquary and Literary Register* 8, part 1 (July 1922): 73–91; 8, part 2 (October 1922): 166–82; 8, part 3 (January 1923): 262–83; 8, part 4 (April 1923): 347–55; 9, part 1 (July 1923): 58–70; 9, part 2 (October 1923): 123–34.

————. "The Cherry at Nuwara Eliya." *TA* 63, no. 4 (1924): 214–15.

————. *Bibliography of Books and Papers Relating to Agriculture and Botany to the End of the Year 1915.* Colombo, 1925.

————. "Papers and Records Relating to Ceylon Mycology and Plant Pathology, 1783–1910." *Annals, R.B.G., Peradeniya,* V, 343–86. [N.p., n.d.].

Pfaffenberger, Bryan. "The Harsh Facts of Hydraulics: Technology and Society in Sri Lanka's Colonization Schemes." *Technology and Culture* 31, no. 3 (1990): 361–97.

Philalethes [pseud.] [R. J. Wilmot Horton]. *Letters on Colonial Policy, Particularly as Applicable to Ceylon.* Colombo, 1833.

Phillips, W. W. A. "The Present State of the Game and Wildlife in Ceylon." *Journal of the Bombay Natural History Society* (15 October 1929): 942–46.

————. "The Distribution of Mammals in Ceylon with Special Reference to the Need for Wild-Life Sanctuaries." *JRASCB* 32, no. 86 (1933): 315–26.

————. *Manual of the Mammals of Ceylon.* London, 1935.

Pieris, Ralph. *Sinhalese Social Organization: The Kandyan Period.* Colombo, 1956.

Pimental, David. "The Ecological Basis of Insect Pest, Pathogen and Weed Problems." In J. M. Cherrett and G. R. Sagar, editors, *Origins of Pest, Parasite, Disease and Weed Problems*, 3–31. London, 1977.

[Planters' Association of Ceylon]. *Jubilee of the Planters' Association of Ceylon, 1854–1904.* Colombo, 1904.

[————]. *Planters Association of Ceylon, 1854–1954.* Colombo, 1954.

[————]. *Proceedings of the Planters' Association of Ceylon for the Year Ending February 17, 1874.* Colombo, 1874.

"Planting Notes from Badulla [Historical]." *TA* 4 (1884–85): 430.

Plâté, Ltd. *Twenty Five Views of Kandy and Up Country.* Colombo, n.d.

Pouchepadass, Jacques. "British Attitudes towards Shifting Cultivation in Colonial South India: A Case Study of South Canara District, 1800–1920." In David Arnold and Ramachandra Guha, editors, *Nature, Culture, Imperialism: Essays on the Environmental History of South Asia*, 123–51. Delhi, 1995.

————. "Colonialism and Environment in India: Comparative Perspective." *Economic and Political Weekly*, 19 August 1995, 2059–67.

Power, E. R. "On the Agricultural, Commercial, Financial, and Military Statistics of Ceylon." *JRASCB* 1 (n.d.): 42–50.

Prabhakar, R., and Madhav Gadgil. "Maps as Markers of Ecological Change: A Case Study of the Nilgiri Hills of Southern India." In David Arnold and Ramachandra Guha, editors., *Nature, Culture, Imperialism: Essays on the Environmental History of South Asia*, 152–84. Delhi, 1995.

Prakash, Om. *European Commercial Enterprise in Pre-colonial India.* Cambridge, Eng., 1998.

Premadasa, M. A. "Grasslands." In C. H. Fernando, editor, *Ecology and Biogeography of Sri Lanka*, 99–131. The Hague, 1984.

Preu, Christoph, and Walter Erdelen. "Geoecological Consequences of Human Impacts on Forests in Sri Lanka." In J. G. Goldhammer, editor, *Tropical Forests in Transition: Ecology of Natural and Anthropogenic Disturbance Processes*, 147–64. Basel, 1992.

Pridham, Charles. *An Historical, Political and Statistical Account of Ceylon and Its Dependencies.* 2 vols. London, 1849.

Private Life of a Ceylon Coffee Planter, The. Colombo, n.d.

Pretzsch, Jurgen. "Chances and Limits of Tropical Forest Management from the Socio-Economic View: Status Quo and Perspectives." *Plant Research and Development* 47/48 (1998): 88–97.

Pyne, Stephen. *Vestal Fire: An Environmental History, Told Through Fire, of Europe and Europe's Encounter with the World.* Seattle, 1997.

————. *World Fire: The Culture of Fire on Earth.* New York, 1995.

Quammen, David. *The Song of the Dodo. Island Biogeography in an Age of Extinctions.* London, 1996.

Rajan, Ravi. "Imperial Environmentalism or Environmental Imperialism? European Forestry, Colonial Foresters and the Agendas of Forest Management in British India, 1800–1900." In Richard H. Grove, Vinita Damodaran, and Satpal Sangwan, editors, *Nature and the Orient*, 324–71. New Delhi, 1998.

Rajaratnam, S. "The Growth of Plantation Agriculture in Ceylon, 1886–1931, *CJHSS* 4, no. 1 (1961): 1–20.

Rambo, A. T. "Primitive Man's Impact on Genetic Resources of the Malaysian Tropical Rain Forest." *Malaysian Applied Biology Journal* 8 (1979): 59–65.

Rangarajan, Mahesh. *Fencing the Forest: Conservation and Ecological Change in India's Central Provinces, 1890–1914*. New Delhi, 1996.

———. "Environmental Histories of South Asia: A Review Essay." *Environment and History* 2 (1996): 129–43.

Raven-Hart, R. *Heydt's Ceylon (1744)*. Colombo, 1952.

———. "The Great Road." *JRASCB*, n.s., 4, no. 2 (1955): 143–212.

———. "Four Sinhalese Roads." *JRASCB*, n.s., 7, no. 1 (1959): 88–92.

———. "The Great Road II." *JRASCB*, n.s., 8, no. 1 (1962): 141–62.

———, translator and editor. *Travels in Ceylon, 1700–1800*. Colombo, 1963.

Redman, Charles. *Human Impact on Ancient Environments*. Tucson, 1999.

Reid, Anthony. "Humans and Forests in Pre-colonial Southeast Asia." In Richard H. Grove, Vinita Damodaram and Satpal Sangwan, editors, *Nature and the Orient*, 106–26. Delhi, 1998.

Renton, Vantosky. *Coffee Blossom and Other Verselets*. Colombo, 1911.

"Retirement of Mr. Green, Ceylon Government Entomologist." *TA* 40, no. 2 (1913): 81–82.

Ridgeway, West. *Administration of the Affairs of Ceylon, 1896 to 1903*. Colombo, 1903.

Rigg, C. R. "On Coffee Planting in Ceylon." *Journal of the Indian Archipelago and Eastern Asia* [Singapore] 6 (March 1852): 123–42.

Roberts, Michael W. "Indian Estate Labour in Ceylon during the Coffee Period, 1830–1880." *Indian Economic and Social History Review* 3 (1966): 1–52, 101–36.

———. "The Paddy Lands Irrigation Ordinances and the Revival of Traditional Irrigation Customs." *Ceylon Journal of Historical and Social Studies* 10 (1967): 114–30.

———. "Grain Taxes in British Ceylon, 1832–1872: Problems in the Field." *Journal of Asian Studies* 28, no. 3 (1968): 809–34.

———. "Grain Taxes in British Ceylon, 1832–1878: Theories, Prejudices, and Controversies." *Modern Ceylon Studies* 1, no. 1 (1970): 115–46.

———. "The Impact of The Waste Lands Legislation and The Growth of Plantations on The Techniques of Paddy Cultivation in British Ceylon: A Critique." *Modern Ceylon Studies* 1, no. 2 (1970): 157–98.

———. "Irrigation Policy in British Ceylon During the Nineteenth Century." *South Asia*, no. 2, (1972): 47–63.

———. *Caste Conflict and Elite Formation: The Rise of the Karava Elite in Sri Lanka, 1500–1871*. Cambridge, Eng., 1982.

Rogers, John D. *Crime, Justice, and Society in Colonial Sri Lanka*. London, 1987.

Russell-Wood, A. J. R. *The Portuguese Empire, 1415–1808*. Baltimore, 1998.

Ryan, Byrce. *Caste in Modern Ceylon: The Sinhalese System in Transition.* Brunswick, N.J., 1953.

Sabonadiere, W. *The Coffee Planter in Ceylon.* Guernsay, 1866.

Salmon, C. S. *The Ceylon Starvation Question.* London, 1890.

Samarasekera, H. T. P. "'Tropical Agriculturalist'—Its Agricultural Content." *TA* 112, no. 1 (1956): 5–10.

Samaraweera, Vijaya. "A Catalogue of Nineteenth Century British Parliamentary Papers Relating to Ceylon." *Ceylon Journal of Historical and Social Studies,* n.s., 2, no. 2 (1972): 170–75.

———. "Ceylon's Trade Relations with Coromandel During Early British Times, 1796–1837." *Modern Ceylon Studies* 3, no. 1 (1972): 1–18.

Santiapillai, Charles, M. R. Chambers, and N. Ishwaran, "The Leopard *Panthera Pardus Fusca* (Meyer 1794) in the Ruhunu National Park, Sri Lanka, and Observations Relevant to Its Conservation." *Biological Conservation* 23 (1982): 5–14.

Senadhira, Adrian. *History of Scientific Literature of Sri Lanka.* Colombo, 1995.

Senaratne, S. D. J. E. "Some Weeds New to Ceylon." *Ceylon Journal of Science: Section A* 12, no. 4 (1947): 211–15.

Senanayake, F. R., M. R. Soulé, and J. W. Senner. "Habitat Values and Endemicity in the Vanishing Rain Forests of Sri Lanka." *Nature* 265 (1977): 351–54.

Seneratna, J. E. "Patana Burning with Particular Reference to Pasturage and Wet Patanas: A Preliminary Note." *TA* 98, no. 4 (1942): 3–16.

Seneviratne, Sudarshan. "'Peripheral Regions' and 'Marginal Communities': Towards an Alternative Explanation of Early Iron Age Material and Social Formations in Sri Lanka." In R. Champakalaksmi and S. Gopal, editors, *Tradition, Dissent and Ideology,* 264–312. Delhi, 1996.

Senewiratne, S. T., and R. R. Appadurai. *Field Crops of Ceylon.* Colombo, 1966.

Silva, A. T. Mahinda. "Chena-Paddy Inter-relationships." In B. H. Farmer, editor, *Green Revolution? Technology and Change in Rice-Growing Areas of Tamil Nadu and Sri Lanka,* 85–91. London, 1977.

Silva, K. T. "Malaria Eradication as a Legacy of Colonial Discourse: The Case of Sri Lanka." *Parassitologia* 36, nos. 1–2 (1994): 149–63.

[Sinclair, Arthur]. *How I Lost My Wattie or Life in Ceylon and the Coffee Planting Experience of an Auld Scotchman.* Colombo, 1878.

Sirr, H. C. *Ceylon and the Cingalese.* 2 vols. London, 1850.

Siriweera, W. I. "Floods, Droughts and Famines in Precolonial Sri Lanka." In *Modern Sri Lanka Studies,* special K. W. Goodawardena felicitation volume, 79–85. N.p., 1987.

———. *A Study of the Economic History of Pre-Modern Sri Lanka.* Delhi, 1994.

Skaria, Ajay. *Hybrid Histories: Forests, Frontiers, and Wilderness in Western India.* New Delhi, 1999.

Skeen, William. *Mountain Life and Coffee Cultivation in Ceylon—a Poem on the Knuckles Range, with Other Poems.* London, 1868.

Skinner, T. *Fifty Years in Ceylon.* London, 1891.

Snodgrass, D. R. *Ceylon: An Export Economy in Transition.* Homewood, Ill, 1966.

"Sleepers on the Railway." *Ceylon Forester* 3, no. 5 (1897): 350.

Somasekaram, T., M. P. Perera, M. B. G. de Silva, and H. Godellawatta, editors. *Arjuna's Atlas of Sri Lanka*. Dehiwala, 1997.

"Some Account of the Natural Productions of the Island of Ceylon, Particularly in the Environs of Colombo; By a Gentleman Now Resident on the Island." *Asiatic Annual Register* (1800): miscellaneous tracts, 1–6.

Soubeiran, J.-L., and Aug. Delondre, *De l'introduction et de l'acclimatation des cinchonas dans les Indes Néerlandaises et dans les Indes Britanniques*. Paris, 1868.

Speculum. *Ceylon: Her Present Condition: Revenues, Taxes, and Expenditure*. Colombo, 1868.

Spence, H. R. *Report of the Conservator of Forests*. CAR. Colombo, 1903.

Spencer, J. E. *Shifting Cultivation in Southeast Asia*. Berkeley, 1966.

Stark, N. "Man, Tropical Forests, and the Biological Life of a Soil." *Biotropica* 10, no. 1 (1978): 1–10.

Sterndale, Robert A. *Natural History of the Mammalia of India and Ceylon*. Calcutta, 1884.

Statement of the Present Position of the Coffee Trade, with Reference to the System of Adulteration Now in Practice, A. London, 1851.

Steuart, James. *Notes on Ceylon and Its Affairs During a Period of Thirty-Eight Years, ending in 1855*. London, 1862.

Still, John. *Jungle Tide*. Edinburgh, 1930.

Stockdale, F. A., T. Petch, and H. F. Macmillan, *The Royal Botanic Gardens, Peradeniya, Ceylon, 1822–1922*. Colombo, 1922.

Stockdale, F. A. "Soil Erosion." *TA* 61, no. 3 (1923): 131–40.

———. "The Chena Problem and Some Suggestions for its Solution." *TA* 66, no. 4/5 (1926): 199–208.

Story, H. *Hunting and Shooting in Ceylon*. London, 1907; reprint: New Delhi, 1998.

Subrahmanyam, Sanjay. *The Portuguese Empire in Asia, 1500–1700: A Political and Economic History*. London, 1993.

[Suckling, H. J.]. *Ceylon: A General Description of the Island, Historical, Physical, Statistical, Containing the Most Recent Information*. 2 vols. London, 1876.

Sukumar, R. "Ecology of the Asian Elephant in Southern India. II: Feeding Habits and Crop Raiding Patterns." *Journal of Tropical Ecology* 6 (1990): 33–53.

Sullivan, Edward. *The Bungalow and the Tent*. London, 1854.

Super, John C. *Food, Conquest, and Colonization in Sixteenth-Century Spanish America*. Albuquerque, 1988.

Suppiah, R., and M. Yoshino. "Some Agro-Climatological Aspects of Rice Production in Sri Lanka." *Geographical Review of Japan* 59, no. 2 (1984): series B, 137–53.

Tanna, Kaju J. *Plantations in the Nilgiris: A Synoptic History*. Madras, 1969.

Tennakoon, S. B. "The Centenary of the Botanic Gardens, Hakgala, 1861–1961." *TA* 117 (1961): 193–201.

Tennent, J. Emerson. "Report of Sir J. Emerson Tennent on the Finance and Commerce of the Island of Ceylon." In "Ceylon: Reports on the Finance and Commerce of the Island of Ceylon, and Correspondence Relative Thereto." *British Parliamentary Paper*, session 1847–48, vol. 42.105, paper no. 933.

————. *Ceylon: An Account of the Island.* London, 1860.

————. *Sketches of the Natural History of Ceylon.* London, 1861.

Thambyahpillay, G. "Agro-Climatological Significance of the Factor of Rainfall Variability in Ceylon." *Agriculture* 3 (1960): 13–26.

Thomas, Keith. *Man and the Natural World: Changing Attitudes in England, 1500–1800.* London, 1983.

Thunberg, C. P. *Travels in Europe, Africa, and Asia.* London, 1794–95.

Thwaites, G. H. K. *Enumeratio Plantarum Zeylaniae.* London, 1864.

Tinker, Hugh. *A New System of Slavery: The Export of Indian Labour Overseas 1830–1920.* London, 1974.

Tomalin, H. F. *Report of the Conservator of Forests* for 1914; 1915.

Trimen, H., et al. "Pioneers of the Planting Enterprise in Ceylon: G. H. K. Thwaites." *TA* 14 (1894–95): 75–79.

Trimen, Henry. "A Systematic Catalogue of the Flowering Plants and Ferns Indigenous to or Growing Wild in Ceylon." *JRASCB* 9, no. 30 (1885): 1–137.

————. "Remarks on the Composition, Geographical Affinities, and Origin of the Ceylon Flora." *JRASCB* 9, no. 31 (1885): 138–59.

————. *A Handbook of the Flora of Ceylon.* 5 vols. London, 1900.

Troup, R. S. *Colonial Forest Administration.* Oxford, 1940.

Tucker, Richard P., and John F. Richards, editors. *Global Deforestation and the Nineteenth-Century World Economy.* Durham, N.C., 1983.

Turner, F. J. S. *Report of the Conservator of Forests.* CAR. Colombo, 1911–12.

Tyssul Jones, T. W. "Deforestation and Epidemic Malaria in the Wet and Intermediate Zones of Ceylon." *Indian Journal of Malariology* 5, no. 1 (1951): 155–56.

Tytler, R. B. *The Position and Prospects of Coffee Production As Affecting the Value of Ceylon Coffee Estates.* Aberdeen, 1879.

Uragoda, C. G. *A History of Medicine in Sri Lanka.* Colombo, 1987.

Van de Graaf, W. J. governor of Ceylon. "Memorial to His Successor (1794)." *Ceylon Literary Register* 1 (n.d.): 302–4, 309–12, 318–20, 326–28.

Van Gorkem, Karel Wessel. *A Handbook of Cinchona Culture,* trans. Benjamin Daydon Jackson. London, 1889.

Vanderstraaten, J. L. "A Brief Sketch of the Medical History of Ceylon." *JRASCB* 9, no. 32 (1886): 306–35.

Vanden Dreisen, I. H. "Coffee Cultivation in Ceylon." *Ceylon Historical Journal* 3 (1953): pt. 1, 31–61; pt. 2, 156–72.

————. "Plantation Agriculture and Land Sales Policy in Ceylon, the First Phase, 1836–1886." *University of Ceylon Review* 14 (1956): 6–25, and 15 (1957): 36–52.

————. "Some Trends in the Economic History of Ceylon in the 'Modern' Period." *Ceylon Journal of Historical and Social Studies* 3 (1960): 1–17.

————. "Some Aspects of the Financing of Commercial Companies in Nineteenth Century Ceylon." *University of Ceylon Review* 18 (1960): 213–22.

————. *The Long Walk: Indian Plantation Labour in Sri Lanka in the Nineteenth Century.* Delhi, 1997.

Villiers, Thomas. *Mercantile Lore.* Colombo, n.d. [c. 1940].

Walker, A. M. *Report of the Conservator of Forests*. CAR. Colombo, 1891.

Walker [Mrs. Colonel]. "Journal of a Tour in Ceylon." *Journal of Botany* 2 (1840): 223–56.

Wall, George. "Introduction to a History of the Industries of Ceylon." *JRASCB* 10, no. 37 (1888): 327–49.

Ward, H. M. *On the Morphology of Hemeleia Vastatrix*. London, 1881.

———. "On the Morphology of *Hemileia Vastatrix* Berk. and Br. (the fungus of the coffee disease of Ceylon)." *Quarterly Journal of Microscopial Science* 22 (1882): 1–11.

———. "Researches on the Life History of the *Hemileia Vastatrix*, the fungus of the 'coffee leaf disease,'" *Journal of the Linnean Society* 19 (1882): 299–335.

Watson, Andrew F. "The Arab Agricultural Revolution and Its Diffusion, 700–1100." *Journal of Economic History* 34, no.1 (1974): 8–35.

Watts, David. *The West Indies: Patterns of Development, Culture and Environmental Change Since 1492*. Cambridge, Eng., 1987.

Weatherstone, John. *The Pioneers 1825–1900: The Early British Tea and Coffee Planters and Their Way of Life*. London, 1986.

Webb, James L. A., Jr. *Desert Frontier: Economic and Ecological Change Along the Western Sahel, 1600–1850*. Madison, 1995.

Weerasooriya, Wickrema S. *The Nattukottai Chettiar Merchant Bankers in Ceylon*. Colombo, 1973.

Werner, Wolfgang L. "Structure and Dynamics of the Upper Montane Rain Forests of Sri Lanka." In J. G. Goldhammer, editor, *Tropical Forests in Transition: Ecology of Natural and Anthropogenic Disturbance Patterns*, 165–72. Basel, 1992.

Wesumperuma, Dharmapriya. "Land Sales Under the Paddy Tax in British Ceylon." *Vidyodaya Journal of Arts, Sciences, and Letters* 2, no. 1 (1969): 19–35.

———. *Indian Immigrant Plantation Workers in Sri Lanka: A Historical Perspective, 1880–1910*. Kelaniya, 1986.

Wharton, Charles H. "Man, Fire, and Wild Cattle in Southeast Asia." *Annual Proceedings Tall Timbers Fire Conference*, no. 8, 1968, 107–67.

White, Arnold H. *Coffee Culture in Ceylon. Manuring of Estates*. Colombo, 1875.

White, H. "Legislation in Ceylon in the Early Portion of the Nineteenth Century." *JRASCB* 14, no. 47 (1896): 95–101.

White, Harold A. *Hand-book to Cinchona Planting for Ceylon Planters*. Colombo, 1877.

White, Herbert. *Manual of Uva*. Colombo, 1893.

Whitmore, T. C. *An Introduction to Tropical Rain Forests*. Oxford, 1990.

Wickramagamage, P. "A Man's Role in the Degradation of Soil and Water Resources in Sri Lanka: A Historical Perspective." *Journal of the Natural Science Council of Sri Lanka* 18, no. 1 (1990): 1–16.

———. "Large Scale Deforestation for Plantation Agriculture in the Hill Country of Sri Lanka and Its impacts." *Hydrological Processes* 12 (1998): 2015–28.

Wickremeratne, Lakdasa Ananda. "Grain Consumption and Famine Conditions in Late Nineteenth Century Ceylon." *Ceylon Journal of Historical and Social Studies*, n.s., 3, no. 2 (1973): 28–53.

Wiersum, K. F. "Tree Gardening and Taungya on Java: Examples of Agroforestry Techniques in the Humid Tropics." *Agroforestry Systems* 1 (1982): 53–70.

Willis, John Christopher. "The Royal Botanic Gardens of Ceylon, and Their History." *Annals of the Royal Botanic Gardens, Peradeniya* 1, part 1 (June 1901): 1–17.

Willis, John Christopher. "A Sketch of the Agriculture of Ceylon." *TA* 24 (1904). *Agricultural Magazine Supplement* 16, no. 1 (July 1904): 59–60; 16, no. 2 (1904): 131–32; 16, no. 3 (1904): 205–6; 16, no. 4 (1904): 279–80; 15, no. 5 (1904): 353–54; 16, no. 6 (1904): 425–26.

————. *Agriculture in the Tropics.* 3rd ed. revised. Cambridge, Eng., 1922.

Wilson, Christine. *The Bitter Berry.* London, 1957.

Wimalaratne, K. D. G., editor. *Guide to the Sources of Asian History: Sri Lanka.* Dehiwala, 1997.

Yoshino, M. M., and R. Suppiah. "Rainfall and Paddy Production in Sri Lanka." *Journal of Agricultural Meteorology* 40, no. 1 (1984): 9–20.

Yule, Henry, and A. C. Burnell, *Hobson-Jobson: A Glossary of Colloquial Anglo-Indian Words and Phrases, and of Kindred Terms, Etymological, Historical, Geographical and Discursive.* 4th ed., edited by William Crooke. New Delhi, 1984.

Index

A

abolition of slavery: in British empire, 76
acacia, 144
Adam's Peak, 108, 133
agriculture: low surplus, 25; constrained by exercise of political authority, 32; production checked by inadequate transport system, 33; extraction of surplus, 34; planting schedules, 35–36; crop protection, 36–37; nineteenth-century British efforts to improve highland, 59; "scientific agriculture," 80; expansion of Kandyan, before 1800, 148. *See also* chena; cinchona; coffee; rice; tea
agro-ecological zones: contemporary, xvii; nineteenth-century, xvii; map of, 9. *See also* Dry Zone; Intermediate Zone; Wet Zone
Allagalla, 105
altitude: and agro-ecological zones, xvii–xviii
Ambagamuwa, 77
Andes, 116, 117, 118
Anuradhapura, 16
arboretum, 104
areca nuts, 18, 68
areca tree, 67
arrack, 18
Assam, 133, 135
Australia, 4, 53, 115, 116, 143, 144
ayurvedic medicine, 41, 45, 48, 52, 56, 148

B

Badulla, 40, 59
Baker, Samuel: on the healthful effects of deforestation, 51–52; efforts at ecological transformation in upper highlands, 65–66
bandicoots, 65
Banks, Sir Joseph, 56
barley, 54, 64
Barnes, Governor Edward: orders for the Royal Botanic Garden at Peradeniya, 57; plantation at Gannaruwa, 61, 145; horticultural experimentation at Nuwara Eliya, 64; policies toward coffee producers, 69
beans, 53, 65
beer, 54
Bengal sholl, 59
Bennett, J. W., 59
Berbice, 80
beriberi, 52, 55
Bertolacci, Anthony, 51
Bintenne, 29, 68, 98
biodiversity: elevated levels of floral and faunal, in highlands, 10–11; in forests, 23; contemporary appreciation of, 52; and mountain cap reserves, 141; loss of, 148–49
Bird, George, 60–61
birds, 60, 65, 69, 86, 87, 143
Bombay (Mumbai), 118

Borneo, 11, 115

Bos gaurus: and expansion of chena, 13; local extinction of, 21

Bos indicus: varieties of, 43

botanic gardens, 54, 55–56. See also Hakgala; horticulture; Royal Botanic Garden at Calcutta; Royal Botanic Gardens at Kew; Royal Botanic Garden at Peradeniya

Brazil cherry, 59

British East India Company, 57, 117, 133

Brownrigg, Governor Robert, 57

buffalo: physical description, 21; and patana pasture, 22; paths cut by, 22; and rinderpest, 28–29, 93–95; agricultural virtues of, 37, 42–43; dry grain straw for fodder, 40; traction for plowing, 43–44, 60; leopard threat to, 46; forest pasture constraint on natural growth, 89; absence of, on coffee estates, 98; high prices for, 98; hunting of wild, 102

"bug." See insect infestations

Burma, 115, 142

Burnand, J.: 1809 observation concerning agriculture, 32–33

C

cabbage, 56, 65, 66

cacao, 137

Calcutta. See Royal Botanic Garden at Calcutta

California, 115

Camellia sinensis. See tea

Campbell, Governor Colin, 64

Canton, 63, 133

Cape Colony, 54, 55, 56

Cape of Good Hope, 56, 59

capital: flows of, to Sri Lanka, 77; villagers with access to, 106; flight of, in aftermath of coffee blight, 115

cardamom plant, 42

carrot, 56, 65

cashew nuts, 18

cassava, 18, 42

cattle: British policy toward, imports after Great Rebellion, 28–29; agricultural virtues of, 37; dry grain straw for fodder for, 40; leopard threat to, 46, 100–102; imported for meat, 55; manure, 82–83; and forest pasture, 89; volume and value of imports, 96; coast and native, compared, 97–98. See also Bos gaurus; Bos indicus; rinderpest

Cattle Disease Commission, 98

central highlands: physiographic description, 4

Ceylon Literary and Agricultural Society, 59

chank shells, 19

cheetahs, 66, 67

chena: early history of, in association with Iron Age implements, 12–13; dependence upon, after rajarata period, 16; field clearance, 38–39; determinants of fallow periods, 38–39; Sri Lankan and Indian practices of, compared, 39; difficulties of quantification, 39; soil erosion caused by, 40; Sinhala terms referring to, 50; expansion into forest barrier, 66–67, 68–69; and growth of coffee exports, 69–71; stigmatized as destructive practice, 71; impact on, of "Waste Lands" Ordinance No. 12 of 1840, 73; continued expansion of, 141; ecological impact of, compared to monocrop plantations, 149–50. See also forest barrier

chili pepper, 18, 54

China: political interventions in Sri Lanka, 16

cholera: first epidemic in British period, 29; and migration of South Indian laborers, 92; 1845 mortality in Kandy, 92

Christie, Thomas, 55

cinchona: experimental trials at Peradeniya, 116; early efforts to establish, in Eastern Hemisphere, 116; initial chemical results, 119; expansion of, planting, 120; propagation techniques, 121; drainage, 121–22; additional agronomic challenges, 122; bark-harvesting techniques, 122–23; proliferation of subvarieties, 124; Dutch practice of continuous selection, 124; brief domination of world market by Sri Lankan exports, 127; role of, in opening lands at higher elevations, 128

Cinchona ledgeriana: transmission to India and Java, 123–24; Dutch diffusion of, 124; arrival at Peradeniya and Hakgala, 124–25; success in Java, 125–26

Cinchona officinalis: promising introduction, 118

Cinchona succirubra: promising introduction, 118–19

cinnamon: early exports to India, 18; Portuguese exports, 18; Dutch monopoly efforts, 18–19

Cleghorn, Dr.: his role in transfer of cinchona, 117–18
clove tree, 42, 137
coconut palm, 18, 36, 55, 61, 68
coffee: introductions to Sri Lanka, 17–18, 60; 1835 estimate of production, 35; naturalization, 60; old Dutch plantations, 60; plowing of, fields, 60; first plantation at Gampola, 60–61; Barnes' plantation at Gannaruwa, 61; production at Peradeniya, 61–62; sale of seedlings, 61–62; exports of, encouraged by British policies, 69; de Soysa's "hybrid model," 69; extent of Kandyan coffee lands 1812–1845, 70; "mania," 77; "West Indian" model, 80; planting patterns, 80; Kandyan method of harvesting, 80; agronomic calendar, 90; imperial tariffs, 96; Liberian plants introduced, 111; rot, 116
coffee blight: initial appearance, 108, 111; anti-fungoid treatment, 112; patterned deforestation implicated in spread, 115; probable origin, 116; extent of spread, 116
coffee-leaf disease. *See* coffee blight
coffee plantations: abandonment of, during 1840s, 84; rat attacks on, 85; ecological vulnerabilities, 86; expansion of, and conflict with Kandyan villagers, 87; pulp production on, 88; incursions by villagers' buffalo and cattle, 89; lack of corporate resistance to expansion of, 106; higher agronomic limits for, 108; profitability of, 111; abandoned, as centers of disease transmission, 112; decline in profitability of, owing to coffee blight, 112. *See also* capital; transport
Colombo, 29, 54, 55, 56, 57, 61, 63, 86, 88, 94
Colombo Observer, 115
Colombo Observer and Commercial Advertiser, 94
conifers, 143, 144
Corbet, R. J., 118
Cordiner, James, 93
cotton, 20, 35, 38, 39
coolies. *See* South Indian laborers
cowrie shells, 19
credit: extended by Indian merchant bankers, 34, 74; rates of interest in Kandyan period, 34
Crown Timber Ordinance No. 6 of 1878, 139
Cuba, 80

currency. *See* monetization

D
dairy farms, 141
Dambadeniya, 16
Dambulla, 28
De Bussche, Captain L., 56
deer, 21, 28, 45, 46, 47, 56, 65, 85, 102 *See also* sambhur deer
deforestation: cumulative effects of early, 15; and disappearance of springs, 88; ideas about impact of, on human health, 104; efforts to stem environmental consequences of, 140–41. *See also* chena; forest(s)
Department of Agriculture, 146
Deraniyagala, S. U., 11
De Rosayro, R. A., 20–21
De Silva, W. A., 48
De Soysa, Jeronis, 69
dhoney, 90
Dickman, Henry: advocacy for "forest reserves," 105
diet: regularization of British colonial, 53; comparative examples from New World societies, 53; of military and civilian populations, 54–55
Dolosbage, 64
donkeys, 96–97
D'Oyly, Sir John: on Kandyan hunting rules, 46; issues permit for forest clearance, 67
drainage: coffee fields at Peradeniya, 61; via vertical drains, 84; of cinchona trees, 121–22
dry grains: planting of, by early cultivators, 13, 14; in Kandyan highlands, 33, 1835 estimate of production, 35; straw of, as fodder, 40. *See also* chena; kurakkan; maize
Dry Zone: described in comparison to Wet and Intermediate Zones, 7–8; early human presence in, 11; formation of larger settled communities in, 13–14; fire use in, 15–16
Dumbera, 105
Dutch East India Company, 19, 26. *See also* trade; vegetables

E
Eastern Africa, 116
economic opportunities: seized by Kandyan

farmers, 67–69; for Kandyan laborers, 74. *See also* chena; coffee

edge habitats: of patanas, 20–21, 22; use of, by Kandyan villagers, 41; and human-wild animal interactions, 45; and horticultural initiatives in upper highlands, 65–66; on coffee estates, 79, 85–86, 87; and scrub typhus, 93

elephants: Sri Lankan, compared to South Indian, 11; adaptation to highlands, 15; exports of, to India, 18; feeding habits, 22; paths through highlands, 22; raids by, and villagers' defense against, 47–48; use of, for plowing, 60; and horticultural initiatives in upper highlands, 65–66; rogue incursions, 85; hunted and exported during Kandyan period, 99; nineteenth-century exports, 100; estimate of population decline, 100

elevation: and agro-ecological zones, xvii–xviii

erosion. *See* soil erosion

estates. *See* coffee plantations; cinchona; tea

eucalyptus, 143, 144

experimental station for tropical agriculture, 145

F

fauna: endemicity of, 10–11; spatial distribution of, 11; displacement of large animals through land clearance, 12–13, 15; European efforts at naturalization of imported, 53–54, 64; migration routes of small, 85–86; habitat loss, 148

female infanticide, 32

Ferguson, John, 115

fertilizer: ash, 37, 81; jack-leaf fall, 61; dolomite mixture, 82; animal manures, 82; humus, 83; from human excrement, 83; green manures, 84; low quality of, from coffee pulp, 88; use during coffee blight, 112

Fiji, 115, 116

fire: and early ecological history, 12–13; and malaria, 12; and evolution of grasslands, 14; in *rajarata* period, 14, 147; adaptation to, by flora, 15; and hydraulic works, 15; and chena, 38–39; in forest clearance, 67, 77–78; controlled first burn, 78–79; difficulty of control, 79; and soil erosion, 81. *See also* chena; coffee

Fletcher, Major, 30

flora: endemicity of, 10; retreat of endemic, before fire, 15; Sinhala-speakers' classifications, 48–50; European efforts at naturalization of,

53–54; beginnings of Sri Lankan participation in great intertropical exchange, 57; transfer of, to highlands, 63, 66

Florida, 115

fodder. *See* grasses

Forbes, Major J., 99

forest(s): variations, 23; floral community associations, 23; and highland streamflow, 23–24; Sinhala terms referring to, 49–50; British perceptions of, 50–52; auction of, 69–70, 71–73; restrictions on government sale, 71, 140–41; highland clearance of, 77–79. *See also* deforestation; reforestation

forest barrier: strategic importance, 19; symbol of Kandyan independence, 67; revision of rules governing, 67; disappearance of, 142. *See also* chena

forest conservation: early official colonial notices concerning, 139–40

forest gardens, 41–42

forest pasture: implications of reduction in, 88–89; conflict over access to, 89

Forest Ordinance of 1885, 142–43

forest reserves: government discussion concerning, 141–43

fruits: efforts at naturalization, 54–56, 57, 59, 64, 66

fungal infections. *See* plant diseases

G

Gallaway, Captain, 102

Galle, 51

Gampola, 60–61

Gannaruwa, 61, 145

Gardner, George: and seeds for horticulture, 59; and sugar planting, 62; views on tea, 64; alarm over threat of species extinction, 104

gathering: ecological impacts of, 12

gems, 18

gold, 74

Gondwanaland, 4, 10

goyigama: in Kandyan social order, 25; tribute paid by, 34; and chena, 39

grain. *See* dry grains

gram, 35

grasses: colonization by, after fire, 12; *Andropogon schoenanthus* [lemon grass], 22; *Chrysopogon zeylanicus,* 22; poor nutritional quality, 22; *Panicum maximum* [Guinea

grass] as fodder, 82; influence of clean weeding on colonization, 84; *Panicum barbinode* as fodder, 85. *See also* weeds
Great Rebellion of 1817–1818, 27–29, 31, 59, 66, 67, 68, 148
Green, E. E., 145
green peas, 56
Gregory, Governor William: on extent of highland deforestation, 140–41
grubs. *See* insect infestations
guava, 18
Gulf of Mannar, 11, 12, 13, 89, 116

H
Hakgala: creation, 118; sale of cinchona seedlings, 118; end of cinchona experiment, 125; experimentation with exotics, 143, 144. *See also* cinchona
Hangurankette, 69
Hantenne, 79
Happutella, 105
hares, 85
Hemileia vastatrix. See coffee blight
hides, 99, 102
Himalayan Mountains, 4, 10, 133, 143
honey, 41, 45, 49, 71
Hooker, J. D., 116, 140
Hooker, W. T., 57
hops, 54
horns: trade in, 99, 102
horticulture: and botanic gardens, 54–55. 56; at Peradeniya, 57–59; Barnes' experimentation at Nuwara Eliya, 64; in upper highlands, 65–66. *See also* botanic gardens; vegetables
Howard, Dr. J. E., 119, 125
Hull, Edmund: views on deforestation and human health, 104
hunting: ecological impacts of low intensity, 12; Kandyan practices, 45–46; Kandyan law concerning, 46; impact of, with rifles, 99; of elephants during Kandyan period, 99; British policy toward, 99; by highland farmers in British period, 99, 100; legislation to control, 100; impact on leopard population, 100–102

I
immigrants. *See* migration
India. *See* southern India

insect infestations: brown "bug" damage, 86; search for antidotes, 87; "grub" as chronic problem, 87; scale bug, 115; on tea plantations, 144–45
Insect Pest and Quarantine Ordinance No. 5 of 1901, 145
Intermediate Zone, 7–8, 11, 14, 16, 147
Inter-Tropical Convergence Zone, 7
irrigation: in early agriculture, 14–15; and collapse of *rajarata* civilization, 16; and settlement patterns, 30; for paddy cultivation, 35–37. *See also* water
Iron Age technologies, 12–13
ivory, 11, 19

J
jack trees, 42, 61, 68, 78, 103
Jaffna, 16, 18
Jaffnapatam, 29
jaggery sugar, 62, 67
Jamaica, 80
Java, 5, 60, 80, 116, 117, 118, 120, 123, 124
Jayawardena, Jayantha, 102
jungle fowl, 86

K
Kaduganawa, 105
Kaluganga River, 141
Kalutara, 56, 63
Kandy, kingdom of: emergence, 17; ecological impact, 20; political evolution, 26–27; 1803 British invasion of, 27; initial *Pax Britannica*, 27. *See also* forest barrier
Kandyan Board of Revenue Commissioners, 27, 68
Kelaart, E. F.: on rats and coffee plantations, 85
Kelani River, 141
Kerr, William, 56
kitul palm, 55, 62
Knox, Robert: observation concerning low productivity of Kandyan agriculture, 33; observation concerning Kandyan hunting, 46
Kotte, 16, 17, 20
kurakkan, 35, 38, 39, 40, 47
Kurunagala, 28

L
land sales: acreage sold, 1833–1886, 72; in upper highlands, 108

land tenure: as key to economic growth, 32–33; as key to conflict over auctioned land, 71; "Waste Lands" Ordinance No. 12 of 1840, 71–72
Lear, J. G., 63
lantana, 84
lemon grass. See grasses
leopards, 21, 46–47, 66, 67, 102
lime, 81, 82, 83
livestock: British prohibitions against slaughter, 29. See also cattle; rinderpest
Longden, Governor J., 141
Low Country Wet Zone, 11

M
Macau, 56
MacDowell, General, 55–56
Mackenzie, Governor James A. S., 63
MacNicoll, 118, 121
Madagascar, 8
Madulsima, 111
Mahaweli River, 28, 62, 78, 108, 141
maize, 35, 38, 40, 53
Malabar coast, 18, 85
malaria: and forest clearance, 12, 16; and abandonment of *rajarata* zone, 16; attributed to forest effluvium, 51–52; idiosyncratic ecological dynamics, 105
Malaysia, 8, 12, 13
Maldive Islands, 19
malt, 54
mamoty: and soil breakage, 81; weeding with, 83; used for "grubbing out," 87. See also soil erosion
manioc. See cassava
manure. See fertilizer
Markham, Clements: on forest clearance and desiccation of water courses, 103; and the transfer of cinchona seeds, 117
Marshall, Henry, 30; observation concerning female infanticide, 31
Mascarene Islands, 104
Maskeliya, 108
Matale, 98
McIvor, William, 118, 123
migration: prehistorical, from India, 4; historical, from India, 12
migrant laborers. See South Indian laborers
monetization: of precolonial Kandyan economy,

34; British period transformation in currency use, 73–75
monkeys, 86, 102
monsoons, 7–8, 21. See also winds
Moon, Alexander, 56, 63; on horticultural prospects for Royal Botanic Garden at Peradeniya, 56–57
Morice, Arthur, 133
Morris, Daniel: efforts to combat coffee blight, 112; comments on cinchona at Hakgala, 122
mulberry, 59
murrain. See rinderpest
Muscat, 96
Muslims: as merchants, 17; and poultry farming, 45; as cartmen, 82. See also transport
mustard, 35

N
Narlandé, 39
naturalization. See coffee; fauna; flora; fruits; vegetables
Nawalapitiya, 142
Nayakkar dynasty: eighteenth-century rule, 26–27; succession crisis, 27
nelu, 85
New World crops: introduction of, 18
Nilgiri Hills, 117, 123, 124
Normansell, H. F., 57, 59; early experimentation with tea, 63–64
North, Governor Frederick, 55, 56, 60
Northwestern Province, 98
nutmeg tree, 137
Nuwerakalawiya, 30
Nuwara Eliya, 28, 39, 57, 63, 64, 65, 75, 141

O
oats, 54, 64, 65
Ondaatje, W. C., 59
onions, 66
Ootacamund, 117, 118, 120, 123
opium, 133

P
paddy. See rice
Panabokke, C. R., xviii
papaya, 18
Parke, Major, 79
pasture. See forest pasture; patanas

patanas: classification systems, 20–21; as source of food, 21; biological productivity of, 21–22; re-working of upper highland, for agriculture, 65; poor quality of natural pasturage in, 89

Peliyagoda, 55

Perera, N. P., 20

pig rats. *See* bandicoots

pineapple, 18

pine, 143, 144

plant diseases, 36, 40, 135, 144–45, 148. *See also* coffee blight

plantains, 66

Planters' Association of Ceylon, 144

Polonnaruwa, 16

polyandry, 31

poppy, 59

population: early enumerations of Kandyan, 30; lowered nutritional status of Kandyan after Great Rebellion, 29–30. *See also* female in-fanticide

Portugal fig, 59

Portuguese: political interventions by, 17; efforts at naturalization of flora and fauna, 18

potato, 18, 56, 59, 64, 65, 66

Proterozoic era, 4

pruning: as prophylactic measure for coffee trees, 79; haphazard experimentation with, for coffee trees, 80; of tea bushes, 137

pulping mills, 88

Pussellawa, 57, 64, 103

Q

quarantine: to prevent the spread of smallpox, 29; to prevent the transmission of plant dis-ease, 145

Queensland, 116

quinine: early trial, 116–17; high cost, 117

R

railroad: completion of, from Colombo to Kandy, 108; fuelwood for, 141; demand for crossties, 143–44

Railway Department, 143

rainfall. *See* monsoons

rainforests. *See* forest(s)

rajarata civilization: ecological foundation, 14; collapse of, 16

rajakariya: release of native coffee growers from

obligation, 69; use of by British for road-building, 28

Rajawella, 105

Rambo, A. Terry, 12

Ramboda, 64

rats: attacks on coffee plantations, 85

Rebellion of 1848, 106

red ants, 87

reforestation: by exotics, 125, 143–44

Regulation No. 2 of 1822, 68

reservoirs. *See* water storage

rice: introduction of wet, 14; and *rajarata* civili-zation, 14; terraces, 30–31; 1835 estimate of production, 35; planting seasons, 35–36; re-turns to seed, 36; agronomic vulnerabilities, 36–37; storage techniques, 37 recycling of by-products, 37; field preparation, 37. *See also* ir-rigation

rice imports: for South Indian laborers, 90

rice production: in South India, 90–92

rifles, 102

rinderpest: early nineteenth-century epizootics, 28, 65, 93–94; in Nuwara Eliya, 65; South Asian regional reservoir, 91, 93; introduction to Sri Lanka, 93–94; dynamics of infection, 94; 1841 epizootic of, in combination with hoof-and-mouth disease, 94; economic im-pact of, 95; evidence on varied regional mor-tality, 98; impact on draft animal prices, 98

roads: lack of, to highlands in Kandyan period, 19; construction of, to Kandy, 28; construc-tion of, to Nuwara Eliya, 28; importance of, in rinderpest outbreaks, 98; new round of support for, in 1860s, 108

Robinson, Governor Hercules, 133

Rogers, Major Thomas, 100

Royal Botanic Garden at Calcutta, 55, 57, 64, 118, 133

Royal Botanic Gardens of Ceylon, 56

Royal Botanic Gardens at Kew, 123

Royal Botanic Garden at Peradeniya: horticul-ture, 57–59; coffee production, 60, 61; as cof-fee plant nursery, 61–62; sugar experimentation, 62; tea experimentation, 63–64; experimentation with exotic trees, 144; and applied scientific research, 144–46; research at, leading to creation of specialized tea institute, 150. *See also* Hakgala

Russian empire in North America, 53

S
salt, 66, 67
sambhur deer, 21, 28, 65, 93, 94, 102
scrub forest. *See* chena
scrub typhus, 93
seed degeneration. *See* vegetables
sesame, 35
shade trees: value of, for coffee, 80
sheep, 53, 54, 55, 65
shelterbelts: as protection against wind, 79; effects of absence, 115
siltation, of paddy fields, 88
silver, 34, 74
Sinhalese: solidification of ethnic identity, 13–14
Sitavaka, 17
Skinner, Major Thomas, 102
shifting agriculture. *See* chena
slash-and-burn agriculture. *See* chena
Slave Island, 55
sloth bears, 102
smallpox: 1819–1820 outbreak, 29–30; and migration of South Indian laborers, 92
social order: in highlands, 25–26
soil erosion: caused by chena, 40; caused by patterns of coffee planting, 81–82; caused by weeding, 83–84; and vertical drains, 84; lack of, after topsoil loss, 104; and tea planting, 137–38; range of options limited by, 150–55
soils: formation of, 4–5; exhaustion of, by chena, 13; in forests, 23–24; unsuitability for sugar, 62; enrichment through biomass burning, 78–79; ecological impact of plantations on, 81–82; exceptional stability of subsoils, 104
Soils and Agro-Ecological Environments of Sri Lanka, xviii
southern Africa, 116
South Coorg, 116
South Indian laborers: consumption of rats by, 85; wages of, 90; average annual arrivals, 90; arduous migration, 92; new pattern of permanent residence on estates, 137
southern India, 11, 12, 13, 27, 84, 93, 124, 137
squirrels, 86
Straits Settlements, 115
stream reservations. *See* water courses
subsoils, 139

sugar plantations , 62
Sumatra, 11
sweet potato, 42
syphilis, 19

T
Tamil: early Hindu communities, 13; birth of new ethnicity on tea estates, 137. *See also* Jaffna; Jaffnapatam
tanks. *See* water storage
tariffs. *See* coffee
taro, 42
tavalams, 94. *See also* transport
taxation: paid to Kandyan authorities, 32–33; lack of, on chena lands, 68; exemption for coffee lands, 69; commutation of, in grain, 74
tea: "China tea," 63; from Assam, 63; planting at Nuwara Eliya, 63–64; Gardner's lack of support for, 64; importation of hybrid Assam, 133; rise to dominance, 135; leaf blight, 135; versatility of, 137–39; growth pattern, 139
temperature, on island, 7–8
Tennent, J. Emerson: on economic opportunities for Kandyan laborers, 74
Thistleton-Dyer, W. T., 125
Thwaites, E. J., 125
Thwaites, G. H. K.: on protection of endangered plants, 104; advocacy for diversification of export economy, 111; on use of manures during coffee blight, 112; botanical intuition concerning cinchona, 120; on radical stumping of cinchona, 123; support for tea initiatives, 133. *See also* Hakgala; Royal Botanic Garden at Peradeniya
timber: protection of, suitable for construction and carpentry, 68; general lack of selection of, after felling, 78; economic value of, in upper highlands, 139–40; cutting of, for railway fuelwood, 141; demand for, on plantations, 143; demand for crossties, 143
tobacco, 18
toddy, 55
tomato, 18
trade: ecological impact of Portuguese and Dutch maritime, 17–19; external, of Kandyan kingdom, 26; patterns of, in highlands, 33, 66; between highlands and coast, 67; in hides

and horns, 99, 100, 102; in meat, 100. *See also* cinchona, coffee, tea

transport: of coffee, 95–96; costs of, using imported coast and native black cattle compared, 97–98

Trimen, Dr. Henry: and cinchona, 125; opposition to villagers' efforts to grow tea, 135–36; new focus on exotics at Hakgala, 143; and "native flying bug," 144–45. *See also* Hakgala; Royal Botanic Garden at Peradeniya

turnip, 56

Tropical Agriculturalist, 146

Turnour, George: on highland markets, 33; on potato cultivation, 59; as advocate of restrictions on sale of government lands, 71

Tytler, R. B.: and shadeless coffee plantings, 80; on the effects of a burn, 81; and his fertilizer preparation, 83

UV

Udavattekelle, 49

Up Country Wet Zone, 11

Uva Province, 20, 27, 29, 31, 40, 66, 69, 98

Veddyas, 14, 49

vegetables: production of, in chena fields, 39; Dutch efforts at introduction, 53–55; Moon's assessment of production prospects, 56–57; problems with seed degeneration, 57–59. *See also* botanic gardens; horticulture

village settlement: in highlands, 10, 30–31, 37, 87

Vincent, F. D'A.: on limits of natural tree vegetation, 23; on shelterbelts and coffee blight, 115; on extent of chena, 142

VOC. *See* Dutch East India Company

W

wages: to Kandyans for land clearance in upper highlands, 65; and new economic opportunities, 74; and returns to chena labor, 89; to South Indian migrant laborers, 90. *See also* economic opportunities

Ward, H. Marshall, 112, 114. *See also* coffee blight

"Waste Lands" Ordinance No. 12 of 1840, 72. *See also* chena; land tenure

water: fresh, from surface flow, 8; influence on distribution of human and faunal populations, 10; large-scale control, 14; and forest cover, 23–24; in Kandyan highlands, 30–31, 37–38; diversion of, for estate use, 88. *See also* drainage

water courses: early suggestions for protection, 88; 1848 legislation concerning, 103; stream reservations, 138–40

water pollution: through dumping of coffee pulp, 88

water storage: destruction of tanks in Uva, 31; shallow surface reservoirs in Dry Zone, 8, 10

water buffalo. *See* buffalo

Watson, J. G., 57, 63

weeding: deep cut and shallow cut, 83; with scrapers, 83–84; practices of clean, compared with plantations in southern India, 84; on tea plantations, 139; abandonment of clean, 150–51. *See also* mamoty

weeds: growth of, after land clearance, 83–84; *Bidens pilosa*, 84; *Sonchus arvensis*, 84; *Ageratum conyzoides*, 84; *Mikania scandens*, 84

Wellase, 29

West Indies, 54, 55, 60, 62; plantation agriculture, 76, 77, 80; soil erosion and deforestation, 104, 142

West Indian planters: predilections for standardized agronomic practices, 80

Wet Zone, 7–8

wheat, 53, 64; efforts at introduction in maritime zone, 54; in highlands, 59

Wilderness, 133

wild pigs, 21, 85, 102

Wilmot-Horton, Governor Robert, 99

winds: kachchan, 7; and tree stress, 79. *See also* monsoons; shelterbelts

Wright, Henry, 79

XYZ

yams, 42; West Indian, 59

Yattipalata, 66

yaws, 19